AS IF
IT WERE
LIFE

A WWII DIARY
FROM THE
THERESIENSTADT GHETTO

PHILIPP MANES

Edited by Ben Barkow and Klaus Leist
Translated by Janet Foster, Ben Barkow and Klaus Leist

palgrave
macmillan

First published in Germany in 2005 as *Als ob's ein Leben wär* by Ullstein
Buchverlage GmbH.

First published in English in 2009 by
PALGRAVE MACMILLAN®
in the United States—a division of St. Martin's Press LLC,
175 Fifth Avenue, New York, NY 10010.

Where this book is distributed in the UK, Europe and the rest of the
world, this is by Palgrave Macmillan, a division of Macmillan Publishers
Limited, registered in England, company number 785998, of
Houndmills, Basingstoke, Hampshire RG21 6XS.

Palgrave Macmillan is the global academic imprint of the above companies and has companies and representatives throughout the world.

Palgrave® and Macmillan® are registered trademarks in the United
States, the United Kingdom, Europe and other countries.

Images courtesy of Mrs. Jackie Greavett

ISBN: 978-0-230-61328-7

Library of Congress Cataloging-in-Publication Data is available from
the Library of Congress.

A catalogue record of the book is available from the British Library.

Design by Newgen Imaging Systems (P) Ltd., Chennai, India.

First edition: December 2009

10 9 8 7 6 5 4 3 2 1

Printed in the United States of America.

CONTENTS

ACKNOWLEDGMENTS

We are grateful to the following people who made valuable contributions to this book.

First and foremost, Dr. Gertrud Nolterieke, who transcribed the original manuscript, a huge labor of love, and Helen Gregory, a researcher of great skill and tenacity, who collected much material about the inmates of Theresienstadt and solved numerous puzzles.

The staff and Board of the Wiener Library, London supported us wholeheartedly and helped generously at all stages of the project. We particularly want to thank Jane Wilson for her tireless help.

Several volunteers of the German organization Aktion Sühnezeichen Friedensdienste and the Austrian Gedenkdienst helped greatly. We particularly want to thank Nikolaus Deutsch, Gesche Heidom, Daniel Bäumer and Dominik Knes who helped with the present edition.

Mrs Jackie Greavett, the granddaughter of Philipp Manes and owner of the original manuscript, has been unstinting in her support for this project.

We would like to thank Victoria Glendinning, who guided the project at a critical stage. Ivan Mulcahy, literary agent, gave us invaluable help and support.

English-PEN's Writers in Translation program funded a sample translation which helped us to find a home for the book. We are grateful to English-PEN's Andrea Pisac for her help.

Finally, we owe a special debt of gratitude to our editor at Palgrave Macmillan, Alessandra Bastagli and her team.

Eva Manes died in 2004 at the age of 95 and did not live to see the publication of her father's writings. This book is dedicated to her memory.

EDITORS' INTRODUCTION

The posthumous writings by prisoners in Nazi ghettos and concentration camps occupy a special place in the literature of the Holocaust. They speak to us with an immediacy and authority that cannot be matched by any memoir written after the events it describes, which is, consciously or unconsciously, influenced by later knowledge and experiences. Philipp Manes did not write a memoir; he wrote about what he lived through and observed where and as it happened.

Such writings can pose problems for today's reader. They may contain factual errors because of the author's limited access to information sources or because he wrote while under great trauma or stress. In the writings of Philipp Manes, however, there are surprisingly few such errors. He wrote not knowing how his story would end. By contrast, it is impossible for modern readers not to be conscious of Philipp and Gertrud Manes's tragic end from the beginning.

Philipp Manes was a man of his time, not ours. Our judgments of him need to be historically informed and sensitive. Today, some of his opinions may appear "wrong" or politically incorrect. However, when considered from the perspective of his background, his social and cultural milieu, his economic circumstances, and his personal experiences, it is clear that his opinions and attitudes are not particularly unusual.

* * *

Philipp Manes was born in Elberfeld, Germany, on August 16, 1875. His family had lived in the Rhineland since the eighteenth century, pursuing various trades. In 1886, Manes's father, Eduard, moved the family to Berlin, where he established himself as a fur merchant, starting his own company, the Eduard Manes Fur Agency.

After leaving school and working as a business traveler for a time, Philipp Manes joined the publications department of the New Photographic Society in

Berlin. He traveled all over Germany, interviewing prominent artists and writers before their photographic portraits were made. He eagerly accepted the opportunity to travel outside Germany, and some of his long visits to London would remain among his cherished memories. This (roughly the first decade of the twentieth century) was perhaps the most formative period of his life, giving him a taste of the wider world and igniting a lifelong interest in literature, music, and the theater. In 1910, Philipp answered his father's call to join the family firm and went on to become a successful fur dealer himself.

By this time he had been married to Gertrud Elias for six years. Manes was a dedicated family man, but a strict and demanding father. For instance, he carefully controlled which books and plays his four children were allowed to read.

During World War I, Manes was drafted into the German army and sent to the Russian front. He became a sergeant and was awarded the Iron Cross. His main assignment was to organize and run a number of bookshops behind the front. He later described this period as the most interesting time of his life.

During the years of the Weimar Republic, Manes became very active in the fur-industry trade associations. This all came to an end the day after the so-called *Kristallnacht* ("The Night of the Broken Glass"), November 9–10, 1938, when Jewish businesses and synagogues all over Germany were attacked and destroyed, and many Jews were killed and arrested in a state-organized pogrom. His daughter Eva persuaded him that there was no hope left and that he should dissolve the business.

By the outbreak of war in 1939, all four of Manes's children had left Germany. Although Philipp and Gertrud had encouraged them to emigrate, the loss was a bitter blow for them, adding to the misery being caused by the anti-Jewish measures in force at the time. Manes's health deteriorated. His one refuge and consolation was writing.

Manes was an enthusiastic diarist and writer. The titles of some of his unpublished manuscripts, which now form the Manes Collection in the Wiener Library, London, demonstrate his strong desire to document his life. There are the two-volume *My Life* (1899–1915 and 1918–1940); *Memories of My Youth in Berlin and Encounters with German Artists*, two volumes about the war bookshops; and a four-volume study called *The German Fur Industry and Its Associations 1900–1940*. There is also a thought-provoking collection of essays, *Way and End: Destinies, Experiences, Thoughts*, in which he discusses issues such as Antisemitism and Zionism. From 1939 until just before his deportation in 1942, he wrote war diaries in order to record his and Gertrud's experiences and thoughts for their children. They are a testimony of the life of a Jewish family during the first years of the war.

During this period, Manes and his wife lived in a small apartment in the center of Berlin. In spring 1942, Philipp was called up to work in a factory that manufactured nuts and bolts. In July 1942, his property was confiscated, and he and Gertrud were deported to the Theresienstadt ghetto.

* * *

In the late eighteenth century, in Bohemia, not far from Prague, the fortress of *Theresienstadt* (called *Terezin* in Czech) was built as a garrison town for the army of the Austro-Hungarian Empire. It was, in October 1941, designated as a collection point for Jews from Bohemia and Moravia (today's Czech Republic), as well as for Jews from Germany and territories occupied by Germany. Only certain classes of Jews from Germany were sent to the Theresienstadt ghetto: older people, veterans who had been decorated during the First World War, and men and women who were well known outside the Jewish community. Later it was also to serve as a showpiece, a "model" ghetto, in order to disguise the Nazis' extermination plans.

The first Jews from Prague, the so-called "building commando," arrived at Theresienstadt at the end of November 1941 and included many members of the later ghetto leadership. Initially, they hoped that the ghetto would become a self-sufficient community, allowing the Czech Jews to survive the war. This hope was shattered by the arrival of the first transports from Germany in the summer of 1942, which increased the ghetto population beyond a sustainable level. The number of inmates reached its zenith in July 1942—up to 58,000 people were living in a town that had been built for 11,000 inhabitants, at most.

Although they were dismal, the facilities—especially the medical ones—were better in the Theresienstadt ghetto than in the concentration camps. While large numbers of people died there, it was not a place where many Jews were murdered—for that, they were sent on to death camps, mainly Treblinka and Auschwitz. One hundred and forty thousand men and women were incarcerated in Theresienstadt between 1941 and 1945. For about 88,000 of them, it proved to be the antechamber to a death camp; 33,000 people died in the ghetto, chiefly from illness and malnutrition. Nineteen thousand inmates survived the war.

Deportation to Theresienstadt decreased in the first half of 1943, and a period of relative stability followed. In the spring of 1944, the SS ordered a "town beautification" program as preparation for showing the ghetto to the International Committee of the Red Cross as a model Jewish settlement.

The history of the preparation for the visit of the Red Cross is long, complex, and confusing (Manes's account reflects this). It seems that Heinrich Himmler, the SS chief, decided in May 1943 to allow a Red Cross visit to Theresienstadt, to counter stories of atrocities in the camps and ghettos. In the summer of 1943, as part of the preparations for the visit, a form of currency was introduced, and the ghetto was officially designated a "Settlement Area." The SS command post in charge of Theresienstadt was also renamed, becoming the "Department." During the winter of 1943/44 activity seems to have slowed and even stopped, but in spring 1944 preparations picked up speed.

In order to reduce the overcrowding, the SS deported about 17,500 inmates to Auschwitz, where they were kept alive in a special camp, called the Theresienstadt Family Camp, in case the Red Cross wished to visit them. The Red Cross visit took place in June 1944. The following month the Family Camp was liquidated and its inhabitants murdered. The deportations had, temporarily, created somewhat better conditions for those remaining in Theresienstadt.

Autumn 1944 saw the last wave of deportations from Theresienstadt, until only 11,000 inmates were left. By the end of April 1945, about 14,000 prisoners from other camps were brought into the ghetto; thousands died there from infectious diseases. In May 1945, Theresienstadt was liberated by the Red Army after the SS had, just a few days before, already turned it over to the Red Cross. The last inmates left the ghetto only in August 1945.

When it was still under German control, the Theresienstadt ghetto was under the authority of the Central Office for the Settling of the Jewish Question in Bohemia and Moravia (*Zentralamt für die Regelung der Judenfrage in Böhmen und Mähren*), which was in turn under the Reich Security Main Office (*Reichssicherheitshauptamt*) in Berlin. The ghetto had three SS commanders: Siegfried Seidl (November 1941–July 1943); Anton Burger (July 1943–February 1944); and Karl Rahm (February 1944–May 1945). Czech police acted as guards.

A Jewish self-administration was responsible for internal matters, including accommodating and feeding the inmates, and also had to prepare the lists for deportations.[1] It reported to the Nazi-appointed Council of Jewish Elders. Its chairmen were Jacob Edelstein (December 1941–November 1943); Paul Eppstein (November 1943–September 1944); and Benjamin Murmelstein (September 1944–May 1945).

Few of the inmates of Theresienstadt were aware that it was a stage post to the death camps in the East. Unlike larger ghettos, it was almost hermetically sealed, and reliable information about the fate of the Jews did not reach the inmates. At least some of the Jewish elders had partial information about the exterminations, but chose to suppress this. Thanks to a large number of educated people with academic and artistic interests, the ghetto developed a remarkable cultural life, in which Philipp Manes was to play such a significant role.

* * *

Shortly after arriving in Theresienstadt, Manes was summoned by the commander of the Ghetto Watch, which was a kind of internal Jewish police force. He was instructed to take charge of a new auxiliary force, to be called the Orientation Service (later renamed Auxiliary Service of the Ghetto Watch). This group was at first supposed to assist inmates who got lost and couldn't find their way in the ghetto, but it soon grew into a general law-and-order/social-services unit, and then developed into "this funny mixture of police station, theatrical production company, adult education center, and concert agency," as the musician Willi Durra described it in a farewell letter to Philipp Manes. What had grown out of modest talks in the garrison stables was developed by Manes into a lecture series by the Manes Group, which eventually set up over 500 events, including lectures by the most eminent scholar-inmates, readings of Goethe's *Faust* and Lessing's *Nathan the Wise*, choir performances, and musical entertainment, providing spiritual nourishment for an educated audience starved of mental stimulation and hope.

The Orientation Service was closed down in February 1944,[2] although lectures continued throughout the summer. Manes then embarked on a series of interviews with prominent inmates, including Georg Gradnauer, a social democratic politician of the Weimar Republic who had been Germany's Minister of the Interior; the chemist Arthur Eichengrün, who had a role in the discovery or isolation of the chemical compound that forms aspirin; and Elsa Bernstein, granddaughter of Franz Liszt, wife of the lawyer and writer Max Bernstein, and friend of Gerhart Hauptmann.

Because of their length, these interviews cannot be included in this book. In the original manuscript, they intercut the descriptions of the transports rolling out of Theresienstadt for Auschwitz. Even at this point, Manes did not fully understand what Auschwitz was, although it was clear that he dreaded it more now than he had a year or 18 months earlier, when he had believed the Nazi propaganda—that in the great ghetto of Birkenau, deportees from Theresienstadt were building new, permanent lives.

Manes desperately needed a distraction as he watched the ghetto being emptied by the transports to the East, knowing that, despite the official pronouncements, his and Gertrud's time was approaching. The interviews Manes conducted helped to take his mind off the deportations and provided the illusion of normalcy and the hope of a future. This hope was extinguished on

October 28, 1944, when Philipp and Gertrud Manes boarded the last transport to leave Theresienstadt for Auschwitz.

* * *

Philipp Manes wrote this account in nine notebooks, making few corrections. He seems to have intended it for publication, to record what happened and to document the achievements of Jewish people both in the organization and administration of their community and in the cultural arena. There are three more volumes in which Manes's friends pay tribute to him in poems, letters, and drawings, only some of which are included in this book.

Manes clearly describes the main subject of this chronicle on the title page of his manuscript: Orientation Service; Auxiliary Service of the Ghetto Watch; Lecture Series. By calling this text *Tatsachenbericht* (Factual Report), Manes announces an intention—he will rely on the power of facts, the power of truth: He will not interpret, judge, embellish, or cover up.

In her book *My Years in Theresienstadt*, the poet Gerty Spies wrote: "Toward the end of the time in Theresienstadt the old gentleman spent every free hour at his bare table in the garret, which, with its modest triangular eye-like window, gave light to his ongoing work: He wrote a diary. Everything that had happened during his long time there, his artistic work, the work of others, the people he met through his art: his pen captured everything in detailed reports. We always saw him writing, if we saw him at all. Often, in his absence I left a little mug with wild flowers on his desk, which I had picked for him stealthily against regulations on the bank of the moat."[3]

Philipp Manes wrote a brief memoir, *Last Days in Berlin*, in April 1943. Its simple narrative struck a chord with many readers who recognized the experience of forced departure from home to an unknown future, shared by so many deportees or refugees. This memoir now forms the prologue to this book.

Work on the Factual Report began in February 1944. At this time, Manes, devastated by the dissolution of his beloved Orientation Service, suddenly found that he had time on his hands. Being a creative man and a compulsive writer, he put this time to use, setting out to document the work of the ghetto. He begins with a retrospective of the early days in Theresienstadt, starting where *The Last Days in Berlin* ended. Later, as the Factual Report moves closer to 1944, it evolves into a diary of his last months in the camp.

Manes's story of course also reflects the mood in Theresienstadt. Part 1 covers the time when some inmates still hoped to build an acceptable life in the ghetto. In Part 2, this hope has died and been replaced by a long year of dreary imprisonment. Part 3 is divided into two sections. Section I describes life under the somewhat better conditions for the prisoners remaining in the ghetto, which were gained at the expense of those who were deported to the East. In section II, the ghetto is being drained by the transports and becomes a ghost town filled mainly with old people. Manes wrote until just before his deportation; his Factual Report breaks off in the middle of a sentence. He did not live to see the chaos at the end of the war. Theresienstadt's final liberation is briefly sketched in the epilogue.

Occasionally, Manes left a space on the page for adding information, especially figures. Wherever possible, we filled in these spaces using other sources and indicated the new material by the use of brackets, which we also used for some explanatory additions. Parts of the original text have been rearranged for readability and to try to maintain a chronological sequence.

We have not attempted to edit the manuscript as one might a fictional narrative. Manes wrote to document what he regarded as important events and encounters. He did so under immense pressure and often in a state of anxiety about his immediate safety and the longer-term prospects for his wife and himself. He wrote things down as he saw them or recalled them or reflected on them. On occasion this makes the chronological sequence hard to follow, particularly when he describes things from an earlier period and compares them with the current situation.

There are recurring themes such as the weather, nature and landscape, people, food, and the plagues of lice and bedbugs. Some obvious repetitions have been removed, but Manes's representation of the daily rhythm of ghetto life and the often mundane preoccupations of the inmates have been preserved.

Major cuts include the biographies; sections containing information that Manes took entirely from other sources, especially where these are available publicly; some nostalgic and repetitive reminiscences of his earlier life and about theatrical shows and performers from prewar Berlin; and finally, the many poems written by fellow inmates, often into his manuscript. Translations of these poems cannot convey the same nuances and emotions as they do in the original.

* * *

On October 27, 1944, the day before his deportation to Auschwitz, Manes wrote on the first page of the last volume of his manuscript: "Please send these notes to Mrs. Fanny Franck or her daughter Mrs. Ilse Schieschke, Starnberg near Munich [...]." The non-Jewish Fanny Franck was the wife of his oldest and closest friend, the Jewish physician Adolf Franck, to whom he had given his earlier manuscripts before being taken to Theresienstadt.

Manes gave this manuscript, together with other writings by Gustav Hochstetter, a fellow inmate who had died, to Lies Klemich, who had been a friend of Hochstetter's. It is thanks to the courage of Mrs. Klemich that the papers survived. Ill and mostly bedridden, she hid the papers under her mattress until her liberation from Theresienstadt. At the beginning of January 1947, after a period of severe illness, she managed to visit Hochstetter's wife, Hildegard, who had not been in Theresienstadt, in her house in Brandenburg, which was at the time in the Russian occupation zone. Mrs. Hochstetter contacted Adolf Franck in Munich, then part of the American zone, only to find out that it was impossible to send a parcel from one zone to the other. By that time, however, Franck had been in contact with Manes's children, who had also established communication with the Jewish Committee for Relief Abroad in London, which finally delivered the papers into the hands of Manes's daughter Eva in May 1948.

About ten years later, Eva Manes contacted Dr. Alfred Wiener, the founder and director of the Wiener Library in London, about the possible publication of her father's writings. Wiener read the manuscript but could not find any interested publishers. Disappointed, Eva Manes retrieved the papers and kept them in her home at Burford in Oxfordshire, England. In 1995, she finally deposited the Factual Report, along with her father's earlier writings, at the Wiener Library, where the collection occupies 16 boxes in the library's archives. It remains on loan and is the property of Mrs. Jackie Greavett, Eva Manes's niece and the granddaughter of Gertrud and Philipp Manes.

* * *

H. G. Adler, the historian of Theresienstadt, called Manes charming because of his enthusiasm and cultural interests but also ignorant of the fundamental evil of the SS. Indeed, some paragraphs in this book read strangely: Was Manes really blind to the intentions of the Nazis? Other inmates underscored Manes's clear-mindedness and his fighting spirit.

As an assimilated Jew, Manes held views of the world and society that did not differ much from those of his fellow Christian citizens. In his nonpolitical attitude and "Prussian" sense of duty, he was typical of the educated German middle class of the time.

Manes's generally positive view of prominent political figures of the Weimar epoch and some isolated remarks in his writings lead us to conclude that he was as loyal to the Republic as he had been to the monarchy that preceded it. At the beginning of the Third Reich, he had at first hoped for a peaceful development, in which the future of German Jewry would be secure, in spite of the restrictions that had been placed on them. But this soon changed. We cannot establish exactly when he realized that the so-called restrictions would be followed by the end of Jewish life in Germany. In any case, not only did he insist that his children emigrate, but he also considered emigration for himself and his wife.

Over the years, Manes became more conscious of Judaism and reflected on anti-Semitism. He now lived with an inner conflict, which is apparent in his writings during the first years of the war. Again and again, we find patriotic passages and even appreciative remarks about the German military and Hitler. However, in *Way and End*, his book of essays, he grieves over the fact that no one in Germany said "J'accuse," as Zola had done in France during the Dreyfus affair. "Today," Manes wrote in April 1942, "we recognize the danger; we know about the instruments of power of the [Nazi] party and its fanatical determination to implement what is the basic law of National Socialism: The Solution of the Jewish Question." Here, he also expressed sympathy for Zionism and highlighted the contribution of Jews to German culture. He took this unresolved inner conflict with him to Theresienstadt. He saw his work there in the Orientation Service as serving the Jewish community and arising from a moral imperative. He felt that the lecture series was a Jewish contribution to German culture.

Manes never abandoned his hope of liberation and tried to keep this hope alive in his fellow prisoners. He may sometimes have given in to wishful thinking. In a sense, his attitude was not unlike that of a conservative German Christian, who for too long could not believe what was happening in the name of his country. One can perhaps accuse Manes of being too trusting, but he was far from ignorant. Moreover, we must not forget what would have happened if the SS had read his words. It took real courage to write what he did.

✷ ✷ ✷

As a boy, Manes loved to dress up, to watch school parades, and even to attend Catholic church services—he cherished the theatricality of such events. He may have found his business life rather unexciting and dull. In Theresienstadt, he seized the opportunity to revive his love of the theater. He found something like fulfillment and was admired as a creative organizer, an impresario who brought art and culture to a starved audience. Although his life was marred by the loss of his family and his home, property, and civic rights, he found, in the dismal surroundings of Theresienstadt, a high degree of self-realization—paradoxical as this may sound. His personal feeling of accomplishment may have been a motive for his sometimes shockingly positive descriptions of the ghetto and the Nazi authorities.

Can the work of Philipp Manes be described as a sort of spiritual resistance, or did he in some way assist the Nazis by keeping the ghetto inmates passive before they were led to the slaughter?

In his book *Rethinking the Holocaust*, Yehuda Bauer surveys the vast literature on the Holocaust and writes about Jewish resistance, making use of two concepts against which we can measure the work of Manes. The first is expressed in the Hebrew word *Amidah*, which translates literally as "standing up" or "standing up against." Under this heading, Bauer includes activities such as smuggling food, mutual self-sacrifice, and efforts to strengthen morale through cultural, educational, religious, or political work. Bauer's second concept is "the sanctification of life," by which he means acts that did not just promote physical survival but also gave meaning to life.[4]

Manes would probably not have wanted to be called a resistance fighter. Yet, a case can be made that he was one—at least in the spiritual sense. He raised the morale of both his speakers and his audiences. He helped them remain psychologically intact when they might otherwise have quickly deteriorated—and this by itself fits Bauer's definition of resistance.

But he also did something more radical, which arose, paradoxically, from his own conservative personality. In the face of the Nazis' onslaught, he refused to yield what they most wanted to strip from him—his identity as both a Jew and a German. To some it may seem a weakness or a perversion: a group of Jews worshipping Goethe in a Nazi ghetto. But by example and through his work, he helped a large number of victims maintain the integrity of their identities. Might there not be something heroic in his refusal to give up either of the twin pillars of his identity? When he eventually went to his death, he did so as a great Jew and, perhaps just as tragically, as a loyal and patriotic German.

There is no evidence to suggest that Manes had much religious feeling, but he felt very much part of the Jewish community in a cultural and historical sense, particularly once the Nazis had seized power. In Theresienstadt, religion became more central in his life, after he met eminent Jewish thinkers. He witnessed a spiritual rebirth in many of his fellow inmates, and this touched him profoundly. He was proud that his lecture series was a vehicle for that process, and he shared their growing religious conviction.

One of the key figures of Theresienstadt, the rabbi and scholar Leo Baeck wrote a short essay about his experience in the Theresienstadt ghetto, which was published in March 1946. He did not mention any names, but the following lines can only refer to the circle Manes created:

[I]n the sheltering darkness of the long evenings, they were together in the cold and gloomy attic of a barrack, close under the roof. There they stood, pressed close to each other, to hear a talk about the Bible and the Talmud, about Plato, Aristotle, Maimonides, about Descartes and Spinoza, about Locke and Hume and Kant or about days and problems of history, about poetry and art and music, about Palestine of old and today, about the Commandments, the Prophets, and the Messianic idea. All those hours were hours in which a community arose out of the mass and the narrowness grew wide. They were hours of freedom.[5]

BEN BARKOW, KLAUS LEIST,
June 2009, London

Editors' note: This book takes its title from a poem by Leo Strauss, written in Theresienstadt, *Als ob* (as if). The poem satirizes the superficial sense of normalcy pervading the ghetto.

PROLOGUE
LAST DAYS IN BERLIN

On July 13, Mama's birthday,[1] which we celebrated quietly, I came home incredibly tired from the factory[2] and slept for an hour. At seven o'clock the doorbell rang. I opened the door and a man handed me a thick envelope on which were written the words: "From the Jewish Community." I didn't pay much attention to it. I simply thought it contained lists for us to use to do an inventory.[3]

At eight o'clock I went back to bed. We had to get up at 4:30 A.M. on the dot to be able to eat our thick morning soup in peace, and for me, in particular, to gather the strength I needed for the hard work at the drill press. At ten minutes to six, I was, as always, in the changing room, putting on my blue worker's uniform. I slipped into my wooden clogs. I had grown accustomed to their clanking, and their weight no longer hindered me.

I greeted the nice foremen, who sat at the window smoking a cigarette, and exchanged a few words with the young women who stood at the nearby machines. Then the siren sounded, and the gears began to turn. The noise filled the room as I switched on my big heavy machine and put the process in motion.

I knew the many steps of the production process by heart. I no longer needed to study the drill's operating instructions on the boards, written in machine type, to avoid mistaking the sequence and making that *one* false step that would render the whole job worthless.

I was already producing the minimum hourly quota and was proud of this accomplishment. As a 67-year-old who had always been clumsy with his hands, it made me happy to have become a skilled worker turning in flawless brass parts, so that not one was returned by quality control.

The breakfast break was at 8:35 A.M.; we sat in the women's changing room. Aside from three older people, the workers were all young women and girls; some were only 15 years old. We ate the bread we had brought, and drank the hot coffee that was always handed out on time by the helpful Miss Schulz. During the break, everyone talked about the "fate of the Jews," as it was referred to at that time. The workers came from all over the city, and so one heard stories that otherwise would have remained secret.

My neighbor, an efficient woman whose husband and son were also employed, knew the current news about the evacuations and often gave lively descriptions of the latest transports. I told her about the envelope. "God help us!" she exclaimed in horror. "That means evacuation." I was so frightened that I didn't know how to react. "Go to the boss immediately. He should let you go home and get the documents, so he can claim you for the factory."

I went home and saw that the cover letter indeed stated that we should be ready for evacuation at eight o'clock on the morning of Tuesday, July 21. This page had escaped my attention the evening before. The boss brought the letter to the personnel office, and a claim was submitted. I was sure that it would be successful and that I would be allowed to stay. Otherwise, what would have been the point of going to all the effort of training me?

On Wednesday and Thursday, I worked ten hours, as usual.

We ate lunch, which was delivered by the Jewish community in large containers […], with gusto, and the conversation was as animated as ever. At home, I made no preparations whatsoever. I did not want to make life more difficult for us. The days remained unusually warm and dry.

The factory hall faced north, and it was not hot. Working there was tolerable since a fresh breeze wafted through the room. No one was required to maximize their output, and because of that the pace was not as hectic as it usually is in factories where piecework is required. My 19-year-old blond foreman, Grabowski, treated me as though I was his father, and never became impatient during the initial difficulty of training me. I am still grateful to him for that today, and also to both of his older colleagues.

We often chatted about his future when the boss was out of sight, and he always welcomed my advice. Aryans were not allowed to speak to us more than was strictly necessary, but he didn't take the rules so seriously. There was only one policy about which the factory boss was strict. We could not leave our workstation early, and not without having cleaned it first.

On Saturday we performed general maintenance on the machines, and that took a whole hour. I would sweat quite a bit doing this; bending and emptying out the machines was a great strain. But I learned how to do all of it, and gladly undertook these tasks. But at the end of the day I was totally worn out, and no good for anything. […] Another awful thing was that we were not allowed to sit on the tram, no matter how tired we were.[4]

Friday arrived. At ten o'clock [I] was called in to see the boss, who told me that my appeal had been rejected: I could go home. In the meantime, I had tried to get used to the idea of evacuation and had managed to do so surprisingly well. Soberly, I told the foreman the news; he was deeply upset.

The news spread quickly on the factory floor. The women and girls cried, and there was a feeling of great despondency in the air. I calmly cleaned my machine, as I did on Saturdays, so that it could not be said of me that I left things untidy. Brief handshakes all around, wet eyes, and moving words of farewell.

I walked slowly out of the room, past the yard piled high with trash. I was stopped at the gate: "Evacuated!" [I said] and the reply came, "Take care" and "All the best."

Then, on the street, where carefree children played, I glanced back at the house at number 1, at the bay window where in 1892 my mother stood every morning and waved to me as I set out for school.[5]

For as long as I had worked at F. Butzke & Company, I had looked in that direction and imagined my mother's loving face. Feeling that her loving eyes were upon me made my walk through the yard easier. A long good-bye here, too. A painful, albeit short, period of my life came to a close.

Thus began the last three agonizing days of our life in Berlin, which are now behind us like an evil nightmare. What can I say or report about them? It is indeed too painful to describe these busy hours during which we separated ourselves from property, possessions, and people.

It still seemed inconceivable that we had to give up our entire estate, leave behind everything that we had acquired over the 37 years of our marriage. Every object held a loving memory, every picture told a story, and every piece of furniture was like part of the family. All our possessions were to be appropriated by strangers. They would go through all the drawers and cupboards and throw out things that were worthless to them—our cherished possessions. Inconceivable.

We began to clear things out and give them away. Everything was quickly sorted. Takers were found for my last books, my notebooks, those brown volumes that my father had collected when he was young, all the notepaper, the good office stationery, the tableware and glassware, and all the kitchen equipment. Thus, our apartment was quickly emptied. [...]

I sat at my desk, my beloved desk, my faithful companion for 37 years, which still had marks on it made by Annemarie.[6] I wrote farewell letters to all my friends and stuck our last photos inside the envelopes. They should get them by Wednesday, when they would no longer be able to contact us.

Our last night at home came and went. We got up at 6 A.M. Our luggage had already been taken away the day before. We waited to be picked up by the police. Our home was spick-and-span. Everything tidy, clean.

I went from room to room. Here, the painful farewell to Walter and Lilli. There, I said my good-byes to Annemarie. Over there, Eva embraced us for the last time. There Rudolf's large picture looked out of its silver frame.

In the bedroom, my picture, taken in Hamburg in 1897, the last thing my mother saw [before she died].

Out in the corridor, the old portraits of the Manes grandparents, once kept by Aunt Ida in New York and brought back. [...]

The kitchen was clean and empty. In the corridor, the white wardrobes, still filled with odds and ends. The ornaments that the children had given to us for our silver wedding anniversary. Out on the balcony, the planters filled with sedum that [Gertrud] had been so proud of—empty. The chairs that we sat on so often had been bought by Walter as a set. And the tables, one of which had belonged to Grandmother Elias. In the small room, the beautiful mahogany music box, the sofa that Walter had left behind. What should I say about our possessions from among which we were going to be picked up, like criminals with no will of their own?

At 9:30 A.M. there was a loud knocking at the door. I opened up. Gestapo officers, with two Jewish helpers. Our hand luggage was taken away. I went with the men, who were perfectly polite, as they inspected all the rooms. They looked in the cabinets and asked if there was any food that might spoil. We hadn't left any behind.

I forgot the cash box with 100 Reich marks in it. It will make someone's day if they find it. The last minutes in our home.

The men urge us to leave. "It's time," they say. Without looking back, we go out. The door is locked and the keys surrendered to the caretaker, who is afraid to say good-bye.

There is a moving van parked in front of our building, and we climb up some steps in the back. The truck lumbers into motion. It has to pick up more passengers who, like us, are being evacuated. First, we go to Magdeburgerstrasse, then to Stettiner, toward Martin Luther Strasse. Frightened elderly people board at every stop, and we try to give them courage.

We even found a couple, [called] Brie, we often saw him in the hall, and as it happened, he knew Arnold Heilbut. At another apartment, it turned out that the man who was to be deported had taken his own life, which he evidently thought was the better choice.

We sat in silence. We had been driving around the western part of the city, and it was now three o'clock. Finally, we reached our destination for that day, the Jewish community's Old People's Home on Grosse Hamburger Street.[7] We were registered and assigned to rooms.

We arrived too late for lunch, and it wasn't until evening that a [food] ration was handed out. After the day's excitement, we fell asleep early, wanting to wake up reasonably alert the next day. We were cut off from the world, not allowed to go outside or send any more mail.

From the back windows we could see ancient graves with weathered, half-sunken stones. The obelisk of Moses Mendelssohn's grave rose high behind its railings as a call not to despair.[8]

Later, as I walked down the corridor, I had a most affecting and stirring reunion. Mrs. Oberländer, my good mother's unforgettable nurse, saw me and took me in her arms. I cried inconsolably, releasing all of my pent-up emotions for the first time. In my mind's eye, I saw Lichterfelde, where I had so often spoken with this gracious woman, asking her to do a favor for Mother. She always consoled the severely suffering, broken woman, and held her lovingly in her arms.

The door to my mother's beloved room opened before me, and I saw her in her armchair. All that I had guarded so carefully was now forever scattered to the wind. I often sat on that chair that we kept in the little room, to collect myself, to reflect. [...] A reunion such as this can be both moving and upsetting. Emotions erupt like lava that was locked inside because we couldn't control it. Fixed and steady on the outside; in the dark hours of the night, we can cry by ourselves, the tears falling slowly.

The old people's home has become a beehive. Down below all the hand luggage and suitcases that we had been allowed to keep piled up. Policemen and Gestapo officers were everywhere. We did not know what awaited us, when or how the journey would continue.

Previously, we had trembled in the large room at the synagogue on Lützowstrasse when we heard about evacuations—of the long march through the freezing cold or rain to the remote station at Grunewald.[9] How arduous it was for the elderly to drag themselves along; they panted under the unaccustomed strain. We had heard of cattle cars, where large vats were used when nature called. There was talk of being crammed into open cars in temperatures that were well below zero. Questions went back and forth. Everyone had questions or claimed to have news from the most reliable of sources. But the leader could only tell us to remain calm; we would reach our destination in a safe, orderly manner.

We wandered up and down; people stood in groups everywhere. One was surprised to meet an acquaintance; connections were discovered in conversations. I carefully read the plaques on the doors, honoring the sponsor who had given his name to a room. The plaques were often a hundred years old, and the whole row of famous Jewish families, whose grandchildren may have already been baptized, formed the list of "benefactors" engraved in stone.

The rooms had been stripped of any coziness. There was no traditional-style furniture to provide a safe setting for rest at the end of life's long journey. The comfortable upholstered chairs by the windows, once decorated with flowers in bloom, were gone. No wrinkled, dear faces now gazed down on the narrow street that leads from the north to Unter den Linden. Gone; all gone.

At the entrance below was a crush of people; those too frail to travel were being examined to determine whether they should remain behind. The head doctor paced gravely through the multitude, seeing no one, and deaf to any appeals.

✶　✶　✶

The food was good and plentiful. On the last day, my favorite dish, broad beans, was served. Mrs. Oberländer, that good woman, gave me three portions, and with that I had, indeed, had enough.

In the afternoon our luggage was searched. I could safely have brought my fountain pen; the fingers of the officials did not search too deeply. They were quite humane, and even made some little jokes. Then, the meeting with the officials of the Jewish community, to whom we signed over our bank accounts.

In another room, we were given the official written notification that our property was to be confiscated because of "communist activity." We accepted this humiliation in silence. Then, we were supposed to hand over our watches. I kept mine. Our passports were stamped "Evacuated from Berlin on July 23." With that, our life as citizens in Germany ended.

Now, there was only one formality left: the departure. We were finished with the authorities. In the afternoon we were told to be ready early the next day. Wake-up call at three o'clock, drink a coffee, and get ready for the departure.

We went to bed early. But sleep did not come for a long time. The agitation of the previous days' events was still churning. Events replayed in my mind like a movie.

And I dreamed of everything that we had lived through in the last years. The children appeared before us, protectively, wanting us to go with them. My parents called out not to forget them or leave them alone. I did not know what to do to fend off strangers who wanted to tear us apart. I took a gun and hammered away with the butt. The blow hit. I heard the sound of it and woke up. Outside in the corridor, the knocking from door to door: "Three o'clock. Get up!" Still tired and sleepy, we roused ourselves. It was the dawn of our last day in our homeland.

When we were ready, we had hot coffee, and there was still plenty of bread left. We filled our bags with our odds and ends. Soon the call came: "Come down for the departure!"

On the stairs, we were given sandwiches. Mrs. Oberländer was downstairs, shaking our hands and speaking a kind word to each of us. Outside, the new day was dawning. It was raining.

Calm and silent, we left the building that for two nights had been our last home. The foliage of the trees in the cemetery greeted us through the open gate. *Moses Mendelssohn, there below the earth—that at first did not want to receive you, which honored your departure from this life as befits a prince of the spirit—my last thoughts were of you.*

Policemen blocked the streets and led our sad procession to Monbijou Platz. Over on the right was the cheery little palace, a jewel preserved from the time of Friedrich the Great. Over there, I suddenly realized, stood the old house in which we took dance lessons: the Friedberg boarding school.

We boarded the waiting tram. It followed a route that was, for me, like the Stations of the Cross. Hackescher Markt. I saw Seemannstrasse in the gray dawn. Neue Promenade, Kronprinzenbrücke, Museumsinsel, Singakademie, the University, […] Hedwigskirche, 10 Werderscher Markt, our old house. Dönhofplatz, Krausen Strasse, Jerusalemstrasse. There, in front of the Scherl publishing house, Eva and I had waited for the bus. Kochstrasse, Wilhemstrasse, the Anhalter station.

We boarded without needing to show a ticket. The first platform on the right. A mountain of luggage. Everything had to be stowed in the exits and aisles. The young helpers formed a line to quickly load the suitcases.

We found a place for eight in a compartment. Outside, other passengers glanced at us and quickly moved on. We were not allowed to be at the window; we had to stay inside, although we would have liked to have seen if, perhaps, any of our friends had come. No one dared.

Oh, great hall, who has seen me a thousand times and more, now you cast an old customer out into the unknown, as a consignment, a slave, expelled from the society in which we had been allowed to live, protected by law, undisturbed.

Now there are no more rights and laws, only steely power, and with a stroke of the pen our citizenship was extinguished. We were cast out of the lives that we made for ourselves, working for 50 years to see our business crowned with success. Our property was taken, and now here we are with the few effects that we can carry with us in bags and backpacks.

A lurch, and we were on our way.

Karlsbad [south of the Tiergarten], Lüzowstrasse, and Yorckstrasse greet us on the right. The old, familiar names glide by, my beloved Lichterfelde.

My thoughts flew toward the quiet square out there at Weissensee,[10] shaded by a thick overhang of willow trees, stalwart and green, and covered with the mighty bushes of sedum, which guard the sleep of my parents. *You, my loved ones, I can no longer visit you.* How I would have liked to have laid my head on that sturdy trunk and wept, to rinse the pain from my soul! That would indeed have been the bitterest parting. I would have had to make my way by foot, there and back, since vehicles were forbidden to us. But walking would have been impossible after the physical exertion of the week.

On Sunday I could only lie and rest, in order to be fit for work again on Monday. As little conversation as possible, only sleep. The calm atmosphere on our balcony did me good. The green vine and the towering trees enclosed our quiet kingdom, and its peace was only rarely interrupted. The neighbors took it upon themselves to turn down their radios. But visitors could not be refused. They "did not want to disturb" but did, in fact, take away my rest. And, oh, how quickly seven o'clock came, when I had to prepare myself for the night!

The steeple of the red church greeted us. We left behind the familiar stretch just past Lichterfelde and turned left toward Dresden. Now I was no longer interested in the view. I turned to my colleagues in the compartment.

There were Mr. and Mrs. Brie. Mr. Lippmann, a senior government-planning official with his wife and daughter, introduced himself. There was also another lady.

We men began a conversation: One wanted to know what was going to happen. Opinions were exchanged. We agreed to paint our future life as plainly and simply as imagination permits. Not the comfort of the Old People's Home, but a "camp" with all those attributes: confinement, filth, dejection, and imprisonment.

But Theresienstadt had been described to us as a paradise—for which our fortunes had been sacrificed. That was what people had said in the small room where a table had been set up for officials of the Jewish community. They persuaded those being deported to transfer their property and bank balances to the community. They told us that on the next day everything would be seized by the State and could only be saved by transferring it immediately. The community would secure these endangered assets and put them to good use. One enthusiastically signed the forms and left the room with a good feeling.

Now I owned nothing. My account at the Dresdner Bank no longer existed. I had never taken the monthly 300 Reich marks. I wanted to save it to live on until the end of the war. As long as I was employed by Petkowitsch[11] and earning my weekly 60 Reich marks gross, I had enough to get by and did not need to withdraw money from my account. I sometimes earned a bit extra, and so did not need to skimp. But what could one spend in Berlin anyway, since all food was rationed, and the Jews were barred from making almost any purchase and allowed only the barest essentials of life?

While I had the afternoons off, I went shopping at the food market. Everything cost pennies, and for a couple of marks one could buy so much that it was difficult to carry it home alone. Recently, the market only sold food like potatoes, carrots, lettuce, and I occasionally got given something extra. The delicious prepared salads that we had had during the winter, which helped us to stretch the evening meal, had long ago disappeared from the markets.

Our friendly fishmonger—I wonder how he is doing?—mostly stood before empty barrels. Pickles were a rarity, and even mustard was scarce. Red cabbage was available maybe twice in the winter and only when you got given one secretly. Only the bread rolls called "cobbler's apprentices" were saved for us by the baker. They tasted wonderful in the evenings and provided a nutritious meal. We did all right with the bread ration, because Mama knew how to divide it up so that we were never without.

After Lichterfelde, the train turned and took us along the Doberlug-Dresden route. *You, thoughts, do not conjure up those years.* I had traveled for the company to the capital of Saxony, with lampshades for Friedlaender, and stayed at the ancient "Stadt Halle" hotel on Schlossbergstrasse. My father had recommended it, because he had stayed there when he was young. Dresden, the city that I loved, because it offered me so much that was beautiful!

*   *   *

The train rushed across the plains. In the carriage we were not talkative; we were consumed by our own thoughts, which were difficult enough. After two hours the hills of Kötzschenbroda appeared. Soon we saw the houses of Dresden-Neustadt, where we stayed in the station for almost two hours on a siding.

We were not allowed to leave the car, which was being guarded by the Schupo.[12] The promised warm food did not materialize. An attempt to drop postcards into a mailbox failed. Departure. The passenger train slowly churned into motion. We crossed the Augustus Bridge, saw once more the panoramic bank of the river Elbe, the Hof Church, the Church of the Cross, the opera house. A quick glance at Schlossstrasse, the Hotel de l'Europe—the first stop on our honeymoon.

Gone, gone. The suburbs, with their gardens, passed by. Then the Elbe on the left, which would accompany us along the entire route.

Over there, Schandau, situated below the foothills of the mountains, greeted us. Sendig Hotel, the two four-sided towers that flanked the buildings. We stayed in the one on the right on our honeymoon. Mama and I looked out the window, took each other's hand, and stared at the place where we were so happy.

The massive fortress of Königstein emerged. The mountains moved closer together, the Elbe narrowed. All the famous names of Saxon Switzerland are evoked here, the grotesque forms of the Elbe sandstone mountains, the border. Today, there is no border anymore.

But now we have left the old German soil. We are in a strange land. Small places soaring high in the mountains. Beautiful, the varied contours of the wooded heights. The area was charming, with flowers and fruit, the darkness of the tops of the forests. Leitmeritz—we would soon be at our destination.

After a few minutes, a small station: Bauschowitz-Theresienstadt.

Part 1

1942

On July 23, Berlin transport I/29 arrived at Bauschowitz. The 100 passengers were lined up three abreast. Young people wearing stars carried the luggage for those who could not. The suitcases were loaded onto cars, as were, in the end, the disabled. Those of us who were fit enough to walk, slowly started down a street that led through a nice, clean neighborhood. There, for the first time, we saw Czech signs next to German ones. The residents paid no attention to the passersby; after several months, they were used to the sight. It was a hot day, and we soon felt the weight of our backpacks. Our hands were full holding our bags, and walking was increasingly laborious. The chain of people stretched out. Soon the guides urged us to hurry. "Look over there. The red roofs, rising over the dark green of the trees, are the barracks of Theresienstadt. We're almost there." But the road wound and snaked quite a lot, and every additional 100 meters of the unfamiliar walk was a torment. The Czech country police, in their neat uniforms, were indifferent to us, though they seemed to have sympathy for the plight of us older people. No angry word was uttered, despite our snail-like pace.

At last, like magic, we saw walls and ditches straight ahead. That such a fortress should still exist—almost 200 years old, well preserved, the masonry like new; the deep, wide ditches of the ramparts, lush green underneath! Then the walls came closer together, meeting above a narrow passage guarded by inhabited casemates, the Bauschowitz gate. We passed through, unsuspectingly. Now, Theresienstadt—the ghetto, our new home—took us in. As we walked, we saw well-dressed people, pretty young women, and happy children on the streets.

One could live here, we thought. It seemed that we had not been lied to in Berlin, when the community officials spoke of the "paradise of Theresienstadt" and congratulated us because we had been privileged to come here instead of being sent to Lublin.

The street went on forever.

Still no end to the torment. Dusk falls. Then our guides cried out—we have reached our destination: the Aussig barracks.

We hear the word: *Schleuse.*[1]

We didn't understand. We were received into a semicircle of casemates, from which sloping passages led upwards. They broadened out into impressive, wide, long rooms with walls that seemed to be a meter thick. Tables: on one side the gendarmes; on the other, us. Now the *Schleuse* began. We understood quickly what it meant, and watched, shuddering, as the experienced hands searched every bag, backpack, and basket, taking away every valuable item. Medicine; scissors; blade sharpeners; and, to our horror, carefully filled thermos flasks—cognac, the last strengthening reserve; chocolate; and cookies—all disappeared in a flash.

With fearful hearts we sat on the few narrow benches, waiting to see where our exhausted, broken bodies could finally come to rest. If only we could lie down, stretch out, and sleep! No feelings of hunger or thirst, just sleep. Suddenly again, a command: "Take your things. Now, into your quarters."

So we marched again. *This is how it must be, we are prisoners. We have no choice but to obey.* Everyone got ready, painfully slowly; our luggage, now lighter, was picked up, and in the last gray of a day that was so long and painful for us, we stumbled outside into the street. We saw low, single-story houses; mighty squares of barracks; a beautiful church set on an open square; and, again, houses—but no other people. Then, we stood in front of the gate of one of the barracks. We passed through it with the happy thought that perhaps we had reached our destination, finally, finally. We saw nothing more. We were shown to a first-floor room with some wooden bark stacked against the walls: our quarters for the night.

We did not question, we said nothing. We lay down immediately, still in our clothes, using our backpacks as pillows, covering ourselves with our coats. *Lie down, don't think, sleep.*

But the long-awaited sleep did not come quickly. We still trembled with the emotions of our difficult farewells. We had been separated from everything on which our life had been built. Ownership of property and money, to the last penny, had been put in the hands of strangers; we had gone abroad without so much as one coin left in our purses. The clever ones, however, had stashed bills in secure places so that later they could buy ghetto bread and artificial honey to improve the monotonous diet, as well as the hotly desired cigarettes (everything had its price, depending on the supply).

An electric bulb weakly illuminated the room, which had been whitewashed to create an impression of cleanliness. A refreshing breeze wafted in through the open windows as 50 of us slept fast and soundly. We did not feel the harshness of the accommodation, we lay there, left to our own thoughts that drifted ever further away, to our children...Oh! If they only knew that their old parents were stretched out here on the floor, covered by their coats, possessing nothing more than what they had carried with them! But then sleep, the great restorer, finally came and took me up into the great army of those who, for the first time, slept on the hard floor in a 200-year-old barracks, sunk into dreamless nonexistence.

✳   ✳   ✳

In July, daybreak comes early. Despite our exhaustion, the room stirred as soon as the dull light filled it. The natural needs of the body made themselves felt, demanding that we go out. Going outside was a journey of discovery—to find that quiet and secluded cell. Many gates opened onto the vast courtyard, and people of both sexes, drunk with sleep, seemed to know only one destination. I joined them and arrived at the latrines.

Lasciate ogni speranza...[2]

It was perhaps especially trying for the womenfolk to acclimatize, torn from their Berlin apartments and suddenly faced with the conditions in these barracks, which were perhaps modern in Maria Theresa's time. We men are familiar with this from our time in the military, and it doesn't put us out to be constantly in public, etc. The esthete, however, finds it difficult to stomach and endure, and wanders around despairingly. That does not help him. He must line up and wait his turn.

The sun had risen. We looked around the room. The older people were still lying in rows by the wall, and the middle of the room was filled with people lying down. We had been placed in a stable—this was clear from the mangers and hayracks that were built in at intervals and the iron rings for fastening the horses. And so the stable was now our home. It remained our home for the following week, which passed very quickly.

The camp routine began. The first difficulty: the morning wash. A few lucky people were in possession of a bowl, and those who managed to borrow one could wash at the fountain. We men were not embarrassed. We bared our chests and washed off the dust and sweat of the past three days, which had been such a great torment. A colorful life unfolded. Over on the other side there were approximately six stables, full of people who had been here for a longer period and had received their luggage. They aired their bedding upstairs in the arcades—it made a lively, many-colored picture, reminiscent of Italy.

We were told to get hot coffee from the kitchen counter, and, standing in line, this first offering of the ghetto proceeded quickly. We still had bread from Berlin, and so we breakfasted in the cool, fresh air, sitting comfortably on planks.

At nine o'clock, the bureaucratic machinery began turning. Lists were prepared in order to distribute ration cards and to send our personal data upstairs.

At ten o'clock, we were told to assemble; the block elder wanted to greet us and tell us the rules of conduct. A young, very handsome, well-dressed man introduced himself as Fritz Janowitz and spoke to us, as we listened earnestly. He described the ghetto, its institutions and authorities, the duties that awaited us, and what we could expect. He spoke to us with warm heartfelt words to give us courage—we should face all difficulties with some sense of humor to bring some lighter tones to the oppressive gray of our surroundings. Above all, we must have patience, patience, and more patience. The unfamiliar must be accepted. Unpleasantness, which could arise at any moment, could be overcome by arming oneself with indifference and assuming the proverbial thick skin.

The first rule for staying healthy, Mr. Janowitz advised, was to not drink water from the fountain, but to save some morning coffee instead. For the time being, we were confined to the barracks. We were not allowed to go out, but the courtyard offered plenty of space. And now, we should use the next few days to settle in. We had full board, and everything we received was gratis, so there was nothing to worry about.

And with that, he said, "God bless you."

This speech was repeated in each of the four stables. Afterwards, groups of people stood around everywhere, animatedly discussing and analyzing what we had just heard. [...] The inhabitants of the stables across the way, all old people who had formerly been residents of Stettin, Kassel, and Hamburg, came to make the acquaintance of their new neighbors, to ask for news of the outside world, and to tell us about how things worked in the ghetto.

Sitting in the warm sun was very pleasant. Sitting peacefully for the first time, one could finally be alone to gather and organize one's thoughts and try to arrive at clarity, and get a glimpse into the future. One had to remind oneself that it would be days before the authorities registered and filed everything, because allegedly there were [...] people in the ghetto.[3] It was, therefore, understandable that we would have to wait quietly until we were moved to the old people's homes. Then we would see.

The morning crept by slowly, like the shadows on the buildings across the courtyard. The atmosphere was lively; the narrow staircases were full of people carrying their briefcases importantly, who had business in the offices upstairs. The two small neighboring courtyards had nothing special to offer, and did not entice one to stay. Where to sit? There were no benches or chairs anywhere—only woodpiles afforded an uncomfortable opportunity to rest. If they were all occupied, one had to wander about, waiting for a chance to sit. People tried to squeeze into the small area around the two trees, which were each approximately 30 meters tall. Men and women were still lined up, waiting to complete their morning toilette. This was the one opportunity several hundred people had to wash themselves; hence, the business took until lunchtime. Oh, delicious word: lunchtime.

Yesterday, we had waited in vain for a hot meal at the station in Dresden, expecting it to be served by the [Jewish] community as usual, but we were unlucky—there was nobody in sight. The deserted platform was patrolled by an armed guard, who walked gravely up and down. We could see down Pragerstrasse, Dresden's main shopping street, where I had so often walked in the past decade. Every house seemed to wave at us like an old friend, and the Hotel de l'Europe seemed to ask, "So, why don't you come back to me?"

It was lunchtime. Our stomachs had already rumbled for a while. Being outdoors in the fresh air makes one hungry and full of anticipation. We lined up on the second floor, which was equipped with two pots, one for soup and one for a stew. It was 20 minutes before we were all served. We moved forward with the steaming bowls, went back to our woodpiles, and, under the lovely sun, ate our first meal in the ghetto.

We could not claim that we were sated, but we still had bread from Berlin and we ate that for "dessert." In the cool stables people took a comfortable afternoon nap—of course, the flies were a mighty nuisance, and it was never really quiet because it was so crowded, but the coolness of the thick, stone walls made the hour's rest feel quite refreshing.

In the afternoon we received our ghetto transport number, the importance of which we only realized much later. The numbers given to us in Berlin were canceled and replaced by the Roman numerals I–XXIX. We would live and die under this designation from now on. No document was without the main number and our personal identification number. Mine was 2215, i.e., the number of people who had arrived in the ghetto from Berlin.

[…]

Our luggage and identity cards had to be re-labeled. After this formality, we were full-fledged ghetto inmates.

The afternoon went by quickly. We received three days' worth of bread rations and thought about what the safest way to store it might be. We had nothing; our backpacks were the only possible place we could store something. At night they served as hard pillows, although that would change since we were supposed to get our luggage the next day, affording us a little more "comfort," and reminding us of home when we would fall asleep and could slip under the blanket that had given us its protection since our wedding. The "evening meal" consisted of coffee, with which we ate bread.

Already, we had a worrying grievance—the bread was not dry enough because producing it for such a huge number of people did not allow enough time for it to settle. It became moldy. When it was cut open, green flecks of mold, reaching deep inside the bread, were revealed. True, the moldy bread could be exchanged, but that involved a lot of running around and endless waiting. And you would not receive the right quantity.

The Berlin bread donated from the [Old People's Home on Grosse] Hamburger Strasse was finished. Now we had to be careful with our ration and try not to consume it according to our appetite, for it was only every three days that we got our beloved bread.

[...]

The bread ration was increased automatically once one started working and then again if one were promoted to the category of "hard laborer." But this privilege was only for the young, not for us, who for the most part were over 65 years old. Also, the other allocations increased accordingly for the laborers.

The sun went down in a cloudless sky, turning the day pleasantly cool. There were many groups in the courtyard, eagerly discussing the news of the day. The right side[4] could go out freely, and they heard all kinds of things about the outside world from new transports who had just arrived. Reshaped by the go-betweens, the news came in, more or less distorted, depending on the temperament of the narrator. But it was nevertheless a lifting of the curtain, a chink in the wall that separated us and cut us off [from the outside world]. *Let us first really settle in, and then we will also have rights, after all, we are in the ghetto, in the Jewish city, that is intended to be an old people's home for us.*

Every day brings newcomers; they all want to be initiated—impress upon yourselves the word from the morning speech: patience.

One gets tired from doing nothing. The old people were already asleep inside the stables. A nurse made the rounds, asking if anyone was in need of help, and administered longed-for sleeping powder, valerian drops, and, where necessary, a consoling word. And that, especially, did a lot of good.

The moon rose over the high and mighty roof of the barracks and brightly lit the square. No more light anywhere before the vast expanse. Here and there, a stable inmate strayed to the second courtyard, obeying an urge and not his own will. Inside, in a corner, a conversation was under way. I stretched out next to my wife. A squeeze of her hand, a goodnight kiss—these things convinced me that we still slept together.

I woke up at 4:30 A.M. I was used to getting up at this exact time in Berlin, on the dot, and to be alert, in order to be in the changing room of the F. Butzke factory at ten minutes to six, ready to change into the blue overalls. [...] I sprang up, horrified. Had I overslept? Would I be late?

A glance at my surroundings told me that I could calm down and lie down again, which I did more than gladly—in Berlin, unfortunately, I didn't get enough sleep for months at a time, even if I went to bed at 8 P.M. on the dot.

[...]

I couldn't rest for more than an hour—I was grateful for that much—because the room became active. Two very old women who had spent the night on the floor, completely helpless, called out for help. They were 82 and 86 years old and mentally sound, but it was only with assistance and effort that they were able to get out into the open to sit in the sun for a few hours.

The first job on getting up was to get hold of a washbowl, for the necessary cleansing. For eight days we had gone without our usual bath—when would we be able to climb into a bathtub here? How long would we have to loaf around in the courtyard, which had already become too small for us, with nothing to do, counting the arcades, conducting useless conversations? When, how, and would we ever find our way back to a civilized life?

In the midst of these musings, the seventh hour drew near, when people would make their pilgrimage to the second floor, where the steam of the mighty kettle wafted out of the windows in thick clouds, announcing, "The coffee is hot."

*   *   *

Again, a hot day. Really, the weather stayed the same for months. It never rained. No thunderstorms brought a much-needed freshening of the air, but we were tormented by endless clouds of dust. The courtyard, which was paved only at the edges, not in the middle, remained the wind's playground. It came from on high to lead its swirling dance and often seemed to carry the dust of hell. When food was given out, there was nothing pleasant about any of this.

The kitchen was up on the second floor. The food was distributed at six improvised booths. Two strong young men brought the soup down in huge buckets—potatoes, noodles, barley in wooden troughs—whatever was on the menu.

When dumplings or *buchtel* (it took us a long time to figure out the difference) were served, runny margarine and sugar were added. Oh, the beautiful *buchtel*, filled with plum jam! How delicious they were! They were large, and when they were given out with coffee as the evening meal, they could almost silence our hunger. We never had them in the following year. Filled *buchtels* were reserved for the summer months of 1942.

There was great excitement in the afternoon: We were going to receive our luggage. A truck drove up, and the distribution began promptly. The owner's name and transport number had been written or sewn onto the luggage in Berlin, so delivery proceeded quickly. With thumping hearts, we all waited to hear whether our name would be called. We saw our bedrolls on the truck, tied up with broad straps, and tried to stay calm in the crowd that feverishly waited for names to be called.

Finally, finally, our bedrolls were handed to us. They seemed intact, and when we opened them, it turned out that the cords had stayed tight, and our only remaining property was secure.

Now we could sleep comfortably in our pajamas, use hand towels, and sleep under the blankets that we had had all our lives: These things are the essence of what a bedroom means in someone's life, varied in shape and form and full of change. Silently, we caressed our lavender duvet with the white cover, our white flannel blanket, and the few other items. How well we would sleep tonight with these as our very close companions!

But we waited in vain for our suitcases containing our linens, undergarments, clothing, books, and the many small things that we had wondered whether to take, and then packed on that difficult last Sunday in Berlin.

[...]

We fearfully asked where the suitcases were. And every day we repeated this tormenting question until we could no longer find the courage to ask it. Our remaining possessions, which we had brought under orders from the authorities, were never returned to us. A year later, one of my bunk mates bought a good shirt in a store—it had my name sewn into it.

Not all of the transports went like this. The people from Hamburg, who had left with an abundance of luggage, received all of theirs intact. Some comrades could successfully apply for a search and delivery of their luggage if they had suffered severe war injuries. That did not apply to me.

And so, during these hot months I had to wear uncomfortable, heavy, winter trousers that were appropriate for cold temperatures of minus 20–30 degrees, and they were the only ones I had. Only later, when I held office, was pity taken on me [and I received lighter ones].

[...]

Unemployed. This word weighed heavily on me, spoiling a beautiful, hot July day. The women could fill the time with chores. There was the room to clean, dishes to wash and dry, and sewing to do. My wife looked after the old and the sick. She saw to it that they received all they were entitled to, and offered them consolation and kind words of comfort.

I had established contacts in the nearby stables, and one afternoon—I no longer recall what possessed me—I asked the elderly people from Hamburg in stable number 13 if it would be all right if I passed the time by talking to them. They responded enthusiastically and brought me a little bench, and so, like the first rhapsodists, I spoke to my audience, who listened, enraptured.

After a few introductory words of hope and solace, I recalled the Hamburg of the years 1897–1898, one of the happiest periods of my interesting life.[5] I painted such a vivid picture of their beloved hometown that many reached for their handkerchiefs and wiped away a tear. Almost an hour went by before I finished. I had to promise to return the next day and speak again, on another topic.

The people from Berlin received me with the same pleasure, and I found enthusiastic and devoted listeners. I shared the memories of my youth, which went back to 1886, and events from the time of Kaiser Friedrich, when I had acted as messenger between my uncle Dr. Sam Schidrowitz, a reporter for the *Times* and the *Berliner Tageblatt* (Kaiser Wilhelm II also mentioned him in his book), and his friend Sir Morell MacKenzie,[6] who was the doctor caring for the Kaiser. Sir Morell MacKenzie sent reports to my father from the Charlottenburg Palace by pneumatic dispatch, and to confuse the spies, I took them to the Hotel Continental. However, here I will write about Theresienstadt, not my memories of almost fabled times.

After this I went around to all the stables in our courtyard and spoke to the inmates. I was happily engaged for four days, and the people asked for an encore. Then officialdom disturbed my idyll. Rabbi Albert Schön sent for me and said: "I listened to you yesterday and was delighted, but you are not allowed to do as you please so freely. Each lecture must be registered with the Leisure Time Organization.[7] Otherwise the authorities consider it a 'forbidden assembly' and punish the organizer and participants. You must bring your request to me in writing to Room 111. All lectures must be registered eight days in advance and then submitted to the commandant for 'approval.'" We shook hands and parted as good friends, and our friendship has lasted to this day.

[...]

At lunchtime and in the evening, Mr. Fritz Janowitz was always around. As the block elder he was in charge of organizing and cleaning the courtyards. He has to inspect the floors of the buildings himself to ascertain whether all the regulations decreed by the (ghetto) police and fire brigade had been scrupulously and thoroughly followed. At the same time, he is the judge when there had been any violations. He is authorized to hand out penalties of prison sentences—of up to eight days. Many authorities are brought together in his office, and [fulfilling] it requires an extraordinary level of knowledge and experience, calm and self-control, and an attitude toward the inmates that is peculiar to the ghetto, and can only be learned here.

I will say more about the problem of "Jews among themselves" later. Any of us who have been in the ghetto for a year and a half could sing a song about it, a discordant song that only rarely featured a melodious verse. Throughout my service I have been associated with so many people of all classes, from the Jewish elders to street sweepers and toilet cleaners, that I can tell a tale or two.

Now we were on the fourth or sixth day of our stay. We still knew nothing of ghetto life. We knew only the courtyard. Contact with the top was taken care of by the helpful Fritz Janowitz, who always had time to answer questions and helped us whenever he could.

In the courtyard, I noticed a small, young woman who, during the day, used a broom with great verve; every scrap of paper and dirt seemed to be a fierce enemy. In the afternoon, we sat together on the woodpiles and began to chat. She introduced herself as Dr. Weigert—previously Stettin—who had lived here for a while with her calm, thoughtful husband. Later she confided that she was the sister of Fritz Haber, the Nobel Prize winner and founder of the *Leunawerke* [Leuna works].[8]

It was through her that our first outing came about: She had a permit, and under her guidance, a group of about 15 people was allowed to tour Theresienstadt. Our hearts pounding, we passed through the gray gates of the barracks. We were checked by rigorous guards and asked for our identification cards, and then were outside. We looked down the street. At its end we saw mountains in the distance; its forests were easy to discern in the sunlight. The city was clearly constructed in the image of a Roman castrum.

Everything seemed made for the defense of the roads leading directly to the gates. The nearby barracks beyond [the gates] rose up to defend the inner city. The houses squeezed together below them almost seemed to be seeking protection. Large streets were indicated by L; the cross streets by Q plus the house number. Therefore Q603 indicated the sixth cross street leading out from the Jäger barracks. Our barracks are in L4 and cannot be missed unless one confuses them with the Dresdener barracks at the end of the street.

We proceeded slowly through the busy streets, which gave an impression of living conditions. The inmates spent the night on the floor; one seldom saw a bed. The only beds were in the rooms reserved for the sick, and they had loose, white covers. The wind blew clouds of dust through the L streets. It was no better in the market square with its beautiful, old official buildings—the tower-ing church with its grand staircase and massive, wooden portals; the town hall; the two command centers.

A small park, thick with chestnut trees, could only be circumvented, not tra-versed. We became acquainted with the other barracks: Hohenelbe, Bodenbach, and Aussig, and the wide, arched Sudeten barracks, which are more modern with long windows and a huge open courtyard. The small Jäger barracks are tucked away; the Hamburg [barracks] are in the center of the town; Hannover, yellow-ochre, across from us. The tour ended. As we went home, we saw two horses' heads, as an emblem above the gate. [...]

After the colorful, busy life outside, our courtyard felt like an oasis, so peace-ful in the light of the late afternoon sun. The old, sometimes very old people sat in the doorways, having traded something for a spot on a little bench, where they could sit and enjoy the peace. They no longer were required to work. For them, the extremely elderly, Theresienstadt really was an old people's home, even if one understood the concept of an "old people's home" somewhat differently back home. It is strange how quickly one was able to accept a fait accompli.

With the relinquishing of possessions, the divesting of all papers and docu-ments, and the transferring of bank accounts to the community, people were transformed. All worries about subsistence were gone. Without money, they had to think of themselves as prisoners serving a life sentence, whose only ambi-tion was to make this sentence as bearable as possible, to try to get more to eat, whether by straight or crooked means.

But this is a chapter unto itself, very grave and not simple at all. When I see the "orders of the day" that are issued every few days and form the link between the "administration" (which is the Council of Elders) and the ghetto; when I read the judgments of the Court for stealing, which ran from three days' deten-tion up to eight months of hard labor, then you would believe me that there is much that must be said in order to understand the impact of ghetto life on the individual.

One would like to believe that in the ghetto every Jew feels a sense of respon-sibility toward the other, sees him as a brother in the faith, someone to struggle for and to help, regarding him with friendship, accepting him, honoring his age, giving him precedence—in short to act as a *mensch* everywhere and at all times, and to respect this as the most important principle and to act on it—but no, that would be wrong. The court rulings and the experiences every day tell a different story.

Here in the barracks, we were still immune to all this. Life outside did not affect us. Each one sat on his own possessions. Those of us without a suitcase full of valuable things to call our own had no need to lock anything up.

There was still enough bread! Only when there is not enough do the dangers of covetousness come out. The elderly did not always eat their entire ration and gladly gave some of it away, and therefore, bread, the most valuable foodstuff, never ran out, and there was no [need] to buy or swap it. Later, when one could get it for money, a market developed. It became the measure of value for everything that one wanted to "purchase." For example, a woman's coat went for two to three loaves of bread, depending on [its] quality and condition.

One prohibition was especially painful and, in the lives of most of the men, deeply disruptive: no more smoking. No rule has been broken so often to this day as this one. The smuggling of cigarettes took remarkable forms, as several court trials attest. But despite higher penalties, large quantities of cigarettes came into the ghetto in parcels that escaped the eyes of the gendarmes, and were sold for a high price. I never smoked and was therefore not interested in this much-sought-after item. But the smokers simply could not live without cigarettes. They were not frightened by the threat of penalties and imprisonment. They had to have them. It is the bitter truth, what I write here. I often saw up to three men smoking a single cigarette together, passing the end from mouth to mouth. Then an entrepreneur created substitute cigarettes made from dried tea leaves and chestnut leaves or other tea surrogates that were later sold in grocery stores—but they [the smokers] continued smoking, whatever the price.

Then there was the prohibition against writing. It was not possible to write letters to anyone in the outside world. The heaviest of penalties would be imposed on whoever attempted it.

Otherwise, the ghetto had its own [Jewish] self-administration—its own court and police. We never noticed the German authorities; it was rare to see someone in uniform. Then we were required to remove our hats and salute every uniformed German and Czech on the street. That rule was strictly observed and regularly impressed upon us.

Since the camp commandant only dealt with the Jewish elder and his immediate colleagues or, from time to time, with the many specialized department heads, we never bore the burden of having to explain ourselves. Since the gendarmes attended to the trucks and transports, we saw them often. They also stood watch at gates and at arterial roads. [But] we seldom saw the field-gray SS uniform.

Another hot day had come to an end. It had brought us many new impressions, and extremely tired, we stretched out on our familiar bedding, which only reminded us of all we had lost.

Mild and refreshing, the quiet night was undisturbed. One soon stopped hearing the loud snorer who was sawing in the corner. The sleepers lay peacefully, knowing that they were in safe hands.

Orientation Service

We must now turn our attention to a man who can be described as the real founder and an inspiration. The block elder, Fritz Janowitz performed this activity. He became the block helper, and later the protector of the Orientation Service.[9]

[...]

As a student, he [Janowitz] joined the Blue/White youth organization and was part of its development.[10] This means that he was inclined toward Jewish nationalism, which is to say he felt fully "aware" as a Jew. Over the years, Fritz Janowitz worked his way up to become the head of the Jewish youth organization in Reichenberg. By 1922 he had already founded the [local] Makkabi Federation[11] and had accomplished constructive and far-reaching work with extraordinary success.

In 1931 his father's business was liquidated, and after its dissolution, Fritz Janowitz went to Prague to work as a sales manager and an organizer. In 1938 he got a job in Zurich. And then, events moved fast. Czechoslovakia mobilized. At this news, Fritz Janowitz immediately flew home to Prague, enlisted, and reported for duty on the same day. What happened next belongs to history. It goes without saying that Fritz Janowitz placed himself at the disposal of the Jewish community and was employed in youth welfare; later, he served with its emergency services carrying out their difficult and responsible work.

As the Theresienstadt project emerged, the Jewish community asked the question: Who would enlist in Theresienstadt voluntarily? On the understanding that their relatives would be protected from deportation to Poland and that they would later be reunited with their loved ones, Janowitz, along with Jacob Edelstein, Engineer Erwin Elbert, Dr. Rudolf Freiberger, Fredy Hirsch, Dr. Leo Janowitz, Captain Josef Klaber, Dr. Walter Löwinger, Engineer Otto Zucker, and others, enlisted. We will often encounter these men in these pages; they all play an important and meaningful role in the history of the ghetto.[12]

Altogether, 23 men created the first corps, and it was with them that the settlement of the fortress Theresienstadt began on November 24, 1941. [...] Those pioneers were called the "building commando." Fritz Janowitz received number 389.

On May 15, 1942, Fritz Janowitz was [...] told to prepare for a new job. He was assigned the position of block elder of the Magdeburg barracks, which housed all the administrative offices [of the Jewish self-administration]. At the beginning of June, Fritz Janowitz assumed the position that he holds to this day.

[...]

At the end of July, Fritz Janowitz came to me to ask whether I would be interested in and available for an auxiliary service, reporting to the head of the ghetto watch: I could find out more in Room 73. I agreed, gladly. Any job was fine with me—wherever they wanted to place me, I wanted to fill the position. I presented myself to the chief of police that afternoon.

Room 73 consisted of a small anteroom, and the office was about six by three meters in size. The boss, Mr. Kurt Frey,[13] sat at a narrow table. He was about 45 years old, very good-looking, with parted brown hair, good blue eyes, and a tight build, wearing a sleeveless leather jacket and trousers tucked into high, laced boots. Engaging, charming, speaking the somewhat strange-sounding German of a Prague native, he conferred with me and then gave me the assignment described below.

By August 1, I was to choose about 10 men who, under my leadership, would, on behalf of the ghetto watch, provide a daily service of helping people who were lost, finding out their *ubikation*[14] and then taking them home safely. Our office would be in the back room of the Magdeburg barracks that housed the ghetto watch, and all lost people would be brought to us there to be taken care of.

This seemed to me to be a very meaningful job, and I declared myself ready to take it on. I promised to put all my skills to use and to justify the trust he had placed in me. With a firm handshake, Mr. Frey formally appointed me to the office, introduced me to his immediate staff, and promised me every support.

Working once again, on a new project. I never imagined that, for the second time in my life, an external power would take possession of me and place me in its service. In 1915, I had been summoned in Kowel in Volhynia (railroad line Chelm, Lublin, Lemberg), a city once again being disputed today, to establish and manage the army field bookstores of the Linsingen Army Group.[15]

In 1942, I now had a similar assignment, also serving the public. My earlier service lasted until March 1919. Who, today, could predict how long the second post would last? In both cases, I was approached and recommended by outsiders: back then, by a doctor in the military hospital in which I found myself, and here, by Fritz Janowitz.

Choosing the men was not difficult. I went through stables 60, 61, and 62 and gathered the men from Berlin. Twelve came forward to volunteer, and I accepted them regardless of their age.

[...]

At 8 A.M. on August 1, we moved into our office, which had just enough room for us to sit on the beds. Aside from us, an official from the lost and found worked there. So there were many people always coming and going. It was like a beehive, our new office, which had not even a table in it.

The first hour went by quietly. We talked to each other about what we had lived through in the last months. At 9:30 A.M. the door opened, and a ghetto watch led in two trembling, crying women: *lost*.

We had to try to calm them down so that we could question them. "We went for a walk and wanted to go home and then couldn't find our house. All the streets look the same. We looked for a long time; we are exhausted, we can't go on. Our relatives will be worried if we don't come home." And the tears flowed.

They had neither their papers nor their *ubikation*. So their particulars were noted and taken to the registry. There, it was not difficult to obtain the necessary information.

But woe betide us if the lost person was a Kohn, Cohn, Meyer, Meier, or Müller or our information was wrong. Then we had to inquire at *ubikations* to ascertain the right one. This time we were lucky. Everything worked out, and two men set out with our charges. We asked the ghetto watch for a map of Theresienstadt and found the shortest route. That afternoon, the ever-helpful Fritz Janowitz took the twelve of us on an excursion through Theresienstadt to explain the city—its buildings and forbidden streets—and to lead us through practice exercises using the map. Now we were ready.

It was two days before it became popular knowledge in Theresienstadt that our service had been established. Then the influx began to swell, and days on end passed without a quiet hour. After a week, my staff were familiar with the work, and no cases were so difficult that they caused us upset.

Two types of people came our way: the normal and the crazy. We were quickly done with the first type if the registry had their identification cards. Then we could quickly resolve their awkward situation.

But the others! One singular case stood out in my memory. One afternoon, a well-dressed woman who seemed about 50 years old was brought in. She didn't know where she belonged. She gave her name, birth date, and place of birth right away. The information was passed to the registry—my man did not return for an hour, when he finally reported that no information [about the woman] could be found. What to do? We renewed our questioning, getting the same answers.

A female on duty was asked to search the woman and found her name and address sewn into her shirt. It was completely different from what she had told us. Laughing, the woman admitted that her name was not what she had said it was. It made her happy that that we had to go to so much trouble—that's what we were there for. She sat at the table, smiling, enjoying herself like a thief after a successful caper. When we brought her home, we discovered that she was a poor insane woman who often did things like this. She was not at all dangerous, though, and therefore had not been put in a psychiatric ward.

Mentally ill people were often brought to us. In such cases we called a doctor for help, who let the experts deal with it. Finding accommodation for the bad cases was not easy. The psychiatric ward would not accept anyone unless we could provide all their data. When we were not able to determine the mentally unstable person's name and the physical examination yielded nothing, we had to keep them overnight.

By nine o'clock each morning, the block elders had to provide the police with a list of people who were missing, which usually shed some light on the mystery. Or, at night, a nurse from the psychiatric ward might come in, wringing her hands, to ask if we had her patient. Or, parents might come in looking for their mentally deficient daughter. We were able to help most of them.

Still, there were cases where help came too late because the missing people had thrown their lives away. In late autumn, an old woman was brought to us [...]. She could not walk and wore nothing but a thin summer dress and shoes. She carried a cane with a pretty, silver, curved end, indicating that she belonged to the upper classes, and held it tightly, not letting it out of her hands. We quickly wrapped her in a blanket, served her hot coffee, and lay her down on a mattress. After a while she came to and was able to whisper her name, but said no more.

That evening, she eagerly ate some soup and went to sleep. The doctor could not do anything. When I looked in on her at six o'clock the next morning, I found her dead. She still held the cane tightly in her right hand. The investigation revealed that she had escaped from the delousing facility, and so had come to this terrible end. She had no relatives here, and since she had died while in our care, we attended her funeral.

Every day I reported the day's cases to our boss, Mr. Frey, and received advice from him rather than instructions. He said we should wear an armband to identify ourselves as public officials. But we still did not have a name. We thought it over and found a name that expressed our purpose: Orientation Service. The name stayed, and we came to be known by that name in Theresienstadt. We have kept it to this day, in spite of the later official name change [to auxiliary service of the ghetto watch]. The name became popular, even more so during the winter when we took over the service at the information desk of the post office.

Obviously, we had to be out and about day and night and, accordingly, were issued special permits. In the summertime, one was only allowed to be outdoors until nine o'clock, and in the winter until eight. The curfew had to be observed most carefully, and there were penalties for those who were in violation. At my request, the head of the mess, Mr. Ernst Pollatschek, authorized me to serve lunch or dinner (from 12 to 2 the registry was closed[16]) to people who had lost their way, who had not eaten and had to spend several hours with us. Coffee was also available.

Two men and a woman took advantage of our hospitality. They came at lunchtime acting very exhausted, and we hastened to give them refreshment. But when their names continued to reappear on our lists, we figured out their trick and shooed them away.

A member of the Council of Elders, Mr. Heinrich Stahl, the 70-year-old former eminent head of the Berlin Jewish community, was very interested in our organization. He spoke with me several times about the service, about the personnel, and asked me not to hire only people from Berlin. The administration wanted the Orientation Service to take on men from all over; so that it would not become one-sided, Czech speakers should also be recruited.

It was a difficult situation, but the boss solved it by "ordering" that six men from Berlin be dismissed and suitable replacements found. The order was carried out, and the six left. They were replaced by men from Brünn, Cologne, Prague, Minden, Vienna, and Hamburg. [...] By mid-August we totaled 16 men.

A new issue arose that needed to be tackled. Of our 40 to 60 daily cases, two-thirds were women. They needed to be examined and cared for; one could not just take them home. The older people were often without relatives, had no friends, felt lonely and abandoned, and clung to the one woman who helped them, who happened to be my wife. From the first, I called on her to help when it was needed, and she stood by, always available. But now the demand exceeded her capacity, and I had to get more help.

[...]

When the influx of strays diminished, the women's section dedicated itself to caring for the elderly and the sick. They took on the task of shopping for the Genie[17] barracks and other *ubikations* and gave help and comfort to those being transported [to the east]. The ladies were active all day, without supervision, and we trusted them completely; they were answerable only to themselves. The system proved itself, and I was never disappointed.

The ladies were also happy in their work. They were aware that their endless acts of mercy were sometimes lifesaving. In August and September 1942, the large, properly organized authority that is now responsible for the overall care for this vulnerable population did not yet exist. All kinds of small groups were active; that's why mine so quickly won prestige and significance.

One might ask why I only mention the "ladies." Because they were indeed ladies, inside and out, in contrast to the so-called helpers who, when they were recruited to assist at the transports, often grossly and reprehensibly abused the trust placed in them. [...]

"Ghetto" signifies a renunciation of or a moratorium on morals. It is completely self-evident that in this place, which in peacetime hosted 2,689 civilians
and 7,014 military in the barracks, and which is now crammed with 45,000 people,
the most crass egoism and an almost animal willfulness must break through.

When hunger triumphed over civilized behavior and tore down all inhibi-
tions, everyone gave themselves to one feeling and one goal: satiation at any
price. Justice and security, property and order simply yielded to this natural
instinct.

Those who have not witnessed how, at the end of the distribution of food,
old people plunged into empty vats, scraping them out with their spoons, even
scraping the tables where the food was served with knives, looking for leftovers,
cannot understand how quickly human dignity can be lost.

[…] Illustration: An excerpt from the camp orders of [ ]: sentenced a man to
six months in prison under harsh conditions. They convicted him of embezzling
watches and valuables entrusted to him by 25 ghetto inmates. […] Sentenced to
prison for five days, with harsh conditions: The convicted man had stolen about
50 decagrams of bread.

[…] The punishment was justified, because as we all knew, since the camp
rules were announced often enough, that having such possessions was punish-
able. Anyone who owned forbidden valuables must suffer the consequences.
That there were still people who reported such incidents to the police falls under
the category of "moratorium on morality."

✳   ✳   ✳

The summer remained beautiful and dry. I cannot remember any rainy days.
The dust was a dreadful scourge. Our courtyard suffered from it, since from
6 P.M. to 8 P.M. it was used as a soccer field. A thousand people stood around,
and both stories of the arcades were crowded with spectators. The young people,
of both sexes, let their legs dangle, happily following the game for two hours.
Roaring applause when a goal was scored, whistling and shouting when the game
did not go their way. The crowd chanted, "Tempo, Tempo," when the game
was boring. These were Czech teams showing their skills on the hard, unyield-
ing ground. Beautiful young people who worked hard during the day, and yet
gladly and eagerly devoted themselves to their beloved game in the evenings.
Such gatherings provide the best opportunity to form an unbiased judgment of
the Jews in the ghetto.

Neither here nor in my many walks in the streets did I see types described
in every issue of *Der Stürmer*.[18] The people from Czechoslovakia, some of

whom had been in the country for 100 years, had assimilated. I never saw so many beautiful, healthy, well-built men and women as here among the Jews in Theresienstadt. Their luminous eyes, high foreheads, straight noses, lean figures, like fir trees, free and confident demeanors, distinguished them, to their advantage, from the Jews from the German cities. The older men also exhibited the same characteristics; they were not in the least like Jews as they are portrayed in certain [anti-Semitic] quarters. Not to mention the children.

I had never encountered such independence. Three-year-olds already gave such assured answers to questions, as if they already had a point of view. Watching the young people playing was a joy; they were capable, brave, and courageous, with quick resolve and flashing eyes—that could quickly flash with anger. No matter where they came from in the whole of Bohemia, they showed no outward signs of a Jewish origin. They are endearing in their liveliness, but it is hard to get to know them. They shy away from the Germans. Until now I have not succeeded in having a conversation with one of the older boys. In the huge melting pot of Theresienstadt it is extremely interesting for the cool observer to see which nationalities achieve the longest resistance to prison psychosis. I believe that I can safely say from experience that it is the Czechs, then those from Berlin; the Viennese have the weakest resistance.

Whoever works hard and does not count the hours will make it through—unless he catches an infectious illness. Those who have too much free time to think will deteriorate. Whoever expects to work, who knows he will be needed and will be used—will not call in sick with every minor illness. Theresienstadt also demands from us older ones our effort and the contribution of all our strength. This is the only way for us to stay on top—activity is the only healing medicine.

Rumors suddenly spread throughout the courtyard that the stables would be vacated, that our nomadic life would come to an end and we would be settled in *ubikations*. All at once we grew to love our stables, our resting places on the floor, even though they were so cramped. The fresh, night air, the nearby fountain, the convenient proximity to the distribution of food, everything that had seemed so unpleasant and degrading, we now held on to, unwilling to give it up. But it was no use. It was announced the next day that we would be resettled in house Q211. The stables were to be taken over by the ghetto watch, and there was nothing we could do to stop it.

We now called our stable number 60 "paradise," from which we would be expelled, in exchange for the hell of a dirty, old, crowded house. The house was described in the bleakest of terms, and that did not help. The younger people of the Transport Department appeared with their carts, loaded up our luggage, and brought it to the rooms of the house. The people from stable 60 were assigned to a large, bright room, located in the front, opposite the right wing of the Hannover barracks.

Then, our first personal tragedy: We were separated from our wives. Men and women had to live and sleep separately. It did not help to protest. It was the commander's orders. And with that *basta* or, as they say here, "It's done." [...]

One could create privacy by piling up luggage or suitcases, *if* one had been fortunate enough to have them returned. In this manner one achieved a small, private kingdom, about 70 centimeters wide. The middle of the room was occupied by a row of people with suitcases piled high behind them. They were the people from the Protectorate or the Rhineland, who had their suitcases. They were lucky—they had everything they needed and could change their underwear, while if we washed our shirts we had to wait in the sun for them to dry.

[...]

My pleasure was boundless when Mr. Frey gave me a bench for two, professionally made by a carpenter, and I finally could sit there "at home."

On both floors at the ends of the corridor were three toilets, wide clay pipes encased in wooden crates, which led directly into a cesspit that was in front of the well. When the horrors of a typhoid epidemic threatened, this source of infection was finally neutralized when the well was closed.

When the attic was occupied, 240 people lived in the house. The bathrooms, which had no flushing water, were in use day and night, and people often stole the lightbulbs from them (they were valuable for bartering). Excuse me if I do not describe the conditions above and below. It was twice as bad when the toilets were clogged and remained unusable for several days. One can not imagine how people allow this to happen, to leave a place that they themselves use repeatedly in such condition. Now multiply this by 50, and it added up to the horrors and atrocities that prevailed here. We set up "toilet guards," but they were powerless.

In autumn there was much digging in the streets. Water pipes were to be laid and, to our delight, sinks and faucets installed. We would no longer need to schlep our washing and drinking water across two courtyards. The procession between the two courtyards went on all day, much to the displeasure of nearby residents, who resented the intrusion.

In spring 1943 the longed-for water pipes were connected to the house. The toilets were demolished and rebuilt. There were ceramic sinks with running water that for the most part actually worked. Nevertheless, standards of cleanliness did not improve, and the situation, caused by the old and the sick, remained unpleasant—in spite of the toilet guards.

On the other hand, in the summer we were surprised by a refurbishment of our living space. Bunk beds were set up, and lying on the floor came to an end.

One morning we were ordered to clear the room and to put all of our possessions in the courtyard. At 9 A.M. a column of young girls, all of them Czech, appeared and began carrying up the pre-cut pieces of wood. They then got to work assembling the beds, and by midday 24 clean, white beds made of rough-hewn boards (a shame, what a shame[19]) stood ready. We thanked the many workers who, even after the hard carpentry work, still sang a cheerful song as they went home.

The four desirable corner beds were assigned on the basis of age. Out of the first settlers, only one is still alive. And how many have died since then! Today perhaps only 25, at most, are still alive from transport I/29.

In such a room…there now lived 24 elderly men, who often lay sick for many days before being taken away or who might spare the men the trouble of carrying them—by dying beforehand. One becomes so immune to human suffering, to dying and death, that one often begins to question oneself—Where is your compassion? Why do you remain cold to the afflictions of your brother lying next to you?

There was a frail old man in our room called Simonsohn, who came from East Prussia. Back home he had been a male nurse and belonged to the *Chevra Kadisha*.[20] He took care of people here, too. Holding a worn-out prayer book in his hands, he stood by the dying, sat with them as their breath ran out or as they, unconscious, murmured unintelligible words, until the end came. Then he closed their eyes and led us in the *Kaddish*.

The man in the bed next to mine died quietly in his sleep one night—he had had a cold for a few days, nothing that would indicate a fatal outcome. When I woke up in the morning, he lay there with open eyes and a peaceful expression. I had to fetch his unsuspecting wife and take her to the deathbed. The next day I got a new neighbor.

Our three beloved stables were set up for the ghetto watch and outfitted with wooden bunks. In the middle stood wide tables with benches, an electric light hung from the ceiling, and there was an electrical outlet that allowed the occupants to plug in appliances for heating and cooking food. Now a colorful happy life began here. The new residents were young; many of them were married and had children. The women were allowed to stay until nine o'clock to take care of the men, and then—it was inevitable—they had to part.

We were given the upper, extended front corridor, two meters wide, to use as office space.[21] This was a temporary arrangement, while negotiations for a suitable room for us were in progress. We made do as best we could; at least we had a table and several benches.

We got along really well with the young comrades of the ghetto watch. They made their electric cooker available to us and often enough gave us their leftover bread; even a bowl of thick soup often came our way.

Our own new room!

The administration gave the orders, and we relocated. The move looked easy on paper but was so hard in practice. This room, number 38, is in the left-hand corner of Courtyard II, next to our stables. It was being used to store empty suitcases and was filled up to the ceiling with them. All kinds of luggage—from elegant Coupé suitcases to the smallest leather hand baggage. Mr. Fric was the master of this chamber; he was very amiable and pleasant, but he always said: "Not this week, definitely the next." It went on like this until the middle of September, and then I called upon Mr. Frey for help.

We agreed that the front room would be immediately released to us, and the back would be left for two weeks in its old state. But that was the deadline. Our own space! Peace, seclusion, security, decent accommodation for overnighters, comfortable rest for our comrades! Now meaningful, happy work could commence. Finally the Orientation Service was stabilized and no longer free-floating.

We weren't quite yet masters of our domain, but we did our best to work around the suitcases. But one good thing came of it. Our comrades got approval to choose suitcases for their own use. At the time this was a great gift, as such suitcases were unobtainable anywhere else.

In mid-September the Service numbered 20 men, four women, and an assistant. This assistant was a very intelligent, tall, picture-perfect blonde, 15-year-old boy from Prague, who had come here with his parents. I met him by chance and liked his bright manner. I requested his appointment from the Youth Welfare Department. Alfred became my adjutant, doing many errands for me. He soon knew his way around all the authorities, brought the lost home, and became indispensable to us. Nimble as a weasel, he completed each task promptly and often found a faster way to get the job done—nobody could refuse a request from this likable young man. Unfortunately we enjoyed his service for only a short while because he had to go to Poland with his parents.

When we were allocated more personnel, we were able to expand the service. Our commander, Frey, assigned us to light sentry duty as well, which would make the old gentlemen happy. It would not be too hard on them and beneficial to their health.

From eight in the morning until darkness fell, we worked to secure the two arterial roads of Bauschowitz gate and the Sudeten barracks, to ensure that ghetto inmates did not have access. The two roads led to freedom. It was so close that we could almost grasp it.

It happened, although very rarely, that foolhardy young people who worked outside the fortress tried to escape from the ghetto. They must have realized, when they thought about it, that they couldn't hide for long even in Prague, and anyway, only one person had ever made it that far. Wherever they went, they were seized by the authorities. But no punishment deterred them from their longing to see their home and parents again. This became overpowering in the younger people, so much so that all concerns were overridden by the dead-certain belief: I can succeed; *I* can do this.

We were allowed to sit on a small bench and thus guard the street. The summer weather was still marvelous and warm, and we could dream away two hours there, seeing the mountain peaks soaring in the distance, the fresh green of the trenches, the fruit trees on the ramparts that soon would bear fruit, though certainly not for us. Sometimes, when the window was open, quiet music wafted outside from the radio in the home of the head of agriculture.

Still, it was better not to listen to the radio, as it reminded us painfully of what we had given up and lost. I was happy to take my turn here. Since we had settled in Room 38, I had had few opportunities to be outside in fresh air. And what better place to sit and be lost in thought than here, where it was quiet. Only rarely did an inexperienced person get lost, becoming startled when the guard called out, "Do not go further."

It was only the sad, never-ending processions of the dead who did not need any permits, going past toward the central mortuary behind the bridge; its chilling corridors opened wide to receive the deceased into their final resting place.

Road duty at the Sudeten barracks was more monotonous. The commanders' cars whizzed by, but the traffic was light because only people who had business in the Sokolowna[22] or the Institute for Bacteriological Research went by. They showed their permits, and that was enough.

In September, we were given a job with quite a lot of responsibility, which sometimes made high demands on our men. It was at the gate of the children's home just behind the park. The German authorities used [the street] Q7 as a thoroughfare; use by the ghetto inmates was prohibited. The guards had to close a barrier when vehicles or people came into view. Passersby would be checked as they went through a narrow passage [created by the barrier]. When someone in uniform approached, the elderly, who never respected the rule, were reminded to remove their hats, lest they be punished.

[...]

The Magdeburg barracks had the best-known and most eagerly sought-out office, the distribution center: Room 76. Anyone in the ghetto who wanted linens or clothing, shoes or gloves, combs or brushes, in short, any item for daily needs, had to come to this room to speak with the appropriate department head.

Dr. Ludwig Freudenthal from Hamburg was the head of this center. He was a noted lawyer and the eminently energetic counsel of all Jewish emigrants.

Victor Janowitz, from Reichenberg, was his deputy. A younger man, he, like his brother Fritz, was adept at organizing and leading large operations. He proved these rare skills in a brilliant way. Out of a mad chaos, he created, in the shortest time, a smoothly functioning, model department that perfectly executed its task of supplying the ghetto with the extremely modest necessities of life.

The diminutive Dr. Altenstein, from Prague, sat at his desk. He used to work for the State; here he became the administrator of estates of the deceased. With the many deaths every day, it was a difficult job, not easy to perform. According to the ghetto regulations, the assets of the dead belong to the community and have to be made available to it. The relatives only have rights to their most personal effects. Useful artifacts can be given to them [the relatives] upon application. The decision lay with Dr. Altenstein.

In every department there was one specialist, and a swarm of women who maintained the many card indexes and prepared paperwork on the items that were handed over. Oskar Fein, from Vienna, the renowned parliamentary stenographer and director of the *Wiener Freie Presse* [an influential newspaper] reigned over everything. He had introduced the compiling of statistics and carried out this most necessary undertaking brilliantly. He was the backbone of this whole large, extremely important section. I will never forget his impressive lecture in Room 38, when he spoke about his background and what he accomplished in his life. Without anyone's "patronage" he achieved a level of success that was not easy to reach, even in Vienna.

[...]

The women in Room 76! One should dedicate a chapter full of admiring words to them. Room 76 was narrow and filled with tables at which men and women worked, most with full file boxes in front of them. In front at the door was a smaller area closed off by a rickety barrier. Hundreds of people waited there for the chance to tell one of the people at the tables what they wanted.

Those who needed shoe-repair coupons had to go to Mr. Arnold, who sat near the barrier. Reaching Mr. Prinz for bed and blanket allocations was more difficult, and accessing Engineer Wolff and his staff—that required the use of the elbows.

It was our job to bring order into this chaos. People had to wait in the corridor, and only as many as could be attended to at any one time were allowed to enter. How could one enter first? Carry a folder under your arm and snap at anyone who tries to stop you, that you are "official." Or, say that you urgently must speak to someone in "private." These tactics were repeated in many guises until the head called a stop.

We did guard duty here for a year, an above-average achievement. It was incredibly difficult to organize hundreds of agitated people in the cold. No one wanted to obey; everyone was "busy" or "working" and had absolutely no time. It is difficult for a Jew to obey—he is his own little tyrant and wants only to command. A Jew rarely accepts orders quietly, without asking "why." As the Bible says, we are an obstinate and stubborn people!

One can study this here on the first floor under the arcades, and one can get to know the Jewish character—the good, often-praised heart. It is better for me not to speak about it because in Theresienstadt most people lost the qualities we were so proud of, extinguished by hunger, grief, and longing. The distribution center was dissolved in the autumn of 1943 because ration cards and shops rendered this beneficial facility obsolete.

∗   ∗   ∗

Our next assignment came from the outpatient clinic, which gives me the opportunity to speak about the medical care in Theresienstadt.

At the helm of the entire health care system are Dr. Erich Munk and Professor Hermann Strauss, formerly Director of the Jewish Hospital Berlin. To give the reader an idea of everything that fell under the auspices of the health care system and everything that was supplied by this large network, I list some of the sub-offices, whose names describe their functions: Blind, War-Damaged, Deaf and Dumb, Singles, Prisoner's Children, Disabled-Hospitals, Nursery, Home for Newborns, Home for Toddlers, Old and Sick People's Care, Disinfestations, Home for Invalids, Infirmary. [...]

This list reveals how brilliantly organized the medical care was, given that it was created out of nothing and gradually brought up to a level that would have made any big city proud. Only the shortage of medicine was the doctors' constant cause for concern. But this had been a problem for a long time in Germany and could not be helped.

The Magdeburg outpatient clinic is located on the first floor. It is a bitter experience for the old or those who have difficulty walking, those transported by stretcher in cases of accidents, and for the ill and the weak who needed to reach the outpatient clinic. It is a bad arrangement. Incomprehensible that in two years a better space had not been found. Even when a recent fire broke out and burned through part of the ceiling, they did not move out but patched it up and stayed. That's Theresienstadt.

The Magdeburg outpatient clinic operated out of three rooms. The first measured approximately 45 square meters. On the side facing the windows were three dentist's chairs with the newest, most modern equipment, just like at home. Placed diagonally across from them were a wax-cloth chaise longue and the mysterious levers, arms, and rails of the radiation machine. The ophthalmologist's chair, with its manual instruments, was near these, and the vision-chart was attached to a cabinet. The ear, nose, and throat doctor sits, in an incredibly cramped space, next to the door. At least the three departments are now separated by linen cloths; in between worked the receptionists. There is also a sink with running water.

Outside, under the arcades, the patients gathered at eight o'clock and were supposed to be lined up by our guards—right and left for the eyes and throat, across for those suffering from dental ailments. About five people at a time were called in; those who were there for the dentist were called by the nurse.

[...]

Something always happens when 6,000 to 8,000 people gather at the same time to receive food. The elderly people fall easily, sustaining both minor and more serious injuries: They may lose consciousness or cut themselves on broken crockery. There is one supreme law in Theresienstadt: Take even the smallest injury seriously and seek treatment immediately. Vitamin deficiency, the monotonous, insufficient food—the total lack of meat and fat (after all, what good is one slice of sausage or meat for the body's well-being?)—affects the heating mechanism in humans. A machine can also function with bad coal—but how well? So it is, too, for the people in Theresienstadt. Someone who is organically healthy can manage on the amount of food rations. But the strength lost after illness is difficult to regain, even when the doctor does everything possible to help the patient get back on his feet.

From the arcades a door leads to an anteroom with small benches where the ambulatory sick wait. For a long time, milk for the sick was handed out in the afternoon through the single window in this room.

Goddess of Hygiene, cover your eyes! Turn away from all these things. And do not look in the next room either. Do not do it. You will not see anything pleasing. To the left of the door, in a room that measures 17 square meters, is a large pharmacy cabinet, from which a pharmacist or young physician fulfills her duties, giving out the prescribed tablets, pills, ointments, and potions. There is an operating table and a chair in the middle. Here patients are examined, cut, and bandaged.

At the window sits the dermatologist, whose job is doubly difficult. Skin diseases, boils, phlegm, inflammation arising from the most minor causes are quite tough to heal because of the shortage of medicines, special ointments, and bandages. Dreadful, the ulcerated arm; the hand itself gets affected. The body defends itself, wants to expel the bad juices and get rid of them.

[...]

In the last little room, the chief doctor and his large office.

[...]

It is not my purpose to describe the hospitals. I only went into those rooms when I visited a sick colleague. There was first a room for the sick who could be treated without major interventions. The hospital itself is quite modern. It has freestanding iron beds and good, white bedding. Many nurses care for the sick, and the best doctors are available.

The most difficult operations were carried out, and if the patient could not always be saved—even if he easily could have been if he'd been at home and well fed—it was simply because of the conditions in the ghetto. The authorities did as much as they could; I experienced this many times. But we should not forget that the world is at war, which explains a lot.

[...]

One type of room must be mentioned because it is close to where we sleep: the warming kitchen. It holds a huge, brick oven, and four women are in charge of the pots that warm the food that is delivered; they also cook potatoes and other nourishing foods from packages that have been donated from Prague, and bake cakes, bread, potato dumplings, and biscuits. It is a task that places high demands on women's culinary talents, because about 50 pots on the stove have to be watched. A tin number hangs from each one to keep them straight.

These kitchens—every barracks and blockhouse has one—are extremely important. Without them one could not procure additional nourishment and seldom hot food and soup to eat. For example, the morning coffee is boiled at night in huge cauldrons and lunch soups as well, waiting in large vats to be retrieved.

If one picks up the coffee prepared at 6 A.M., at 7 A.M. it is no longer hot. So one depends on the warming kitchen in order to at least have something hot in the cold room. How can one work when there is no coffee to contribute a bit of inner warmth to a barren breakfast?

Indeed, the problems that present themselves every day are not insignificant. At home everything happened as a matter of course. Private life went smoothly— from sleeping and eating, to having a bathroom for bathing and washing hands. Here, hand-washing is really difficult. One hunts for a pump and tries to clean as often as possible, as instructed on the posters for the fight against typhoid— without soap, which is delivered only once a month.

Medical skill and the dedication and sacrifice of the nurses have abated the threat of typhoid, but not without many great losses. Recently, some parents told me that they had lost their only daughter, who was 18 years old. She had contracted typhoid while caring for children who were sick with the deadly disease. One could mention many similar cases!

Yet another danger threatened to bring severe hardship into the ghetto—lice and the dreadful petechial fever, which brought back bad memories of Russia. At first, we laughed at the thought. What? We are civilized people: lice? No, we are quite clean; we wash carefully, take care of ourselves, change our clothes, and take them off at night. Nothing like that could happen to us.

We had laughed at the thought in Russia, too, during the world war, but we stopped laughing when the number of deaths increased alarmingly. The authorities in Theresienstadt worked tirelessly, as they usually did when there were big issues to resolve. The battle against the louse began.

Doctors who had been assigned to work only on this issue visited every house, barracks, and occupied space, unannounced. One had to undress. There was a full-body search, including underwear, shirts, and jackets. If anything was found, the person had to go, with all his luggage, his bedding, and his mattress, to be deloused. Not only the person with the lice, but also the people in the neighboring beds had to walk the bitter path. At the beginning of the campaign, it was really a terrible affair to have to carry the cumbersome, heavy luggage. One had to bring provisions and be sure not to forget the food-ration card, which had to last until one returned home the next day.

Later, the delousing could be wrapped up in a single afternoon. One's luggage is picked up and returned. The entire saga is not as exhausting and difficult.[23] It is unpleasant, of course, when a louse is found during the examination, which takes place every 14 days. Lice could be picked up by anyone waiting in a line, at a concert, or at a lecture. No one is safe, neither the high nor the low. Everyone accepts this reality and, therefore, conducts their own inspections every day. It is both self-protection and a responsibility one owes the community, which has to defend itself against the "enemy."

In closing, let me say: The enemy is defeated; the victory has been won thanks to the dedication of those who fought together. Theresienstadt is almost free of lice! [...]

Yet another insect, while not life-threatening, robbed us of our peace: the bedbug. When we slept on the floor, we did not notice this vermin. The minute the beds were built, the assault began at nighttime. The rough-hewn planks made wonderful hiding places. The intersections of the floorboards invited them [the bedbugs] to linger, and they nested wherever there was a small hole. First, they arrived separately, and then in families, and finally, in columns, like an army. Daily inspection, airing, and shaking out [of the bedding] do not help. The beasts slept by day. They do not stay in the bedding but, probably, on the back side of the two mattresses. One has to surrender to one's fate; there is nothing more that can be done. In the living and sleeping area, there is no way to keep things clean, even though the room elder was very energetic.

How should one fight the filth and dirt dragged in on the boots of 24 people three times a day? Cleaning under the beds is a challenge: Shoes, suitcases, the (*pardon*) crockery of the night, and washbowls are all stored there. We no longer have brooms, scrub brushes, and mops; they are completely worn out from overuse.

Twenty-four men—half of them are elderly or sick and cannot clean the room. Most of the remaining 12 have to work. How could cleanliness prevail in such a cramped, densely populated space? Countless decrees demand cleanliness, but noncompliance is the norm.

Conclusion: The fight to prevent epidemics succeeds, but the fight against lice and uncleanliness was never won.

Outpatient clinic. The new duty that had been assigned to us a year ago was no easy task. Every day it was the same: No one wanted to wait. Even though elderly, unemployed men and women had nothing to do, they still did not want to wait and did not organize themselves in an orderly fashion; nor were they disposed to step aside in certain situations, out of respect, so that someone older could go first. None of the above.

Here, as it was in front of the shops or at the post office when ration cards were issued, there was an appalling lack of discipline in the Jews. Each feels that he is better—more preeminent in the group—and demands preferential treatment. [...]

Bread is a daily necessity. One could get it relatively cheaply, as long as the Protectorate[24] could freely send as many packages to Theresienstadt as possible. They were forbidden to us Reich Germans. We never had the same advantages as the Czechs, whose relatives unfailingly sent them the longed-for gifts. We depended on packages of one or two kilos, which seldom came after the bombing had damaged the big German cities, and our friends who were still there were experiencing hardship themselves.

Another source was thefts and misappropriations from supply rooms and bakeries. Despite strict supervision, security, and harsh penalties, it seemed that there was no way to discourage these criminals, who were motivated to practice their shameful craft by their addiction to money and profits, who committed such grave sins against the community.

Those who bought from them used the excuse: We cannot manage; by the third day we don't even have one slice of bread left. We are forced to trade [something for bread] or if that is not possible, to buy it.

Envious, and with a growling stomach, one went to the kitchens in the quarters to heat up some coffee left over from the morning—and saw the Czechs' full pots of food, which had become legendary. Over there, peas, beans, lentils, and rice simmered, and dried vegetables soaked. Canned delicacies were opened, and the smell of baking cakes, made with white flour, was seductive. The aroma of real mocha arose to say that fresh cookies were ready.

It was like this every day, and in every kitchen something was always bubbling and sizzling. On the one side there was abundance and the good life, which was not shared; on the other, endless hunger. There were the Reich Germans who seldom received a package, and the bachelors, without wives to make the food better. If friends from the Reich sent pasta, stock cubes, or powders in various forms from which dishes could be made, then the day's simple menu could be extended, and one got by on what was offered.

At the post office in the great hall, where parcels and packages were well organized and quite quickly handed out, there were large, colorful posters of the joyful recipients of these packages, open to show all the treasures included therein. The inscription read: "Think of those who have nothing! Give gladly!"

My acquaintances and I never felt the effect of this.[25]

Finally, I would always say, and emphasize, that I have sympathy for all those who stray from the right path. They feel defensive in a battle that is not of their own making, bound by laws that they do not recognize, while violence and coercion is the order of the day, but not forever.

[…] Nevertheless, to me this maxim does not ring true: To understand everything means to forgive everything. The ghetto provisions are seriously jeopardized if the administration closes one eye and keeps the other only half open. This is just tilting at windmills.

Some information on the work in the kitchens during the summer of 1942 should be mentioned here. Each evening, the head cook collects from the food store the provisions needed to prepare the next day's foods. The quantities are calculated on the basis of the registered ration cards. In August and September, 9,500 people were supplied with food. The food offered was varied:

- soup with lentil extract (not the whole beans);
- peeled potato, 35–38 decagrams;
- dumplings, rutabaga, called *dorschen* here;
- sauerkraut, millet; as a rare bonus: salami or meat, one slice, 1/2 cm thick;

- doughnuts, fried in fat, once a week; and
- 3–4 times a week in the evening there was only coffee.

And so, one depended on the bread allocation.

In the kitchen, 25 to 30 cooks worked in shifts. One hundred to one hundred and twenty women in a stable sat in long rows, peeling potatoes nonstop, day and night. A once rich, highly educated woman would sit next to a humble woman from the countryside—and they peeled for eight hours. In spite of its monotony, this job was most sought after, because they were given extra potatoes, in addition to what accidentally landed in their pockets.

It was often said in inner circles that if all the food supplies had reached the kitchen, it would be enough to give every ghetto inmate an additional half portion of potatoes. [But there were] countless convictions for burglary and theft from the food store cellar during the night. Even the ghetto watch was powerless to do anything about it.

Food and drink were handed out at eight stalls, three times a day. This was a stressful and difficult task for the men and women doing it. At that time, the portions were measured out at their discretion according to a standard sample portion that stood on the counter. The speed with which the work had to be done resulted in sometimes more, sometimes less being given out, causing outrage—often serious confrontations—and decisive intervention by a member of the Household Commission.[26] Meanwhile, those still waiting for their portions would grumble, becoming impatient at every delay. No one wanted to wait.

We had unheard-of luck with the weather that summer and into the autumn months. It did not rain at all, and only rarely did a thunderstorm bring refreshment. So the distribution of food was carried out without problems. Lining up in the sun was not bad; one only needed to think of the lines at the springs in nearby Marienbad or Karlsbad, and standing became easier. But one thing must be noted: Impatience and intolerance increased with each passing month.

Physicians should be able to explain this: why the grip of nervousness slowly but surely pervades and becomes so blatantly apparent, why most people lose their self-control so that the smallest thing "tips them over." After a year and a half, this overstimulation of the nerves is unbearable. It makes life in the *ubikation* hell—from the time one wakes up, one hears people in other beds arguing over ridiculous trifles. One has to listen to this day after day, without any possibility of escape, and it is no better anywhere else.

Those who take food and unthinkingly complain about the small portion
and poor preparation do a bitter disservice to the people working in the kitchen.
They can cook only what the food store supplies. They have the best recipes—
without the best ingredients. A cart full of bones is delivered, with no meat
on them. With that, soup should be good? Just think, such a small quantity
to make 9,000 portions! There was no variety for three months—nothing but
lentil-extract soup. Probably the factory did not have anything else and sent their
whole stock to the ghetto.

[...]

Dumpling day. At night the kneading of the dough begins and the shaping
of the dumplings, which is done by hand. The workers wear swimming trunks;
they cannot wear anything else in this overheated room. From time to time, they
get some air under the arcades, only briefly. Friends already crowd around with
their bowls raised, just in case there is something to eat.

The strongest young men are chosen to carry full vats and troughs to the
courtyard. It is a hard job. Boiling hot soup, steaming potatoes: A misstep on
the slippery, well-worn staircase, and their hands are burned. The warnings,
"Caution! *Pozor!*"[27] ring out continually. Of course, the staircase is blocked off at
lunchtime, but accidents cannot be totally avoided.

[...]

The vats must be empty and scrubbed by 6 A.M. Filling them for lunch
begins, because the service starts at 11 A.M., an hour earlier for certain categories
of inmates.

The kitchen operates according to an exact, efficient, and interlinking plan.
Nothing is done without supervision. Despite its being a large-scale operation, the
number of servings is not calculated, not exactly, but to within 10 to 20 servings,
more or less, and the food distribution is also calculated with a plus or minus. But
it very rarely happens that there are not enough potatoes so that more must be
freshly cooked. Then, there is only one option for the hungry: to wait patiently.

Ernst Pollatschek, 49 years old, born in Prague and fluent in both languages
[Czech and German], is responsible for the overall management of the kitchen
and for food distribution. From the beginning, he carried out his difficult and
responsible job with four assistants and several helpers, both men and women.
In two years, he developed a unique way of working. Like a sheepdog tending its
herd, Ernst Pollatschek circled the queues. Nothing escaped his sharp eye. Here,
he intervened before a fight broke out; there, he helped an elderly man who had
dropped his bowl and was miserable, to a second portion.

Then, his short mustache bristles. He finally found the traitor who was
stealing food with ration cards that he had found. He rages so that the whole

courtyard can hear his voice. A unique talent: He brings most swindlers—and the number is not small—to justice. He does not rest until justice had been done.

Indefatigable in his service, he never takes a day off; he is completely consumed by his job in Theresienstadt. He is not a simple person. His energetic demeanor makes him a lot of enemies, but those who know him understand that he is only rough on the outside. Those qualities are needed in this kind of job. If not, disorder would result. The "ménage" functions perfectly day after day and to the minute, and for this we have Ernst Pollatschek and the men and women of his kitchen to thank.

[…]

September 21, 1942, was a day that will perhaps have a small place in the history of the intellectual movement of Theresienstadt. It is the day that I presented a lecture in the small Room 38 for the first time, which was open to the public.

Until then, we had had lectures, but only in front of comrades, quite spontaneously, and without a definite program. Those attending talked from 7 P.M. to 8 P.M., when we were rarely required to be on duty, about our own life experiences. Through these personal narrations I pursued my goal of getting to know the people around me better, to hear about their pasts and learn about their characters. These hours gave me this opportunity. It was always a bit surprising to hear about the background of these men.

The rich manufacturer from southern Germany, who had employed 1,000 workers, described his company, its organization, and its extensive foreign connections. He had chosen to stay a bachelor in order to be able to live independently which led him into the wide world. One saw that he was a well-groomed man; he maintained his appearance despite modest conditions. Unlike many, he did not tolerate a single stain on his clothing. He remained full of hope and never stopped believing that things would turn out happily for him. He had made sure that his foreign friends would not forget him. When he was free, he would go directly to America, where he could live comfortably. He did not look like he was 72 years old; his round face was so fresh. Yet, death still took him. He died suddenly of a heart attack after two days of an illness that he had not taken seriously.

The most original in the circle was Jacques Brock, who was a lanky, lean, scrawny bachelor, but very fit and lively. He anxiously tried to make sure that no one discovered his age. But on his 75th birthday, I just had to honor him at the daily roll call, which did not please him. In Berlin he owned a store that sold coats, and after it took off, he turned its management over to his nephew, while he went traveling. He lived the life of a gentleman in London, Paris, and the Riviera.

Then came the change that gave him an occupation that was near to his heart for the rest of his days. He became the general representative for Greater Berlin of the firm Henkell, which produced sparkling wines. Herr von Ribbentrop[28] was his boss, and Brock could not say enough about the efficiency and kindness of Henkell's son-in-law. He himself had been received by von Ribbentrop to the end and assured of protection. But letters containing assurances did not help: He still had to make his way to Theresienstadt with no more luggage and possessions than the rest of us.

These examples show the variety of men who did duty and who could converse interestingly in the evenings. But Brock had more to him; he was secretly a poet and the author of many aphorisms. He never missed a chance to write them down or to read his creations out loud in the evening.

[...]

In four weeks we had said everything to each other that there was to say. Now we needed variety, and I decided to ask my new friends to give evening lectures and to make them available to a larger audience. I opened the series myself and spoke about *From My Life*.

I described old Berlin, from around 1886, and that paradise of my youth, the Garrison Cemetery at the cathedral parish on Gormannstrasse,[29] where as a schoolboy I spent the afternoons from May until the end of September with my friends, the last of whom remained steadfastly loyal to me until his death. As often as I gave this lecture, it was always a pleasure for me to look back on that glorious time of youth. My audience also enjoyed the conversational style, especially about things that now sounded almost like a fairy tale.

On September 23, 1942, a speaker from outside our group, Ludwig Sochaczewer, spoke for the first time. His lectures, *Contemporaries*, ended on September 25. I had met Ludwig Sochaczewer in the courtyards. He was a broadly built, stocky man, young and vigorous-looking, although he was already [72 years] old. At lunchtime, he stood helplessly with his plate, and I invited him to eat in comfort with us. That was how we came to chat and I learned—his name was familiar to me—that he was the famous journalist and features editor for the *Berliner Tageblatt*. More recently, he had been press secretary at the Japanese embassy.

He was a man to whom the personalities shaping the world's tragic fate were surely familiar. In the last four decades, they had all crossed his path—all. He knew those whose names have now stirred the world, and he understood more about politics than any who observed it from afar.

How often we spoke about the past and the future! He remained an optimist. He always had a pocket full of news that he had gleaned from the Theresienstadt "mouth-radio" or from first-class sources. In autumn 1942, things were, after all, very different, and we ghetto inhabitants just wanted to see a light on the horizon, to be able to bear the dreadful burden that constantly oppressed us all.

Ludwig Sochaczewer's life was, based on the short reports that he gave, varied and colorful—he had been all over Europe—and I had a deep desire to hear more about it. He instantly agreed to speak in Room 38. So he was our first "foreign" lecturer, and there was hardly anyone worthier. [...] What that man had experienced and how well he knew how to tell stories. We hung on his every word as he told us about the great in the realm of politics and about art and science. And it was so easy and fluent, so lively and vivid, that one could spend hours listening.

I would have to write a biography of this splendid man to tell everything I learned from him in the months of our friendship. But, oh, he began to sicken in winter. Bowel disease had begun to threaten him, followed by severe disorders of the bladder. He was in the hospital for a long time, bearing the unspeakable pain bravely, but the food was poor, and he could not regain his strength. On February 26 he who had always hoped so confidently for a happy ending fell into a gentle sleep.

[...]

He was the only ghetto inmate ever to have the good fortune to be allowed to speak to his former secretary, who had requested certain information for the embassy. The conversation took place in the commandant's office with the head of the German administration present. The two sat across from each other. He [Sochaczewer] was allowed only to answer questions. They [he and his secretary] were not permitted to shake hands. After the end of the conversation, he had to leave the room and was allowed to stay in his house for the rest of the day. Imagine the dramatic scene: Two people who had loved each other for a decade see each other again after a long separation. They are not permitted to embrace or to say to each other what is in their hearts. He never forgot this hour, and it led to the decline in his otherwise indestructible health.

The next eminent speaker on the list was Louis Treumann, the great Viennese operetta tenor, who on three evenings talked about his experiences and successes in [Franz] Lehar's *Merry Widow*, among other things. He was the first Danilo and probably the best. [But] we were not able to get him to sing. Only once did he do a serious scene from a comedy, and he showed what a great vocal artist he was. He spoke enchantingly, standing—but look out if he was disturbed by noise! Then he would explode.

We learned a lot about the alluring, glittering world of the theater, from the process of creating and putting on plays to the fears and anxieties of everyone involved: Will it be a success? [Unfortunately] Treumann was not able to give the final lecture; the iron curtain lowered quite suddenly. Medicine could no longer stem the tide of his escaping life, and on the day when he was supposed to speak, I could only speak words of remembrance and thanksgiving.

I tried to vary the program to let men from all areas of expertise and knowledge speak.

Dr. [Johann] Weinberger, *The Beginning of Christianity*
Dr. [Berthold] Feigel, *As a Prisoner of War in Russia*
Rabbi Dr. L. Neuhaus, *The Number 13*
Professor Dr. E. Levy, *Bacteriology*
Rabbi A. Schön, *A Day in Jerusalem*
Miss Rabbi Jonas, *About the Talmud*
Franz E. Klein, *The World of Music*
Professor Dr. Emil Utitz, *The Actor's Art*
Dr. Paul Blum, *German Humor, French Esprit, Jewish Wit*

[...]

But I do want to be clear about one thing—this was not just about serious scholarship. Saturday was reserved for humor. Under the heading *Colorful Hour*, I put lighthearted lectures together and presented them to a cheerful audience.

[...]

We held lectures every other day. Desks were removed and put by the door in the courtyard. We got hold of a lectern, and that gave us all the props we needed. Room 38 was changed twice over the course of time. Once, when we took over the second half of the room, and then when the partition was removed, finally making room for 100 listeners.

Now, I could increase the size of the audience to meet popular demand. Word had quickly gotten around Theresienstadt that a kind of cultural community had developed in Room 38. Every month new listeners came, wanting tickets to specific lectures, and unfortunately, I often had to say no.

At least we had a warm room: During the day a stove gave off a cozy warmth. We let it go out in the evening since the body heat of visitors pressed closely together was sufficient.

At the door we made a sort of porch out of two blankets, which kept out the draft. Lighting was difficult. Not only was use of lighting governed by strict house rules, but we suffered from shortage of the necessary materials: wire, frames, screens, insulating tape—and electric bulbs! That was a cross to bear! One never knew what would go wrong. Would it be a short circuit or a switch-off by the power plant?

[...]

The Poetry of Theresienstadt

Some people brought me verses that they had written here. I found some so remarkable that I said to myself that there must be a way to preserve them, so that these good poems could later be made available to the public to promote young talent and encourage creativity. I initiated a competition—deadline: December 20 [1942]—and put an announcement in a circular and also posted one on the notice board.

It was a great success. Approximately 200 poems were submitted, written on all kinds of paper, including—please believe me—toilet paper.

I made the first selection, separating the wheat from the chaff. A lot were unusable, doggerel suitable [only] for club and family meetings, the intentions generally better than the results. Thematically, they were rather one-sided: food, rations, and housing shortages. I chose approximately 40, which satisfied the purpose, and turned them over to the two judges: Professor Dr. Emil Utitz and Fritz Janowitz, who would give each one a grade.

After that I had little peace. The authors were worried about the fate of their "babies" and longed for news of whether they had been accepted. I had to ask them to wait. The distribution center had donated valuable prizes: There were fountain pens for the gentlemen, handbags for the ladies, and other smart items that were desirable in Theresienstadt. The chosen poems, and later everything that was good and worth preserving, were typed on good paper, in four copies.

Then I had a new idea. We could not take photographs in Theresienstadt, but wanted to preserve people and things for the future. This only left drawing. I had the luck to discover an artist from Vienna, Mrs. Henriette Lehmann-Laizner, a thin, delicate, very sensitive lady, who applied herself to the task with eagerness and great joy. She filled the empty space on paper with exquisite, feathery pastel drawings, all with motifs of Theresienstadt: the major buildings—the church, military barracks, the pretty fountain in the courtyard, the mountains, the sheep pen, the picturesque courtyards of the houses, blossoming cherry trees, groups of elderly people, potato peelers at work, the courtyard of the Magdeburg barracks—in short, capturing everything that appealed to her eye with her few green, blue, and brown pencils.[30]

The result was about 100 drawings forming a beautiful and valuable collection. We gave one copy in two portfolios to our commander, Kurt Frey, on May 18, 1943, for his birthday. A second copy was given to Dr. Paul Eppstein, our Jewish elder.

[…]

The Strausses, Leo and Myra, first brought Theresienstadt into the poetry produced here. He, the son of Oscar Straus,[31] was a tall, thin gentleman; his way of speaking was a bit slow, thoughtful and quiet. He was a first-class writer. His "period" poems, as one must call those that originate here—for example, the serious *Give a Sign of Life* and the sarcastic *As If*—are sharp and effectively presented. He wrote many spirited small sketches for his evening lectures; they reveal a French *esprit* combined with Viennese lightness and grace.

His articulate, clever, brilliant, and quick-witted wife dedicated herself to the lectures body and soul; she managed them very skillfully and with great success. She, too, was an author of lighthearted poems. Her poem *The Yellow Star* became very popular, as did many other of her verses.[32]

Another woman must also be praised. She captured the deepest sensibilities, which were informed by maternal kindness and an understanding of both suffering and the joys of a child's soul. She captured the atmosphere of the sick room, the playground, and the bastion: These were the themes chosen by Mrs. Ilse Weber, a nurse in the children's hospital, a small, delicate woman, very dedicated to her profession.

In the summer, she could be seen every day going up to the bastion with a flock of convalescent children, stopping to rest in the large square with the poplar trees. The children sat in a circle around her singing German and Czech children's songs while she accompanied them on her guitar. When she sang her own songs at lectures, she also played the guitar.[33]

[…]

The first Jewish holiday[34] gave me an opportunity to celebrate the occasion with dignity. On the night of Hanukkah[35] our small room was filled beyond capacity because this time there would be a woman speaker, Rabbi Regina Jonas. She lit the first candle and spoke from the heart. She had mastered the art of speaking and knew to avoid hollow pathos. Poems—appropriate to the day— were presented, and after the conclusion we comrades stayed for a long time chatting.

I used the *Colorful Hour* to implement a long-cherished plan. I had found two editions from Insel [publishing company], one of *German Songs* and the other of Bierbaum's *Poetry*, in the library. Now I had what I needed to revive Ernst von

Wolzogen's *Überbrettl*[36] in Room 38. Could I have found a better master of ceremonies than Dr. Leo Strauss, whose father had sat at the piano and accompanied his immortal song, performed by Bozena Bradsky and Robert Koppel, *Cling, Clang, Gloribusch, I Dance with My Wife?*

His graceful wife presented *The Music Comes* and other charming little things. Other artists followed, and so we were able to hear very fine and praiseworthy poems, which today seem a little dusty and faded.

[...]

So-called big nights were:

- Professor Paul Blum's spirited interpretation and rendition of the work of Christian Morgenstern, which revealed its poetic depths.
- Professor Dr. Klausner, a physician from Prague, gave a talk on the theme *About Animals That I Have Learned to Love*. He spoke only from his own experiences, for example, about a vicious, biting, but wonderfully beautiful Alsatian that even bit its master, which he was then supposed to put down. This animal must have known what would happen to him. When first spoken to, he seemed to transform, and in a few days, the transformation was complete. The new master [Klausner] and his dog became inseparable.

A Heine evening, dedicated to little-known works of the poet, was unforgettable. The young actor Franz Karl Stein (unfortunately, he had to go to Poland) recited magnificently from the Paganini scene in the *Florentine Nights*. We listened to Heine for nearly two hours. It was a great pleasure to be taken out of oneself.

And now to the literary conclusion of the year 1942. It occurred to me to give the gentlemen of the administration [the officials working in the self-administration of the ghetto] and also a larger audience a chance to get to know my work. Until now I had had complete freedom to act and to create. I was not accountable to anyone. I did not need any permits and never catered to the general public. Those with an interest in high-quality lectures knew where to find me. I never did any advertising, and Room 38 was not mentioned in the program of the Leisure Time Organization.

[...]

The only condition that had ever been imposed on me was to hand in my weekly program. The commandant's office had to be informed about every lecture. The Leisure Time Organization vetted the themes, to see whether or not they were acceptable, and if they gave their approval, I had a green light.

Year's End: A Contemplative Hour, December 31, 1942

That is what I called the last event at the end of the year, which I wanted to be especially festive. I requested the use of Room 118, a festival and theater hall that could hold 350 people. First problem—sorry, it's already reserved for a performance later that evening. My suggestion—that, since we had four weeks, we could plan things in such a way that we would only need the room from 6 P.M. to 8 P.M.—was ignored. It was only after Mr. Frey intervened that I received permission to use the hall—from 3 P.M. to 5 P.M.

Now we had to plan the celebration itself. There were many problems that were not easy to solve. Who should speak? Who must be invited? The room could hold 200 people sitting, [and] 150 standing. What would come before and after the speeches? I knew nothing of the hierarchy and the protocol of Theresienstadt. I did not personally know the many men of the administration and the Council of Elders, and I had no relationship to the top.

I had only been introduced to the Jewish elder, Jacob Edelstein, in autumn and I took the opportunity to invite him to give a lecture on Zionism; he promised to speak but never did. I was again helped by the block elder who had connections and knew how things worked, and I went to work.

The speakers: Jacob Edelstein would have been happy to speak, but was prevented by a monthlong hoarseness during which he never appeared in public. So I asked his deputy, Engineer Otto Zucker, as well as Rabbi Dr. Leopold Neuhaus, Captain [Joseph] Klaber, and Mr. Fritz Janowitz to do the honors.

An *ad hoc* women's choir was assembled by the conductor Alexander Weinbaum from Berlin to sing festive songs. The program was finalized, showing that I, working on my own, without any official support, was more than capable of doing a valuable cultural service to the ghetto.

And on December 31, 1942, I proved it. A truly illustrious group filled Room 118. The ghetto watch had sent 50 men as a symbol of their support. The heads of the administration, the police, and the rabbinate were present. The men of the Orientation Service sat with their wives on the stage. The choir took its place on the left.

The program began on time. After the choir sang its first song, I spoke words of welcome. Then it was the speakers' turn. Unfortunately, the lectures were not recorded by a stenographer, as they would be later, so I cannot repeat them here.

The "Contemplative Hour" had been just that. Initially, there had been objections to the title: One could not very well announce a "New Year's Eve Celebration" in the ghetto. But when Dr. Neuhaus explained that the intention was to do a retrospective, a looking back at the year that was ending, there was no objection. On December 31, in the final hours of the secular year, we Jews had good reason to reflect on what we had lived through, to seek courage and confidence. We listened to the speakers, and they gave us both.

It is curious that in the ghetto, a Jewish town, the Sabbath is not observed as a day of rest. We worked in the offices and workshops as usual on the high holidays. The authorities demanded that everything be subordinated to the necessity of war; even religious observances should be suspended.

I organized an hour of prayer for comrades on these three days, which despite its brevity, was edifying and uplifting. It is not the length of the prayer but the content, the fervor of entering into the world beyond, contemplating God as the sum of all that is and will be, that gave the hour such value—the satisfying breath of inner peace.

Religious practice is not easy in the ghetto. There is not even one room that is dignified enough to be a synagogue. Why not even a hut was built and made available for prayer is incomprehensible to me: There were enough cut pieces of wood on the woodpile. Synagogues in the attics were impossible to heat, ugly, inappropriate for worship, and did not accommodate all the devout, especially not when one of the great speakers was there. Rooms were apparently needed for other purposes. The beautiful church stood empty; it was neither used nor permitted to be used. The Star of David did not rule over the ghetto, but the cross.

Mors Imperator![37]

Death tore a very unexpected, painful hole in our circle of comrades. Ernst Wartenberger, born in 1873 in Hamburg, Elbe, a blond, stocky man, with a youthful face and a straight posture, was one of the most service-minded comrades we had. The clock played no role in his life, no matter how long he had to work. An enthusiastic soldier, he had reached the level of sergeant, and it pleased him to be able to be of "service" again in his later days.

He enjoyed talking about the war, about his old 76th Regiment, how esteemed and beloved it was. Precisely because he was a Jew, he was held up to his fellow soldiers as an example of loyalty. When someone who had lost his way had to be taken home late at night, it was always Ernst Wartenberger who volunteered for the job.

He caught a cold while at his post at barrier Q7, and since his lungs had not been in the best condition for many years, he came down with a disease that led to his death. I visited him a few times in the hospital. He spoke proudly of the Service and wanted to know what was new, who would be hired, what lectures were planned, how everybody was doing. By my next visit, his voice was weak; he could only speak a few words. He pressed my hand and held it for a long, long time as though wanting to cling to life. By the afternoon he was dead.

He left behind his wife, Jenny, born in 1888, who was a member of the women's section of the Orientation Service. She was extremely efficient and reliable [and] unfortunately had to go to Poland in the spring of 1943.

Mors Imperator! It is worth the trouble to examine his empire a little more closely, even if this is not a happy chapter. In a factual report, it cannot be left out without leaving an incomplete picture of this time. The dedicated work of all those who served the dead and dying deserves to be appreciated.

In the hot summer and in the autumn days of 1942, Death had a rich harvest; it was more than rich. It was the time of the great dying of the old and the very old who, with their broken, weak bodies; their worn, uprooted souls; and their unrealizable longing for their far-off children, could not resist even a mild illness. Torn from their familiar lives, their well-kept rooms, the security of a Jewish Old People's Home, and hospital care with its resources, the elderly found dislocation hard to endure. Old trees cannot be transplanted. But any change can be imposed on people. To die is easy in Theresienstadt. It does not even require a serious illness.

The food one wasn't used to: the heavy bread, given out mainly very fresh during those months; the coffee given morning and night; the ice-cold water gulped down on hot days, despite the warnings—at first one would get only an upset stomach, and then indigestion, reduced or no food intake, a quick loss of strength, and after that, enteritis, the sickness called "Theresiana," and the immediate and last result: *exitus.*

During those months the dying was quite terrible. It seemed as though Theresienstadt was being depopulated, as in the time of the Black Death. And then another sinister guest arrived: typhus! The lice infestation took on threatening forms. One avoided all events in crowded spaces.

We were still at the start of the great campaign against lice, which the Medical Authority led with skill and energy. The entire organization had to be created from nothing. Space, equipment, expertise—everything was lacking; one was unprepared for such a life-threatening situation in the ghetto.

The battle began. The delousing facility was established. Baths for men and women. Disinfection procedure. The [deloused] clothes were hung on portable racks and taken away.

Patients were soaped up and brushed, and then Lysol[38] was poured over them. Having passed the medical examination, they would then usually come into the warm waiting room, where they received two terry cloth robes and waited for their clothes to be returned to them. In the meantime, their toenails were clipped, and corns were removed. Before entering the facility, one had to bring one's bedroll to be disinfected. The transportation section picked up suitcases and mattresses, and returned them two days later. The procedure began at eight o'clock and was completed by twelve-thirty. The bedrolls were ready at home, still hot inside and ready to be used. This was the process.

Women provided the care in the delousing rooms. They helped people undress, hung their things up, escorted them to the shower, and soaped, brushed, and took them to the other treatment rooms. It's funny, when I was in the shower, with hot water comfortably running down my body, a smiling young lady said, "Mr. Manes, yesterday the *Talisman* was marvelous." I must mention that this same woman, as I lay resting, gave me a thick slice of bread as a token of thanks for all the beauty that she had appreciated in Room 38.

It is remarkable what these women, young and old, accomplished in these rooms, the amount of patience they had to have to endure the moods and rudeness of their patients. How they carried out their strenuous duties day after day with a smile. How much trouble they took to help the elderly, who struggled with dressing and undressing. How soothingly and reassuringly they answered a hundred impatient questions. It was truly wonderful.

Here, the love of mankind was alive; "the love of one's neighbors" should have been written over the entrance. If three inmates with lice were found in our room, we comrades in suffering all had to go through the process. Every 14 days the "louse doctor" came to examine every man and the clothes he was wearing.

This is how the lice infestation was defeated. [Yet] even now, people carrying the insect are found, and then the fight continues, relentlessly.

We should thank the authorities for handling the situation with such energy. If they didn't, the result would be typhoid fever and, with that, the destruction of us all. Therefore thanks and thanks again to the medical authorities, the doctors, nurses, and the hard workers in the gassing room,[39] and the disinfection facility.

I have been describing my experience of the "lausoleum" from February 1943. Before then, the process had not been perfect. At first, we had feared the very long, drawn-out procedure, which lasted late into the night. There were not enough treatment rooms. During the endless waiting, many people caught colds. Even though lunch was brought to us, it did not hold us over during a twelve-hour stay. Things are always difficult in the beginning. But now delousing is almost a popular amusement.

Death has arrived. The coroner has attended to its duties. The dead man is wrapped in a blanket, an identification card firmly attached to his feet. The block elder has to fill out the forms and send them over to the authorities. The corpses are loaded onto two-wheel carts and driven to the central mortuary, which is in the casemates in front of the Bauschowitz gate, accessible by long passages.

In the terrible September days, when we mourned up to 30 deaths every day, we stood at our posts as the sad procession of cadavers passed before us, often ten to a wagon. Here, we saw a hand, there, a bare foot—horrible. Worthy of a Goya's brush. We found him later, our Goya. He was Dr. Karl Fleischmann, who stood at the helm of health care; he did powerful drawings that masterfully depicted such scenes.

The funeral ceremony takes place in the front of the vaulted, elongated casemate, where two mighty chestnut trees spread their broad branches out protectively. At the back of the 25-meter-deep hall stands an altar, and piled in front of it are the coffins, stacked in twos, which usually numbered between 20 and 30 at any ceremony. The wagon could not handle more than that.

The mourners lined the road. The coffins are then covered with black cloths. A prayer leader recites the prayer for the dead. The Rabbi speaks words of consolation and reads the names of the dead. Men and women who have done notable service for Judaism are memorialized with a eulogy.

Then four pallbearers come to carry away the coffins, which bear the names and the transport numbers of the deceased, on their shoulders. In the beginning, the corpses were buried in separate graves at the cemetery. When there was no room left, the field in front of the crematorium was used for burials. When there were mass deaths, the coffins had to be lowered into communal pits. For a while, there weren't enough coffins, and the existing ones were reused: The dead were buried on a plank. It was a shuddering, terrible scene, which, fortunately, the mourners were spared.

The wagon [...] proceeds very slowly up to the barrier; the retinue of mourners falls in behind it. It stops; the carriage pulls away from the mourners, turns the corner, and disappears from sight.

The mourners return to the hall to say Kaddish.[40] They are not allowed to go to the cemetery or the crematorium, which are outside the ghetto and therefore not accessible. Nor can they go to the places in which the bodies receive their ritual washing and are wrapped in a shroud made of paper. How can one thank the men and women of the Chevra Kadisha ghetto who perform this gruesome charity?

In those autumn months of 1942, when more than 100 people died every day, it was monstrous—unimaginable—to perform this last labor of love for the dead in those dark rooms. It is hard to think about the 100 narrow bundles lying in rows on the floor, people who had pulsed with life, thriving and vigorous in spite of their old age—who now were literally just skin and bones, terrible remains, lamentable remnants of the person a mother and father had once loved, coddled, and cared for. They were placed on the washing table, and then no human eyes saw them again. When the coffins are taken away, one can see the uncovered corpse through the cracks. Here, Death has no secrets; he is very open, and one takes no notice of him.

The carts roll through the streets. Nobody stands still to let the dead pass by. One does not look. One wants to negate it, not see or hear it. Everyone just wants to focus on their own concerns and not be burdened by those of another.

The names of the dead and the time of the funeral are posted at the barracks. There is no other possibility. If one wants to check [for the names of] one's circle of friends, one has to go to the blackboard every morning. I often found the name of someone I knew just in time to pay my last respects.

In early spring 1943, the crematorium began operating, doing its hard work day and night, and burials no longer took place. Here, too, dedicated Jews dutifully and faithfully performed their task, and I repeat all my words of appreciation. Will they ever receive the reward they deserve? Are they not [like] brave soldiers at the front who put their lives on the line hourly in order to bring the dead to their final rest?

No medals and decorations can be distributed. But hopefully, when the history of Theresienstadt is written, their names will be recorded therein as heroes who selflessly and in defiance of death chose this vocation. When the poor bodies are turned to ashes, their few remains are put into an urn-like, hard cardboard box and brought to the columbarium, which is housed in a deep casemate leading through a long passage in which the [sound of one's] steps reverberate[s]. From out of the semidarkness, one walks between two sections of ramparts to a narrow space decorated with flower beds. In the middle, a steep stone staircase leads to a castellated wall. In front is a modest memorial structure. On its base stands a pillar, which bears a pitcher of tears.

[...]

The distant hall with its brick wall to the right and left of the stairs. The climb seems to lead to infinity; the blue sky can be seen, inspiring prayer and melancholy thoughts of the dead here and the living far away. The columbarium itself may not be entered.

The Dead

1942		Ghetto Inmates
August	2327 +	43403
Sept.	3941 +	51554
Oct.	3096 +	53264
Nov.	2205 +	45312
Dec.	2430 +	47693
1943		49397
Jan.	2473	45747
Feb.	2210	42966
March	1910	43692
April	1285	43651
May	977	43774
June	766	44621
July	623	46132
Aug.	559	
Sept.	430	45635
Oct.	506	40447
Nov.	427	40497
Dec.	530	40145

By December 1943, approximately 28,000 people had died and been taken to their final rest in Theresienstadt. Where will one erect the "grave of the Unknown Jew," the memorial of the Jewish community? Do not we Jews also have the right to our monument to the dead and to tears? What do we know of those who died in Russia and Poland, who chose to take their own lives because they did not want to leave their homeland? Do we not need to create a place where the Unknown Jew rests from the eternal obligation to wander to which our children could make a pilgrimage?

Perhaps their father lies here?

And because thousands do not know the final resting place of their loved ones, there must be a place to bring flowers to, where an eternal flame will burn, dedicated to the memory of European Jews who had to leave their homes for an unknown destination.

Mors Imperator. The skeleton sits on top of the arch [of the] casemate where 30 coffins are waiting for the ceremony to begin. He lets his legs dangle, smokes his pipe, and calmly watches the procession of mourners accompanying the cart. "Ha ha!" he grins and stands up. "You all belong to me. You all have succumbed to me. You all must pass through here."

[...]

We do not want to lay down our arms prematurely; we do not want to be resigned to despair. Did we, as we stood at the front and stared so often into the pallid face of death? We stayed upright. Our sacred love of the fatherland kept us from losing courage. So it should be now. Have our German men not boldly and bravely faced the danger of being taken captive in the world war, the barbed wire, the distance from home? Here we are also prisoners of war, albeit under better conditions. We should always think about this! We have better conditions, a little bit of freedom. And this we want to fight for and maintain.

We have the capacity to bear *Mors Imperator* if we work and do not despair.

That should be the answer for all whose immediate future is in the ghetto.[41]

*   *   *

The year drew to an end. We spent the first half in the comfort of our own home, the second half in foreign surroundings—the ghetto—crowded in with 45,000 strangers. I learned a maxim: Do not look back, only forward. One day we shall be free; the children will ransom us, arrange an exchange. With each passing week, the longed-for goal, for which there is no fixed date, draws nearer. Therefore, let us live only to work and to be active and useful. It preserves our health and gives us the strength to persevere.

What have the last months of the year brought to us?

One day the rumor mill had it that shops stocking the daily necessities would be opened and that a bank would pay ghetto money to all workers according to their position and duties, making cash purchases a possibility.[42] Then another rumor spread throughout the town, and we laughed at it incredulously. A café would be established in the market, with music to entertain customers; coffee and tea would be served.

What the wisest did not want to believe, what we ourselves declared nonsensical, became a reality. At the town hall a big sign appeared: Bank of the Jewish Self-Administration. At a beautiful building, where a similar establishment had been before, the inscription appeared, in large letters: Café.

And on the daily orders there appeared a request for accountants, salesmen from various industries, and waiters to sign up. With that, even the staunchest pessimists were beaten. The ghetto takes a great leap forward. Thanks to the kindness of the German authorities and the energy of the self-administration, the new facilities quickly came to life. The difficult preparations involving months of work were finished. Several million well-printed paper banknotes, in denominations of 1, 2, 5, 10, 20, 50 and 100 krone, were ready in the bank.

Ration forms were given out: One could not let people who were starving for goods buy freely, or the shops would be empty in two days. Therefore, purchases had to be controlled through a system of coupons. Shops were assigned a number of points. If one wanted to buy a coat but did not have enough points, one could apply to the coupon office for special authorization, which was decided after careful scrutiny of the case. A shop for underwear opened first, and then ladies' clothing, a haberdashery, shoes, men's clothing, stationery, luggage, and food. The shops were stocked with property that the German authorities had confiscated and from the estates of the deceased.

Ground rule in the ghetto: There is no private property; everything belongs to the community, the relatives do not inherit, only the ghetto. The survivors only have a right to personal belongings and keepsakes. Clothing and laundry had to be turned in. [Compliance was] necessary for self-preservation, even though it was absurd.

[...]

* * *

We are told at every opportunity that there are *only Jews* in the ghetto. Rank, dignity, office, and former position do not count. We had to give up our titles, and in doing so crossed out the period of our lives before the evacuation, when we had lived according to our own rules.   In the line we are all the same. We stand with our bowls and receive the same portions, the officially prescribed quantity that is posted on the notice board: soup 0.4 liters, potatoes 32 decagrams, etc. But, hand on heart—can people's temperaments be commanded?

The natures of the Berliner or the south German are different from the one of the Czechs. We are all created and molded by our homeland. It has to be said: The Jewish Czech does not love us. He sees us only as Germans. When one discusses this with him, he comes up with a hundred "ifs" and "buts." We are accused of knowing nothing about the culture of a country that is our close neighbor. Even in peaceful times we spoke about Bohemia ironically—Well, what have they achieved? The Gablonz and Reichenberg industries are German. What else is there? Nothing significant.

[...]

Unfortunately, I also know too little about Czechoslovakia to be able to say much about the land and its people. I know only one thing from my own experience—that the Czech Jews are far more patriotic and have a stronger national will than we have. I got to know two large groups: those who are completely attuned either to being Czech or to Zionism. They advance their ideas with purposeful energy and are committed 100 percent. The younger generation is politically aware and has zealously taken part in the great battle for the creation of the Republic. We have nothing like this to show. We German Jews stayed away from politics after the war and lived only to serve our families and to earn money.

Here everything fermented—fiery, even glowing, temperaments, still fiery earth (as the hot springs of Carlsbad attest); the people are ablaze here. It shows in their anger and desire. Their language sings and rings, doesn't flow uniformly like our German. How different it sounds—*ano* for "yes," *prosim* for "please."

They are easily provoked whenever they believe that you are stirring things up or when some little misdeed, neglect, or violation seems to be committed. And in spite of this, the men and women were lovable, because they always take a stance. This pride can also be seen in ordinary people. Even their workers speak differently than ours.

May our living together lead to a better understanding and become a bridge for us in some peaceful time in the future. The time is not yet ripe to speak about this, about how things could be. We still live in uncertainty, in insecurity. We do not know today what tomorrow will bring.

Ours, the fate of the elderly, is not completely opaque. We who are nearly 70, how many more years can we count on? Should we even think about the future? Or should we view Theresienstadt as the end that is intended for us? Is our release imminent, an exchange arranged by our children once peace is finally achieved—life's last gift, the shining goal in the uncertain evening of our existence? Who will decide? Who does not want to unfurl the banner of hopes and dreams?

Austria! Golden Vienna! Blue Danube! All is not gold. Who imagines the golden Viennese heart, the coziness of Vienna, the Viennese humor? I found little of all of that in the people from transport number IV—a bit in the men and almost none in the women. They are characterized, always, by an unusual sensitivity and an aggressiveness that borders on being grotesque. People believe that the eternal "kiss of the hand"—strange that men also exchange this greeting with one another—represents Vienna. But oh! All our affection for the imperial city on the Blue Danube vanishes here, once we got to know its residents better.

[...]

Of course there is a Viennese intellectual elite here, men who are in every respect of high standing and high caliber. I met men and women—and we were on the same wavelength—who possessed the old Viennese culture, not having forgotten or lost it here. I cannot say too much about people in my wider circle, because this picture would be too colorful. Among them were lieutenant colonels, generals, field marshal lieutenants, big businessmen, and educated aristocrats who had been sent here despite being raised in other religions.

We should not forget that there are not just Jews in the ghetto. Among us are men and women who were born as Protestants or Catholics and raised with those beliefs, who had no idea that by descent they belong to the Jewish race. Coming from different environments, adhering to the teachings of their churches, they cannot feel Jewish, yet they had to travel the bitter road to Theresienstadt.

Two examples of this: An elderly lady, who introduced herself as Mrs. W[ach], with the maiden name von Mendelssohn-Bartholdy, came to a "Moses Mendelssohn" lecture. She said she was a direct descendant of Abraham Mendelssohn, the son of the great philosopher.[43] Another lady, Mrs. [Ellie] von Bleichröder, had married the heir to the famous bank.[44]

We even have a clergyman here who has spent many years in a monastery as a monk. Protestants and Catholics established their own places of worship and came together at evening lectures. When they die, they are laid out in a special room, and the appropriate prayers are said. It is only the last part of the road that they walk together.

*   *   *

Something we never dared to hope for was to come about in the near future.

There was an institution: the post office. It reigned in the town hall, which was not accessible to us common ghetto folk. Only the prominent inmates were allowed to write and to receive mail. Then a camp order was announced: Each ghetto inmate would have the right each month to write one card.[45]

How and when? We were directed to the post office information services.

Five hundred cards a week were provisionally issued, and one had to stand in line to get into the post office. It was winter, and some days were bitterly cold.

At the post there was a total failure of organization. The people in charge of setting things up were in no way equal to the task. They did not know how to process and protect the incoming items, thousands of parcels, or how to organize the new card post in a way that would make things easy for the senders.

It must, unfortunately, be said—because where there is light, there is also shade—that the clerks stole a considerable amount, and men in higher positions also misappropriated some of the items that had been entrusted to them. A somber story, these thefts of things that people longed for, which were supposed to help them get through these hard times. Even now, there are scoundrels who steal what loved ones on the outside have sent, at some cost to themselves. For many, it was not the content of the packages that mattered; it was the proof that their loved ones were still alive, still there.

[...]

At an information session about 25 people crowded into a room to listen to a lawyer (he was also a censor) explaining the rules for writing. They were not easily grasped, because each of the listeners believed that he was entitled to send special requests. What we all wanted to write to our loved ones—"send parcels with food"—was not permitted; only the message "cards and parcels arrive safely" was allowed. The people at home had to interpret this to figure out what to do. [...]

The elderly people lined up at the entrance, exposed to the winds that swept through the big square, waiting to receive their cards and the instructions, which they would soon forget. Our requests to hold the session in a larger room to speak to everyone who was waiting so that there would be no need for a line, were not granted because of the thickheadedness of the lawyer sitting there, hiding behind the rules. He would not listen to reason and stubbornly continued his small sessions. The men of the Orientation Service had a tough time with those who waited, rightly impatient. They had to stand for long hours, often in the darkness of a cold, stormy dawn, just to get the longed-for card. Who can know how many people in the square caught the beginnings of a deadly illness? In Theresienstadt no undertaking was marked by such a lack of organization, by such mismanagement, thieving, and fencing of stolen goods, as the post office.

The great change came about when the arrest and dismissal of senior officials brought the scandal into the open. At the beginning of the new year [1943], the entire post-office operation was moved to the vast lower rooms of the Bodenbach barracks. Engineer Ervin Elbert from Brünn created convenient, suitable facilities that were well equipped to cope with the traffic, with serviceable counters for picking up and dropping off. He also overhauled the entire service, providing information, instructions, and help for those who could not write.

Now there was no more waiting on the street, no standing in line for hours to pick up a parcel. One could cheerfully pick up one's mail at an enclosed counter. Parcels are stacked up on tall, ceiling-high shelves. Each has a number that is also on the notification, so it is easy for the clerks to find. The clerk calls out names and carefully examines identification. One acknowledges receipt and can then go happily off with one's treasure.

Only the Protectorate citizens are allowed to receive packages weighing up to 20 kg, and their relatives take full advantage of this privilege. We secretly envy them: Their diets can be enriched, almost as though they were at home.

The bountiful Protectorate sent to its children a lot of bread, potatoes, and legumes. Going through the kitchens of the houses, one saw the pots bubbling over; I never saw anyone share the surplus. Among the many thousands of listeners [to the lectures], who assured me of their gratitude, none, with perhaps three exceptions, thought to give me a treat, some small thing [...].

Initially, the post office carried out its extensive and infinitely beneficial work completely free of charge, since of course in the ghetto one could not, having no possessions, pay for postage. This changed when we were given krone every month and suddenly could spend again. To stimulate the currency and keep it from proliferating in the wallet, it was ordered that all postage had to be paid for.

Small packets were 10 krone; parcels were 50 krone. The revenue from these new sources—the circulation of currency having been accelerated by these requirements—was easy to calculate, as the following figures show:

- 1942—Received: 200,000 shipments; of those, 20,000 parcels and packages
- 1943—Received: 750,000 shipments; of those, 550,000 parcels and packages

It was a great thing when verification cards were introduced on September 1, 1943. One filled them out, and after a few days [they] reached the senders of parcels or packages. Both parties were served by this. The sender saw the handwriting of his loved ones, and we could confirm that each shipment had been received—and thus encourage those at home not to cease their labor of love.

What route does the mail at Theresienstadt take? The place of arrival is the small Bauschowitz train station, which was absolutely not built to handle the large volume of ghetto mail. The facilities may have been sufficient for the small town of soldiers [of Theresienstadt's past], but not for the larger needs of the ghetto.

The mail trains, which ran north to south, dropped the mail off at night. There is no loading platform; the sacks of mail are simply tossed out. During the few minutes the train stops, the bags cannot be carefully handled. If the post train is late, and the sacks cannot be tossed out in time, it can happen that quite a number of them are destroyed when the other quicker trains go through. The shipments are also exposed to accidents in transit. A south German postal service reported that a shipment of 180 packages had been burned in a fire.

The ghetto post can only accept responsibility for the entire shipment once it has been handed over, meaning that it has been placed in its offices.

Then the extensive apparatus aimed at preventing theft goes into action. The packages and parcels are opened by Jewish helpers and searched by the Czech gendarmes. Not every piece [was examined], but as many as possible in the allotted time.

These items are confiscated: medicines, tobacco products, anything written or printed, and stationery. The helpers had permission to take their breakfast from the large packages. As strange as it sounds, this is how it was, and the younger people were not bashful (no more needs to be said). Today, in February 1944, there has been an innovation, welcomed on all sides. In specially converted areas of the post office, packages are opened and searched in front of the recipient. A gendarme monitors the process. He does not interfere; the Jewish helpers still open the packages. But now one received the entire shipment, so enormously important for nourishment, upon which health and survival depend. The processing takes place at four or five counters and goes smoothly, without much waiting. We can be sincerely grateful to all the men and women who work here day and night.

Some numbers: In January 1944, [a total of] 36,922 shipments arrived, weighing 120,000 kg. Of these, 5 shipments were lost. In February 1944, [a total of] 39,944 shipments came in; 9 were lost.

What these numbers meant for the diet in the ghetto is obvious.

Many of the parcels are packed badly. Under supervision, these are repackaged and tied up with string. If it is not possible to salvage them, which is often the case with larger packages, the entire contents are put into a sack and sealed.

Frequently—unfortunately—shipments arrive either without an address or with illegible writing. The mail bags are left out overnight because Bauschowitz station has no storage facilities for the ghetto. If it rains, the adhesive washes off and the wrapping comes undone; the names of recipients cannot be identified. Such undeliverable mail is transferred to the children's hospital, where it works wonders. In this way nothing is wasted, and everything finds a home thanks to the most thorough organization.

[...]

There is one more useful postal scheme to mention: the delivery of letters. The mailboxes are emptied three times a day, and [the letters] delivered quite promptly.

We have now been given another gift. We are permitted to write to the Birkenau[46] ghetto in Upper Silesia. This is an opening-up of our isolation, which cannot be valued highly enough. We are in a position to give and receive signs of life from friends in the ghetto with whom we have lived and worked for over a year. This is like a vitamin supplement of the greatest efficacy. The administration that accomplished this adds another page to the history of Theresienstadt.

* * *

[...] The Christmas holidays [1942] passed unnoticed and unobserved.

In the ghetto it is wished that these days not be spoken of, least of all to talk about how they were celebrated at home. As far as I'm concerned, we who actively planned our entire business around the Christmas celebrations, who in December hoped that our customers would pay their bills promptly, who walked through the streets of Berlin for four weeks looking at the festive decorations in the shop windows, we are not able after 60 years to forget the magic that emanated from our Christmas tree every year. All our childhood memories are bound up with Christmas. Is my generation to blame because our parents did not celebrate Hanukkah? That we know so little of the history and [the] customs of our people?

My wife and I sat together in the evening and talked quietly about the happy times we had celebrated with our four children. I was filled with nostalgia and sad because we had not received a greeting from those who were so far away and because we were alone in this cold room, and could only be with them in our thoughts. [...]

Some comrades had expressed the wish to celebrate the beginning of the new year together. I was happy to comply with this request, on one condition: The entire event should be a New Year's gift to me. I did not want to organize any part of it. That fulfilled their intention. They wanted to show that there was talent among the comrades.

We gathered, together with our wives, at 8 P.M. Commander Kurt Frey and Mrs. Gubot were the guests of honor. We sat at tables covered with white tablecloths. At midnight there was hot coffee and sliced bread contributed by the kitchen. Wilhelm Marburg, our house poet, opened the evening with a spirited prologue. A variety of lighthearted presentations followed, and there was even the première of a short stage play featuring Carl Nasch-Month, the once well-known Austrian actor, [...] and our Mrs. Maria Ziffer.

At midnight I spoke solemn words recalling our loved ones far away. Many a secret tear was shed, and we old ones remained silent for a long time. But then the mood lightened again. We parted from each other at 1 A.M. having shared a really nice, pleasurable evening. The streets were dark. The stars shone with a festive clarity. The air was mild and soft.

1943 had begun; its first hour had already flowed into the sea of eternity. *New year, what will you bring to us, the uprooted and incarcerated?* The anxious question on all our minds as we walked "home" was what will the next 365 days bring? Will we continue peacefully in the rhythm of our work or be hurled into extreme, unknown, threatening circumstances with new goals and tasks?!

"Remain unbowed"[47] should be the motto for 1943.

Part II

1943

The first of January brought no surprises. We shook hands, exchanged good wishes, and spoke of our hopes and fears.

There is no holiday in the ghetto, and our work at the Service proceeded according to the same rhythms and routines as last year. Our office had the advantage of being easy to heat. Our room orderly, Albert Fuß, who had also taken on the night shift, took exemplary care of us. By 6:30 each morning, the area was swept and clean, and the tables and benches were ready for the staff.

Our comrades warmed their coffee, which was seldom hot because the pots had been standing on the stove for several hours. At lunchtime [however], we could enjoy a hot meal, because the stove was at our disposal. Wood and coal were distributed to us every morning, brought in on a stretcher.

The door was protected by a vestibule made with two blankets. My desk was across from it. To the left, on a base that had formerly served as a repository for oats, stood the filing cabinet. Everything I needed was at hand. On January 1, the Service numbered 29 men and 10 women.

Our name had become well-known. On the street, people asked the men with the white armbands for information, directions, or inquired about the upcoming lectures. We were in constant demand. For example, if a roof needed to be repaired and passersby protected from falling tiles, our men stood by. If for some reason there was unusual congestion in front of an office, we were responsible for maintaining order. A headcount was to be taken when food was distributed. Everyone volunteered—because there was the reward of an extra ration.

Spring delivered its calling card to Theresienstadt, as the high mountains sheltered us from the rough winds. We were given the job of guarding the small lawns in the two parks, to prevent the grass from being trampled and to keep the ramparts at the Bauschowitz gate clear. That was a happy assignment for the seventy-year-olds, who loved to be able to spend long days outdoors. It was beneficial to their health. There was only one problem. In the good, pure air, their appetites increased.

Yes, appetite, the motivation behind the most terrible acts in the ghetto. The nourishment with which we were provided was satisfactory but not sufficient. Whoever failed to [evenly] divide his three days' bread ration, who for some reason cut off too much on one of the days, would run out. Many strong men finished their bread in two days, which was understandable considering that one night a week, the menu featured one succinct word: coffee. Even if it turned out to be coffee with milk, it did not satisfy the hunger.

Also, the soup, euphemistically called "lentil extract soup," that for many months we had to consume in both the afternoon and evening, was filling, but not nutritious at all. On two occasions, tins of liver pâté and black pudding were distributed, each of which four people had to share. Oh! If the division was not absolutely even and one of the partners felt cheated—it was the source of many disputes.

So it was with the bread as well. The entire house received a single allotment. Men and women put it on carts or wheelbarrows and delivered it to the building elder, who controlled the quantity. He divided all the bread into portions for each room and knew exactly how much each individual should receive:

S = Hard laborer
N = Normal
L and K (Light and sick) = Not working

The room elder took the bread and sliced it in half. It was divided exactly, with a ruler. Even then, people were not always satisfied. There were plenty of gripers in Theresienstadt, who always found fault with something. Margarine and sugar were given out in equal portions. The sugar was given out in bags, no longer measured out by the tablespoon. This method invited cheating, which was avoided by meticulously pouring the sugar in the supply room, rather than dispensing it in public. Yes, life here is built on a thousand small things—and to spread the white cloth of brotherly love over all of them is not easy.

The Service operated every day according to a schedule. The guard posts were divided into hourly shifts, which always had to be filled. This was often difficult: We had people who got sick, which left us short of personnel. My deputy was the newly arrived lawyer and notary Dr. Max Meyer from Münster. A bit ponderous, a bureaucrat by nature and happy to work; and extremely correct. He quickly fit into the Service and took over all its correspondence.

There was a lot to write: long lists for the central labor office recording how many hours each man had worked. Lists to be sent to the supply office, and special permits for laundry and shoe repair. In short, paperwork took up several hours each day. Daily service reports had to be given to the head of the ghetto watch, which he read and signed. In the morning there was a roll call; the hours were recorded, the day's assignments given out, and everyone could say what was on his mind. I instituted a new policy that caused great joy: I publicly congratulated people on their birthdays with a few well-chosen words. Then the comrades encircled that person and wished him well. Except we could not give any gifts.

Dr. Meyer did not stay in our circle for long. He became ill with a stomach disorder that kept him away for several months. Time and again he tried to keep active; his whole heart was with the Service, where he had found so many good comrades. Sometimes he would come in for two or three weeks, and then his strength would give out. Still, he gathered himself together again. He wrote the admission tickets for the readings, which allowed him to sit still and not strain himself. Unfortunately, even this apparent improvement did not last long. He had to be transferred to the hospital, and there he died [January 29, 1944]. The cause of death was, as we suspected, cancer.

Hugo Weinmann from Vienna took his place. He was a strong, energetic man who had been a cavalry captain in the war and was therefore qualified to command a large group of men.

He took over all the paperwork for me, which by now had become quite extensive. From month to month, the size of our staff increased, eventually reaching 49 men, and a group this size required all kinds of administrative work. There were 24 places to be guarded and, in addition, incidental requests, which we often had to refuse because we lacked the men.

At that time, January 1943, people rushed to join our Service. But the personnel office drew the line, allowing us only to take on men who were over 60 years old because the Service was specifically meant for elderly men who could not be placed elsewhere. In a few exceptional cases, I succeeded in obtaining authorization, if I could prove that I absolutely needed the man and his classification was IV: for light work only. After endless negotiations, the personnel office approved a total of 55 men and 10 women. That was the limit. So this staff had to cover all the assignments as ordered. In the first months of the year, we still had people staying overnight because transports still arrived. Then that stopped, and our "Hotel City Magdeburg" was closed.

I remember that one evening we were assigned about five women who could not be housed anywhere. We were therefore to give them overnight accommodation. My room was occupied, so I prepared a shelter, with hastily prepared straw sacks, in a stable in the first courtyard. "Are we going to a hotel?" asked the ladies, who had just arrived from southern Germany and had been told about the Theresienstadt old people's home. *Of course, ladies, I will take you now to Hotel Magdeburg!* When we arrived at the stable and I told the ladies that this was their lodging for the night, they were not so cheerful. In fact, I had not witnessed such horror in a long time, as it played out here in the semidarkness of the room. I had trouble convincing the crying women that they were in the Theresienstadt ghetto, which had neither a hotel nor a home, and should resign themselves to everything, including the straw sack.

A propos the straw sacks: These were scarce at that time because production could not keep pace with the great demand. In Berlin, we had handed our horsehair mattresses over to the Jewish community, which had promised to send them here "by barge." After half a year and thanks to having a medical certificate, I managed to get two mattresses that finally gave my tired body a reasonably comfortable night's sleep. Our life here is composed of a thousand small things that seem in themselves insignificant, meaningless, but that still play an important role in the difficult life of the Theresienstadt ghetto.

The "Lecture Series of the Orientation Service," as it was officially named, continued along its peaceful, undisturbed path in those first months and became increasingly popular. Doctors, scientists, officials, and department heads came to me to sign up, not only as speakers, but also as listeners and regular visitors. Our audience increased so much in the spring that I decided to schedule the lectures daily instead of every other day.

Now I even received a *stampiglie!*[1] In the ghetto the authorities recognize a document such as a requisition or a message only if it carried a stamp. If one wanted pencils, paper, pens, or notebooks, one had to go to the finance department to obtain authorization from Otto Brod. Only with a *stampiglie*—with State approval, as it were—would he give his consent.

It was through this official transaction that I got to know the brother of the important Jewish poet Max Brod, from Prague. He was a gentle, dignified man, with a calm but authoritative demeanor, highly educated, and knowledgeable, in addition to being a poet. He gave several lectures, and his clear, often headstrong views were met with lively applause.

As for the result of the *stampiglie*—I even received two, Orientation Service and lecture series—it helped very much to smooth difficult roads for me, for example, for the issuance of materials. People crowded into a narrow area to pick up the "necessities of daily living." These were precious necessities, such as a box of matches—a popular barter item for smokers, who gave bread in exchange for fire—or soap, wash powder, brooms, buckets, plates and mugs, toilet paper (when the rolls of toilet paper ran out, a mountain of military records that had been found somewhere were handed out). One had to try to "grab" all these things and wait in line for a long time to get the bare necessities. How often one heard "unavailable"! And then the waiting in line and the battle to find a similar item began anew.

When one puts them together, all these little anecdotes, like the scattered pieces of a puzzle, reveal a true picture of life and the struggles in Theresienstadt. What seemed unimportant to us outside, laughable even, and of no concern to us, has great meaning here—for instance, a fine-toothed comb. It is essential to have one if one is to provide proper evidence of the presence of certain small bugs.

We in the Orientation Service were at particularly high risk of exposure to lice. In the evening, the lecture visitors, unfortunately, sat very close together, filling every corner. Infestation was a possibility at all times. Yet for weeks we were told, "Fine-toothed combs are out of stock and not available." To this day, I do not have one.

Something else. We owned some large and small storm lanterns. The Service used the small ones when we had to bring the lost people home in total darkness; the large ones for emergency lighting in our room. At first everything went well: We were given the necessary fuel. Then, came the restriction: distribution only by the police. The result: lengthy negotiations. Further, fuel could be had only by special permission of the administration. Finally, we had neither fuel nor a substitute. The lanterns remained unused, and we made do with candles—for as long as we still had them. Once candles could be had only on the black market with Czech krone, we had to give them up, too, and when the electric lights failed, we could do nothing but wait patiently. Out of respect for the electric plant, which provided us with the pleasure of light, it should be said that such failures seldom occurred. Why "pleasure"? One treasures only that of which one has been deprived. When we look back at history, has it not been this way in all ages?

In the houses there was only electric lighting in the rooms, hallways, and lavatories. That the [electric lightbulbs] were stolen with frightening regularity is not a surprise. The wattage of the lightbulbs was low, and people with bad eyesight could not read, nor could the sick in the bunk beds.

Light creates, at least during the short evening hours, the illusion of home. Even though there were no tables or chairs, one was happy to have a stool that could be used as a dining table. One sat on the small plank in front of the bed and tried to prepare a midday or evening meal with the bowls, plates, and glasses filled with various contents. What could people crowded together in such cramped quarters do on long winter evenings? By 8 o'clock they had to be in the *ubikation*. The rooms were not heated. It wasn't possible to sit comfortably. One bulb in the center [of the room] provided a cone of reading light.

Most people lay in bed after dinner to keep warm and to rest their old bodies. The light had to be turned off at 9 o'clock. If someone came from work later, he was allowed to turn the light on again for 10 to 15 minutes. [...]

* * *

How had the lecture series developed in the new year? I can answer this question precisely because all events were registered. The first "Colorful Hour" that I presented in 1943 was dedicated to a popular idea—staging the *Überbrettl*.[2] [...] Now, this *Überbrettl* evening was a great success. Mrs. Myra Strauss sang and recited delightfully. *The Husband* and *The Music Comes*[3] seemed as fresh as they were 50 years ago when they were first produced in Berlin. The performances had to be repeated, and I could have done it ten times to satisfy popular demand.

The next major event in the series of talks had a longer prehistory, which I do not want to leave out. I was encouraged [by my audience] to stage small plays as well. I flatly refused to do so. I did not wish under any circumstances to compete with the Leisure Time Organization, which possessed all the necessary equipment to stage performances appropriate to the circumstances in Theresienstadt. Staging plays exceeded my ability considerably—I had ventured into recitals, but not of stage plays. Still, might it not be possible to find a different solution?[4]

The Leisure Time Organization presented some comedies: *Dictatorship of Women* and *The Camel Goes Through the Eye of the Needle*. These were light entertainments, nicely presented in Czech, but they avoided "high art." The directors could not bring themselves to stage a "classic" repertory. And yet it would have been very easy to do because people who were qualified to do them were hanging around idly in Theresienstadt. There was Mathilde Sussin, the noted actress from Berlin, to name just one. Also living with us, unemployed, were Louis Treumann [...], Carl Month, and many other men who had been actors and now had nothing to do. The situation led to a crude joke that circulated in Theresienstadt: "Seeking qualified man for the position of conductor. Musicians preferred."

I couldn't stop thinking about it. Something had to happen—I was expected to take a different route from the Leisure Time Organization. And I found one: to read plays with assigned parts. That was the solution, and it was just right for our small space.

I found actors who were happy to participate in such an undertaking because they longed to be active in their beloved former profession, to perform before the public again, to act and to hear the applause.

Building the stage in Room 38 was a big headache, but the difficulty was overcome with the help of my comrades who knew how to use a saw and a hammer. The room orderly's bed stood by the wooden wall. It was 185 cm long and 1 meter wide, big enough to be used as a stage. A bench of a similar size seated five people. A detachable shelf formed a lectern that was strong enough to hold the books and to withstand the fists of the speakers. We scrounged up some big, red, plush blankets [for curtains], to give the stage a dignified appearance. Our reading stage was installed, and it is still used today. It was later moved to the middle of the room so that both sides could see equally well.

Choosing the plays was not a problem for me. Was there any doubt about what should be presented? Goethe, of course. And if him, then only *Faust*.

I reached for the stars.

[...]

We were fully prepared on the first evening, but my heart was still pounding because I had a reputation to protect. I had risked a lot; I had penetrated into areas that really should have remained closed to me.[5] The theater belonged solely to the Leisure Time Organization. To intrude upon its domain seemed like a sacrilege. But we did not act, we read; it was just like presenting the poems. I took this position and vigorously defended it against all attacks. And there were some. I only chose plays that the Leisure Time Organization had not staged or announced: One could not interpret my activity as competition. But even so, some did.

The premiere took place on January 30, and I can say that it was an unmitigated success. Everything worked out. The two evenings blended harmoniously together, and the audience was thrilled to be reunited with Goethe here in the ghetto.[6] The requests for tickets increased from week to week: I could have easily presented the reading of *Faust* every night for a whole month.

Now I was besieged by actors in Theresienstadt who wanted to participate. Suddenly people thronged my small room and wanted to be a part of the action. So I let them audition and chose from the younger talents, who would gradually take the places of the very elderly.

The younger, transformed *Faust* was now read by his best representative in Theresienstadt—the approximately [30]-year-old Dr. Georg Běhal. Blond, handsome, energetic, and healthy, by day he worked—please, this is the truth— for the transportation department as a potato hauler. He carried the heavy sacks on his strong back to the peeling areas. He had to work on many nights, when the carts had to be unloaded quickly. In the evenings, he sat, radiant with youth, on our readers' bench. He led me to another Gretchen when the first actress became ill and could not speak for months. It was the small, petite, very pretty Mrs. Hana Munk, with the soft, supple voice of the Czechs.

She recited *"Ach neige* (Oh, bow down)" for me, and after that I was utterly convinced that she would make a perfect Gretchen: simple and moving. I was not bothered by the slight unevenness of her language, as coming from her mouth, it had a charming ring.[7] I was really not concerned by her hard pronunciation of the "ch" in the words *Gärtchen* [little garden] or *Milch* [milk]. When the prison scenes were read with such feeling, vitality, and mastery, then all the little misgivings fell by the wayside. And I was proved right. I never heard as moving a Gretchen as Hana Munk, and the public agreed. She was celebrated as a diva, and deserved it, too.

The *Faust* readings became a topic of daily conversation in Theresienstadt, and I was congratulated on the success of my daring feat. A great honor was bestowed upon me when the ghetto watch built its own stage in the ballroom of the Deutsches House—with curtains, electric lighting, and walls created with panels of gray fabric.[8] After an inaugural variety show following the dedication, *Faust* was read twice, over the course of four evenings.

The hall had the capacity to seat over 350 people comfortably; it was the only place in Theresienstadt that was suitable for theater. We improvised other "stages" in attics, but they could not be used in winter since the attics were not heated. These "stage rooms" were used because of an ongoing problem: the shortage of rooms. When, for example, the Jewish elder had to speak officially to the ghetto, he wanted to do so before the largest possible audience. But he could only gather in the attic of the Dresdner barracks, with its large back room. Otherwise, there were just improvised stages, smaller, which had been lovingly set up by those concerned.

It was not until the summer of 1943 that the beautiful ballroom was made available for musical performances. Our commander, Kurt Frey, with his young team of ghetto guards, had completely refurbished the poorly maintained hall. Its appearance had been shocking—it had housed more than 100 people for over a year. He built a model stage: All the benches had backrests, and a "lighting man" sat high up in a berth, looking out over the stage and the hall. The whole house was set up for the work of the ghetto watch—the youngsters had a comfortable place to sleep and their own kitchen with better food than in the mass kitchens. But the best was the separate W.C. with flushing, the height of luxury in Theresienstadt.

On the day of its inauguration, Mr. Frey could look upon his work with justifiable pride. A broad staircase with a half-landings led to the hall. To the left and right was an honor guard formed by the ghetto watch standing tightly, man-to-man, and the smartest young people of the community. The stage was decorated with fresh greenery and was a charming sight. [...]

After a prologue, the variety program began, with the elite sitting above and also in the stalls. Whoever had rank in Theresienstadt was invited. The mood was that of a grand premiere, an evening that would be remembered forever.

Alas, the stage that should have been available to us two nights a week was not ours for long. Suddenly, to everyone's surprise, came an order to clear the hall and remove the stage, in order to put in beds again for 100 people who had been sleeping in cold attics.

Difficile est satiram non scribere.[9] After months of work, they had created, through their own efforts, a worthy hall, a gift to the ghetto—a place where one felt content, that reminded us of what we had lost. Yet the space-allocation section could not find another way to accommodate them in the whole of Theresienstadt. That is how cultural affairs are promoted in Theresienstadt. On the one hand, there was the call for more good events in order to provide a happy, carefree hour now and then for 45,000 people; on the other, the same authorities sabotaged all efforts that might make up for what we lacked.

Now, back to *Faust*. Requests for it increased by the week. My hall held only 100 people. I was forced to create waiting lists. The evenings were sold out a month in advance.

I embarked on a new adventure, which I knew, in spite of all the difficulties, must and would succeed. I selected scenes from the second part [of *Faust*], which my actors knew and which were appropriate for my stage. [...] The three *Faust* evenings stayed on the program indefinitely, and I could have let it play for the whole month, it was so sought-after by both the old and the young. However, he who rests goes rusty. [...]

Likewise, the lectures continued on an upward curve. At my request, Dr. Leopold Neuhaus delivered a series of lectures on the history of religion, entitled *Bible Studies*. Our generation knows so little of the book of books; unfortunately we learned nothing in our youth, because religion was a minor subject, and we Jews were not taught about it in school—in my time, it was left to private initiative. And since there wasn't any, we remained ignorant about Jewish things. It was time to catch up—also [being in] the ghetto imposes certain obligations on us, and it seemed to me that the first was for us old people to learn about Judaism and its history so that we could appreciate what the Jews had achieved in 3,000 years.

Over the course of ten evenings, for approximately an hour and a half each time, Dr. Neuhaus presented this significant series. It was, for us, a revelation. A new, unknown territory was made accessible to us in a way we had never before experienced. At last, and for the first time, Dr. Neuhaus led us from the source to the estuary—we learned what the Bible was, how it should be read and understood, how Judah's religion began, and how it had developed from century to century.

It did not stop with these ten sessions; we were guided ever further. The bearers of important names and their life's work were revealed to us through Dr. Neuhaus's masterful presentation: Moses, Ezra, Saadja Gaon, Rabbi Gershom, Raschi, Maimonides, and, finally, Moses Mendelssohn. Each of these evenings was valuable for everyone. I may say that particularly the lectures about Jewish prophets and teachers won many Jews back to their religion.

In this connection I wanted to summon the words of the first man to proclaim the message of human kindness and tolerance to a world, which, in its position toward the Jews, was positively medieval. I prepared *Nathan the Wise*. The administration definitely did not greet my proposal with immediate approval. On the contrary, they tried to dissuade me from presenting it. In the end, I went along with their wishes on another proposal. Although I did not share their views and could prove them wrong, I did not want to seem obstinate. Thus I could read *Nathan*.[10]

[...]

* * *

If one wanted to have a particular position in Theresienstadt, one did not simply present oneself at the place where the job or position was; rather, one followed the official path, which for many seemed unfair and proved difficult. After a few short days to acclimatize, everyone who arrives in the ghetto has to report to the "Hundertschaften."[11] There he performs every kind of physical labor and is not asked what he was in civilian life.

An appeal court judge from Munich and a lawyer and notary from Berlin have been sweeping the yard in the Magdeburg barracks for weeks. Our best actor cleans toilets at his *ubikation*. A very senior judge has had a most prestigious position as chief of personnel of the entire revenue service and then served as a judge on the Reich Fiscal Court until [he was dismissed for being a Jew]. He has now been sitting for a year in the central labor office writing out index cards. The list goes on and on, but I will stop here.

Once the candidate has worked for a month in the Hundertschaften, he is allowed to apply for a post. First condition: submission of *curriculum vitae* in duplicate. One copy goes to the graphology department, where it is examined and sent to the department that the candidate has chosen, together with a reference or confirmation number. Large departments such as production, provisions, medical, etc. had their own registration for personnel. But even they depended on approval from the central labor office. The personnel office could confirm officials only after each case had been reviewed by the central labor office. If, for example, a lawyer wanted to be employed as an official, but wrote in his *curriculum vitae* that he had been retrained as a "carpenter," he would never work in an office, because carpenters were very rare, and sorely needed.

The organization of the central labor office is a model and covers all ghetto inmates with the exception of the [very] old and those not working. It is responsible for all the workers' needs, and you cannot get a suit or shoe repaired without their approval. In the case of long illnesses, it issues an "allowance," and special rations are available upon request. Theresienstadt is a large work camp that accomplishes a great deal, and its history, which will surely be officially recorded [one day], will show that the Jews proved themselves as workers.

Regarding the *curriculum vitae*. It is hard to determine how often, over the course of a year (despite the shortage of paper), one has to write a CV in looking for a position. It is required everywhere; it is indeed the basis of every official act. When I wanted to recruit new people, I went to the personnel registry [in the central labor office] and was handed a pack of such papers, which I studied. Then I invited potential candidates to an interview, only to find that none of them was right. Ruins, but no men. I looked for candidates for the Orientation Service among the men from the new transports, and by this method, I got good results.

The personnel registry treats every ghetto inmate by the book. They once rejected a man who had proven to be especially good during his 14 days of trial service and also worked well with the comrades. I received a notice that the man could not be confirmed [in his post]. When I asked for an explanation, I was told that his personnel files were not in order. This meant that he had a criminal record, which made him ineligible as an official. One of my people, who had been in the Service for a year, was punished with one day of incarceration for an unresolved issue in the mess. I was immediately told by the personnel registry to let the man go.

The days were getting longer—it was light until 6 P.M. If we got up at six in the morning, as was our habit, we had to turn on the light, but when we went to get coffee, we were able [to see to] avoid the puddles in the courtyards and the worst patches of mud. The rain turned the paved roads into marshes. Especially the passages connecting the houses—they had made openings in the dividing walls, to make the houses accessible from the back—remained in a desolate condition in spite of all efforts.

We were lucky—the winter of 1942/43, unlike the winter of 1943/44, was completely free of snow, and there was hardly a rainy day.

* * *

On March 10 [1943] the 100th lecture was to be held. This first jubilee had to be celebrated. Our reputation demanded it. I went to the Jewish elder Mr. Jacob Edelstein. I had been introduced to him in the fall, and he had promised me a lecture on his pet subject: Zionist issues. Long-lasting injury to his vocal cords had prevented him from delivering his talk. Now I reminded him, and he agreed to speak in Room 218. So now I had the most prestigious speaker for this day, and when Professor Dr. Emil Utitz said that he was also prepared to give a celebratory lecture, I was not worried about the event's success.

[…]

The two hours went by as well as I had imagined. A mixed choir, adults and children, framed the lectures. Professor Ledeč, an excellent violinist from Prague, played Smetana and Beethoven. Both lecturers spoke superbly. Jacob Edelstein, in order not to restrict himself, chose *On the Jewish Question* as his theme. Professor Utitz elaborated on the advancement of culture in Theresienstadt. The hall was filled to capacity, standing room only, and the audience listened attentively to both speakers' presentations.

With kind words of appreciation, Mr. Fritz Janowitz handed me a portfolio filled with valuable drawings by the painter Bertho[ld] Ehrenwerth. *The Hatikwa*, heard standing, closed the wholly successful celebration, which earned many new friends for my efforts. I could be pleased with the 100th lecture.[12]

[…]

Up until April 7, all the evenings went according to plan. Then we suffered a hard blow—the lectures were to be suspended until May 12. One morning in the beginning of April, we were informed of an event that caused both great consternation and great excitement. Five young boys had escaped, just disappeared, and had not reported to work. When all attempts to catch them failed, the German authorities had to be notified.[13]

Is it surprising that in springtime young, immature people are filled with such powerful longing that all reason falls by the wayside? It was easy to imagine being in a runaway's shoes. One was reminded of Karl May[14]: Contemplating and planning throughout the winter strengthen the resolve.

It was possible for the Czechs to disappear among the country folk, [but] not for the Germans of the Reich. Not knowing the language, they could not go unnoticed in the South, even if they succeeded in breaking out, and in the North, it was hardly better. Without identification papers, they will certainly be caught by the gendarmes within a day. From the outset, such attempts are misjudged and doomed to fail.

These boys don't hurt just their own families, [but] the entire ghetto, which has to bear the consequences. That said, the German authorities went easy and did not impose "sanctions or penalties" but instead issued only one decree: All leisure activities are banned. The suspension was valid from April 17 to May 13. It is difficult to describe what this lack of activity in the evening meant to us, how heavily it weighed on us.

[...]

It was lonely in the evenings in Room 38—there were no events of any kind. I refused to undertake anything covert. For me a prohibition is a prohibition, and I would not willingly risk danger if I could avoid it. We are not, and this should be said here, unobserved. There are Jewish spies in Theresienstadt, who for condemnable reasons betray the trust of their comrades. How else could it happen that those in hiding, whose whereabouts are known only to a few, could be found? It was once said that we need betrayal, but we despise the traitor. I fully understand the expression "The end justifies the means." In war, every means is allowed, and therefore informants persist, wretches who make their reports for a reward. I dread to think what the German authorities think of such an individual.

* * *

After the welcome end of the "terrible days without lectures," Senior Rabbi Dr. Leo Baeck [and] *Geheimrat* Professor Dr. Strauß spoke in our room. Both men, who were 70 and 75 years old respectively, attend to their duties with an unusual youthfulness. They speak many times during the week, and the crush of people is remarkable.

Dr. Leo Baeck, honorary chairman of the Council of Elders, has become the most popular speaker in Theresienstadt. His lectures—purely philosophical, rarely religious—are models of crystal-clear exposition. It is a pleasure to listen to him. His lecturing has completely changed since Berlin. Does age bring dignity, clarity, and the art of brevity? One might assume so. The great philosopher Baeck enjoys wholehearted recognition and admiration literally in all circles in the ghetto.

The 150th lecture was held on June 30. Dr. Leopold Neuhaus delivered a talk on the *Talmud* part of his series on religion.

An interesting series of lectures was given by Professor Dr. Maximilian Adler: (1) *Greek Philosophy Before Socrates;* (2) *Socrates and the Sophists;* (3) *Aristotle;* (4) *Plato.*

I must refrain from elaborating on the series of daily lectures that were held starting in July. Each one had its own character, its own quality, was special, and only rarely was there a washout. I could now pick and choose and didn't have to provide a speaking forum to all the second-rate people who constantly urged me to let them demonstrate their skills.

[...]

Now I want to tell the story of a discovery that brought me great joy. One day a real poetic talent came forward, very humble, whose background was reminiscent of that of Hugo von Hofmannsthal. When I announced the Theresienstadt poetry contest, a young man, who was slender and delicate, like a high school student, whose eyes were red and irritated (from a lot of nocturnal official and private writing), submitted a couple of poems. Professor Utitz, who knew and thought highly of him and his intellectual creations, told me about him and asked me, if possible, to support him. His name was Georg Kafka, born February 15, 1921. During the day, he worked at the registry on the card index. [...] At night, if his duties permitted (at the times of departing transports people often had to work through the night), he sat at the typewriter to transcribe his creations.

The verses that he wrote were not voluminous. [...] His talent requires a larger space. He wrote stage plays, and the first one he gave to me was *Alexander in Jerusalem.*

[...]

Unfortunately the young poet was restricted for months, constrained by the pain in his eyes and also by his father's severe illness. His heavy workload is very demanding as well. In spite of this, he has produced a new work. A puppet play: *The Golem.* Maybe I can produce it.

[...]

Now I wish to write about the [...] religious service that was held in Room A6–38. The comrades complained that they seldom had a chance to attend the religious service that was held in various places and in different forms. [...]

As an old established member of the reform community, I had for decades been thinking about shortening the long and tiring religious service, adjusting it to our tastes so that every visitor would be drawn in for an hour. The old prayers, speaking directly to God, would be maintained and spoken alternately in German and Hebrew. In consultation with the rabbis, a mutually satisfactory arrangement would be found.

[...] The Durra choir framed the hour with German and Hebrew songs. The atmosphere was truly devotional, and members of the other two religions attended regularly, often telling us how much they were moved by the event.[15] When we had to give up Room A6, the hour of prayer also came to an end. The director of the Leisure Time Organization did not want it and forbade me to carry on elsewhere.

The ever-increasing [number of] visitors—there was not even standing room left—proved how much the people who came appreciated this hour—it uplifted and gave them peace.

In the ghetto one is allowed to profess and practice Judaism any way one wants. Anyone who does not want to eat bread during Passover gets matzoh. This is a big sacrifice, as one cannot get full on the allotted quantity; it is impossible. Bread, the foundation of our nutrition, can hardly be done without. The person who trades it [for matzoh] anyway goes hungry during those eight days.

But someone who is tuned to the modern sensibility, and wishes to promote devotion through a service aimed at "seeking God," [finds that the men who decide these matters do not see it that way]. Unfortunately, hundreds of "God seekers" are left without the possibility of finding "Him." Wherever there is any form of government—it is always the same—it is carried out according to time-honored practices. Even in the ghetto, where one might assume that everyone can become holy in his own way, this is permitted only by permission of the superiors![16]

A few of the evenings should be highlighted, as they are particularly interesting because of their originality.

[...]

An especially lively evening: *Hasidic Tales of Martin Buber*[17] read by Hugo Friedmann and Alfred Schmitz. Dr. Leopold Neuhaus spoke about the nature of this movement with a wonderful impetus that swept us all away—he himself being a Hasid of eloquence and persuasiveness.

The reverberating and lasting effect of these lectures is that the majority of listeners now aspire to learn more about these Jewish events, to light their own ignorance and to get a glimpse of the major Jewish movements of the past. We know so little about the history of the past millennia that we need—whoever is willing—to take every opportunity to light the darkness. It was from this standpoint that I directed all the lectures. I have the feeling that as a direct result of these lectures on Jewish history and literature, many who were half-hearted, uncertain, or aloof from Judaism were reclaimed as convinced adherents. I will always be very proud of this.

* * *

The first of August was approaching—the anniversary of the founding of the Orientation Service. How should this day be celebrated? That question gave me a headache.

The ghetto watch celebrated its founding day with a parade on the bastion. The entire administration and many guests of honor were present. Commander Kurt Frey led the military section, which marched by briskly in a Prussian style. Then the head of security, Dr. Karl Löwenstein, inspected the front line and gave a speech. I could not celebrate our founding day this way. I needed to strike a note of my own.

At 8 o'clock on August 1, I held a ceremonial roll call, attended by Commander Frey and Mr. Fritz Janowitz. I read out a progress report about our first year of work and unveiled a wooden tablet upon which were recorded the names of all of our comrades who had passed away. A choir sang the song *The Good Comrade*,[18] which sounded poignantly through the room. In the evening, Dr. Martin Salomonski spoke exclusively to the members of our circle and their wives on the theme *Citizen, Jew, Human Being*.

The actual anniversary celebration took place on August 2. It was my idea. Since a large room was not available, I chose for myself: the small third courtyard of our barracks. No one raised any objections.

Parts of the dais from the stage of the Deutsches House were in the courtyard, and we used them. Under the direction of Wilhelm Homburger, the comrades had prepared the program for the afternoon—it was intended as a gift to me. And it was truly a worthy gift, not only for me, but for everyone.

Benches and chairs were placed around the dais for the guests of honor, but otherwise one could only stand. But at the stipulated time, 4 P.M., it was extremely crowded. Approximately 1,200 eager people in the happiest of moods waited expectantly for what was to come. The arcades and windows around the courtyard, up to the roof, were full of happy groups of spectators.

The event began with a prologue, and then the program rolled out, which was really worth seeing: music, singing, recitation, a magician with his instruments, who fooled us with his sleight of hand, the house elder of the Home for the Blind, a private gymnastics teacher with his group of splendid children exercising, the comic duo Bobby John and Morgan, the delightful Trude Frankl, who accompanied herself with a harmonica; in short, every number was an "event."

As always, we had presented something new, distinctive. We had attacked the space problem without giving it too much thought and did not ask whether it was possible for people to stand for two hours, whether the audience would be quiet and orderly. Our invitation was a large poster that we placed above the first entryway, and over a thousand people responded to our call. The acoustics of the courtyard are excellent. When people are quiet, even a softly spoken word and, above all, music are clearly audible. We proved that this courtyard is very suitable for outdoor events. Our listeners appeared most appreciative and enthusiastic.

In autumn, the Leisure Time Organization staged a wonderful event in the courtyard. The Karl Fischer mixed choir sang scenes from *Aida*, and *Cavalleria Rusticana*, featuring soloists. It was overwhelming, an electrifying experience that we, the audience, took home with us. It was part of another, better world—a world that we believed we had lost forever and that, at long intervals, we recaptured piece by piece, creating an imaginary, yet shining, picture.

*   *   *

Besides the Leisure Time Organization, there was another source of spiritual nourishment: the library. It is another miracle, like so many here in Theresienstadt.

The ghetto had a library stocked with about 49,000 volumes, many of which were works of Jewish literature, supplied by the Institute for [ ][19] and libraries in Prague and Hamburg. It was housed in the inadequate rooms of house L306, but one made the best of it and set up bookcases in two rooms. Lack of space and personnel made it impossible to allow all the ghetto inmates to come and borrow books, so a brilliant solution was found. Every house received a box of books to lend out internally; at the end of the month, these books would be exchanged for another box. Likewise, in the hospitals.[20]

Houses where there were people with infectious diseases could not, unfortunately, receive books. Individuals were able to obtain academic books for studying. The members of the Leisure Time Organization received the books they needed as intellectual munition. It was as though an invigorating energy emanated from this store of books. Here was the intellectual nourishment that we had missed for so long.

We found all our favorites from back home, books that we had owned; at times we gently stroked the volumes, feeling the joy of being reunited. Interesting first editions, small volumes of the classics published by Cotta, and French antiquarian books with beautiful bindings tempted us from the shelves. And—a treasure trove for researchers—countless volumes of journals: *The Jew, Menorah,*

East and West, *Allgemeine Zeitung of Judaism*, the *Israelite*, and many more like them. There were the volumes of the magnificent *Jewish Lexicon*, the *Talmud* in translation, an endless collection of Jewish literature in Hebrew, English, and German.

If one only had the time. Here, one saw lined up what a lover of books or a scholar had acquired over a lifetime. Now strangers' hands dug through them, and the precious works were not handled with the care that their value demanded. Still, this source was available and offered itself to us.

Professor Dr. Emil Utitz was appointed as director. Mr. Hugo Friedmann from Vienna was his deputy and the head of circulation. Miss Else Menken was the assistant librarian; dragon-like, she was shrewd, energetic, and she tirelessly watched over the treasures that had been entrusted to her. She knew every book, where it was shelved, was familiar with the contents, and could answer any question. We had her to thank for the library's smooth and successful running in the first year. The Hebraica section was presided over by Mr. Slonitz, a man of extraordinary knowledge in this area.

The crowning achievement came in the middle of the year when the reading room was inaugurated, which stayed open until the evening. There was a carefully chosen reference library providing visitors with useful tools.

* * *

After a long deliberation we got a new assignment: guarding the bastion. The German authorities had decided that the site, which until then had been available only to the young, would now be designated as a recreation area for all ghetto inmates. The bastion was a parade ground, laid out as a quadrangle. On three sides were ramparts, and the fourth side was the long wall of the Jäger barracks. An inner rampart circled the space again and formed, at the edge, a wide walkway for pedestrians.

A mighty poplar tree in the left corner dominated the square. A stage had been built under it, upon which the children often demonstrated their skills in dancing or gymnastics. The youth organization often extended invitations to a performance; these were among the most beautiful in Theresienstadt. Several hundred children from 6 to 14 years old took part, boys and girls all dressed alike in white shirts and dark trousers. How they managed to procure these matching outfits in the ghetto is a mystery.

The children made an excellent impression. They were fresh, fun, frisky, and healthy-looking, with red cheeks and flashing eyes. They carried out the commands to the second; the gymnastic performances were executed with impeccable precision. One must not forget how little time and opportunity there was to practice and how difficult it was to assemble large groups of children into one unit. That they were capable of forming such a large group of children was wonderful. These mostly beautiful children—I could not count ten that were of pronounced Jewish type, and they were definitely not among the Czechs, but rather among the Reich Germans—thrilled the spectators. They gave one the impression that the next generation would be brought up to be healthy, that the ghetto would do everything possible for these children, within its modest means.

The children played soccer up here with such enthusiasm. When the ball came flying at them, many of the lads were agile goalkeepers. They imitated the adults, who played in the courtyards of the barracks with great passion after long hours of hard work. The sight of the Dresdner barracks—two floors crowded with spectators, and the courtyard bordered by a few thousand people—was reminiscent of a bullfight in Spain. Whenever a goal was scored, one heard roaring cheers, gestures of disappointment, and a concert of whistles. And if the fans did not think they were quick enough, "Tempo, tempo" thundered over the square. One lingered here for a few hours, until darkness or the curfew brought the game to an end.

But the most beautiful of all is still a clear, sunny day when one can look far out over the country. Wide, wide is the view. Behind the barracks, a wall of mountains. The houses, lit up in white, climb the left slope, upward from Leitmeritz. The Elbe was not visible, but to the left of the town the chain of mountains retreats into the distance. Some still carry a tower, the last remnant of old castles. The towers are curiously shaped like ninepins. The hills are approximately 800 to 1,000 meters high, with sides that are deeply inclined. In the sunshine, it is magnificent. [...]

*   *   *

Our lives in Theresienstadt are pretty monotonous. The day revolves around one's duties, always the same—the three meals constituting welcome breaks—and the only topic of conversation in almost all the rooms was what there will be for lunch or dinner the next day. The only thing on the minds of the elderly is [their] health. How the young see things, I cannot say because, unfortunately, I have no connection to them whatsoever.

The second theme that dominates the day is: What is happening at the front? We are cut off from the outside world, and officially, it does not exist for us. Yet fleeting news filters in from several sources and passes from mouth to mouth until it arrives back where it started, completely distorted and warped.

For a time, the German *Prager Zeitung* was displayed in the shops.[21] We read the official communiqués and the well-written explanations as well. Foreign news also reached us this way, and we were able to form a rough picture of [what was happening in] the world. We also received old newspapers in parcels and packages. But this source was sparse.

After the newspaper display was stopped, one depended on word of mouth and the beloved and widespread "*bonkes.*"[22] I was not familiar with how they came about; I was never connected with the people who ought to know something. I consciously did not want to become one of those "in the know." Why should I bother to learn about the situation on the front? It would not change my own circumstances. [Besides,] the majority of news reports on the progress of operations turned out to be either false or predictions of things that would not happen for months.

We receive reliable news only when we can speak to newcomers from Germany, who tell us the truth about the air raids. That goes right to our hearts—this is our home, our city; our house in which our children were born, in which our parents had died, where for half a century we had experienced joy and sorrow as citizens, and with the citizens. When we learned which neighborhoods had been badly hit, which streets had suffered, which public buildings had been destroyed, it was as if our own property no longer existed.

Can we Berliners remain indifferent when we hear that the armory is now a pile of rubble?[23] Does it not still stand vividly before our eyes? The atrium with the flags, the guns, the Schlüter masks of the "dying warriors,"[24] the beautifully curved stairs leading up to the Hall of Fame. Didn't we learn history here as boys? The mural by Anton von Werner, the memorial to the kings of Prussia, and under glass, Napoleon's medals and tricorn—didn't they speak to us more convincingly than the boring history teacher who only taught us dates?

Yet, I digress. We hear of the devastation that is being wrought in all the German towns—and I know them all—the old towns on the Rhine, on the Main, in central Germany, on the coasts. And when I imagine the damage to my beloved Munich, to my magnificent Nuremberg, it breaks my heart. When the sirens howl in the night and announce that the enemy is approaching, we anxiously ask ourselves: Which town in the homeland will be hit?

We, on the other hand, stay peacefully in bed. Usually sleep through the alarm. We are safe, for now; nothing has happened nearby: There are no industrial centers in the area. What would it be like if the war were to come closer?

It was regrettable that the official communiqués were withheld from us. Rumors would have been deprived of their foundation if only we had been able to rely on the official reports. We did not want to know anything about the wider world. That would only wake our slumbering longing for our children, so far away. But our homeland is and remains ours, and what evil befalls it also wounds us. We love our parents, honor and respect them even when they chastise us. Should our attitude toward the fatherland be different? Have we forgotten the poems and songs that we learned in school? I have not, and I do not want to.

*   *   *

I have time to myself once a day, when I stroll back and forth along the path behind the Magdeburg barracks for almost an hour. [The distance is] about 500 meters, with the steep rampart rising in the back; on the right is a plateau planted with fruit trees. Mighty old elm trees hide the barracks from sight. In summer it is cool here. In the winter the rampart provides some protection from the bitter winds. There is no traffic. The wide, beautiful gate breaches the ramparts here, opening the path to the central laundry, which could be accessed only by the workers. [...]

Walking to and fro, I can collect my thoughts, make plans, choose the lectures and schedule them in a deliberate sequence. At home, there is no such opportunity. So one must make full use of this midday hour.

In Theresienstadt there is only one set of happy circumstances that preserves one's life: constant work, a well-functioning digestive system, and undisturbed sleep. If these three factors coincide, then existence was easier to endure.

One need only have the courage to close one's eyes to certain things, and to cover one's ears. Not to see how others carry on, who have lost their glued-on veneer [of civilization], not to hear the squabbling and name-calling that every gathering of people brings with it. To preserve equanimity when someone is rude, to smile when you are mistreated in the offices, where all the people think they are demigods, at least.

In Theresienstadt one really has to exercise restraint to not pay someone back in kind. If you do so, there is no end to your troubles. It is unbelievable how much value is placed on "authority"; everyone thinks he is the top, ruling, and not to be circumvented. Woe, if an employee takes matters into his own hands in the interest of [doing] something quickly and appropriately. Woe! Three times woe!

I can tell you a thing or two about it. For a year and a half, I was fully focused on myself. Nobody asked me to be accountable—the Service and the lecture series ran smoothly from day to day. That entire time, I didn't have a single free day. There was never any "complaint" on the part of my superiors.

[...]

My position in Theresienstadt is, if I say so myself, very unusual and certainly unique. Where else in our "self-administration"—which is served by a very large, complex bureaucracy—is there a man who has a superior only in a formal sense.

[...]

✳　✳　✳

It is curious. There is an issue that is not addressed here, and is even fearfully avoided, one does not speak about it or touch upon it, is sealed in the deepest recesses of the heart: the children. We are mostly older people between the ages of 60 and 80, with children in the outside world, on some continent somewhere. Only occasionally does a Red Cross letter, which has been under way for an eternity, waft into our "island of silence." A letter written in Shanghai [April] 1943 was delivered to us in January [1944].[25] We had to write our reply immediately and were not allowed to keep our son's handwriting. We have heard from our two daughters, who live in England, only indirectly, through Switzerland, during the two years we have been here.

When we sit in the kitchen by the cooling stove—there is only enough wood to warm the meals—then we eight people gaze into that small space at the fading embers and nod to one another, lost in the same train of thought: "If our children, who now sit at pretty, covered tables before an appetizing evening meal, the butter dish full, a rich array of cold cuts, the aroma of tea flavored with lemon slices—the cookie jar takes care of dessert—if they could see us cowering on stools without backrests..."

And then the woman in the top bunk, who has been bedridden for the past two days, entered our consciousness and asked, "Where might my son be, who was in Africa?" And the widow of the pharmacist—the pharmacist who, in spite of his will, all his energy, and the greatest confidence in his deliverance, did not make it through (the plans he made, the finished blueprints for a small, comfortable house[26]—he wanted to share with us whatever he still owned). This brave woman had a daughter in Spain and a son in America—her longings are directed there. Then [there is] the young couple—60 is young here—who knew only that their married children were in Poland.

We know that our loved ones, even if they are so far away, are free and safe. In the last years we had taught them to be independent so that they should build their lives without their parents' protection, shoulder their responsibilities, and regard every decision that they had to make as final.

Softness was misplaced. Those who—in the years when everyone knew what was coming, as the exclusion from business and commerce became increasingly widespread—did not show their children in a hard and pitiless way that separation was necessary, and would lead to salvation for both sides, sinned against them. Now our salvation will depend on those "outside"—our children who, as soon as they are financially able, will fetch us to them.

Thus are our thoughts in the ghetto circle—we seldom speak about it. A soft exclamation now and then—"if our children..."—and one breaks off, as though frightened. Perhaps it is possible to bare one's soul too much. I pick up my children's photographs only on their birthdays. Otherwise, they remain locked away for the entire year. I do not want to bring them here from afar, my children, who have already almost vanished for us.

I heard an elderly woman say, "What use are we to our children, outside we would only be a burden? Would it not be better, if some day in the future they find out from the lists—died on such and such date?"

When the dead rise!!

Did we not die to them from the moment we could send no more letters? Three, four years without any news. Was it really so terrible, so shattering, if the children found out from an office that Father passed on this date, and then Mother on that?

Their ashes remain in the columbarium, the temporary room of "eternal peace." There is only one wish that resonated in every parent's heart, though we did not write it to the children: Bury us in the soil of our homeland. Do not leave us in little cardboard boxes in the casemates of the fortress, but make a small place for our ashes where you are, so that you can come visit us, dedicate to us a few minutes of tender recollection. If we remain in your hearts, then we are not dead; then we live on, at least until the instant when you, too, will close your eyes.

[...]

*   *   *

One day, a sort of yellow ball of wool rolled into the courtyard of our barracks, propelled by the wind. Upon closer inspection, it turned out to be a small, adorable, lovable dog that one simply had to cuddle in one's arms. Long, scraggy hair, with ears that stood up, and a funny, curly little tail—this was what Budulinku looked like. He soon became the darling of Magdeburg. He romped around mostly in the second courtyard, all day, loved, pampered, and fed by all the residents.

Extraordinary. People did not give away food because every morsel was necessary for sustenance, but everyone always had something left over for the dog. From month to month, one could observe how the dog grew, how independent he became, no longer allowing us to cradle him in our arms, how he responded to the call of its master. In short, it became a true and proper dog with a good pedigree. There are no animals in the ghetto, so this was a rare and singular event. The owner was proud of his beautiful animal and, in the room where he and his dog resided, gladly shared his love for him with the comrades.

All the love that we could not express was transferred to Budulinku. His eyes lit up when we stroked his fur or when we watched as he hunted for something in the courtyard. If one day he was not running about, people inquired about the state of his health. Budulinku grew up to be a truly beautiful dog. He was respected as a small, protective spirit of the barracks. People pinned their hopes on him: If he lives, then...

The summer passed, and we saw the darling animal less and less often. The muddy courtyard was not the right place for him—he preferred the room; the long corridors allowed him to romp and do his funny jumps. I often saw him up there and thought, "Soon the freedom bell will also toll for you."

But it didn't happen that way. Spring struck the soul of this small dog with all its might, luring him outdoors to the green meadows, the flowing, thunderous water, the broad paths. This bewildered the little guy, who until then had known only the stones of the courtyard. He did not return from this excursion.

[...]

* * *

In this section I will write about the organization that constituted the police force in Theresienstadt, and of which our Orientation Service was a subdivision.

One might have thought that, in a ghetto inhabited only by Jews, each suffering the same fate, there could not be any great issues. We are a community of fate, solely focused on making our lot bearable, not to increase the load. At the end of March 1944[27] there was a poster in all *ubikations* that read:

"On the nights of March 24 to 25, there was a break-in, in the office of the court. Watches and gold wedding rings that were being held there were stolen. A big reward in the form of foodstuffs is promised to whoever reports the culprits."

It was the first time they [the Jewish ghetto police] had turned to the public.

If food, margarine, and bread were stolen from the provision warehouses, the thieves were pursued. Sometimes they were caught, but not always. Jews knew about digging underground channels, which our ever-so efficient Kripo could not infiltrate.

Why was it that everything could be had for money? It could not all come from the parcels from the Protectorate. The Jew of a certain stratum cannot live without trading. He begins with a simple barter and ends up selling his wedding ring. The paths to get money are intertwined—I have neither the time nor the desire to follow them. But when one sees what people have in their rooms, what they eat for lunch and dinner, and compare it to what we have with our 0.4 liter of evening coffee, we sometimes become quite envious. For us, it is just three slices of bread, the first covered with caraway, the second with garlic salt (an undefinable artistic creation), and the last with sugar (oh, we would have happily eaten two more, but we cannot; otherwise, we go hungry on the third day, so we cannot give in to temptation and indulge).

I see it time and again, the good heart of the Jews fails completely in Theresienstadt—the sick do not share in the abundance, even those for whom a gift could have been lifesaving. Here, I speak only of the Czech and Viennese Jews, who received an abundance of parcels. The Reich Germans depend on small parcels and are unable to share the few items they received.

[...]

*   *   *

Kurt Frey took over the command of the ghetto watch and held it until September 1943, when he was appointed to the same job in the big Birkenau ghetto, in Upper Silesia. Kurt Frey was, for us, the best and most understanding boss imaginable. I never heard a loud or even unfriendly word from him. He respected my 68 years, my experience, and my calm, which was still unshakeable at the time. Whenever I went to him in his office, he offered me a seat at once—there was never a command, only a request.

But he could certainly holler at his people when they were slacking off on the job. He would not tolerate it. Then his eyes flashed, and his voice became fierce and biting. But he rarely had such temperamental outbursts. He remained the jovial boss, and because of his fairness, his team would put their hand in the fire for him. What attractive young people he chose when recruiting.

The ghetto watch recruited mainly from among the Czechs or residents of the Protectorate. This race, as far as appearances went, was naturally blessed. The people from those lands were broad, tall, stately, and confident, with handsome, lively eyes. One senses a commanding attitude. They know what they want and how to make it happen.

Under the leadership of a man like Kurt Frey, the ghetto watch was a force to be reckoned with, in spite of its small number, and could be deployed when the authorities ordered it. And it was. This was evident in the two parades organized by the head of security, Dr. Karl Löwenstein.

This reminder of our time in the military delighted us old soldiers of the Great War. A band was even set up that accompanied the formations with spirited marching songs. The spectators in the huge courtyard of the Dresdner barracks clapped and applauded enthusiastically when it played the popular march from the beloved operetta *The Ghetto Girl*, which was, obviously, premiered here!

The last public service of the ghetto watch took place on that day. Once again there was a reorganization—young people were needed in other places more than here in the Service, and they were reassigned to places that had more priority. The age of admission increased significantly […].

We had yet another happy day on May 18, when we learned that this was the birthday of our esteemed commander. Our gift consisted of a portfolio of pen drawings by the architect Jacques Loeb. They were outstanding miniatures of Prague motifs—some of them made using a magnifying glass.[28]

A decorative inscribed address designed and executed by the same artist, which included pictures of Theresienstadt, featured the following text:

For over a year the Orientation Service founded by you has worked happily and joyfully under your leadership. You have made it easy for us, mostly rather old men, to bear this difficult year that brought such unfamiliar burdens. You gave us complete freedom in our work, never controlled us, and demanded no military rigidity, only that we carried out our assumed responsibilities. In this freedom, every man and woman of the Orientation Service accomplished more than was required of them by the unvarying schedule of duties. Wherever you placed us during this long year, we did not ask whether it was easy or difficult; we did it. On a social level, you cared for us, we may well say, in a paternal way. When our wishes could not be fulfilled, it was because they were outside the scope of your power. To thank you with our whole hearts, expressed in this present form, is the purpose of these pages. May the content of this folder remind you of the year in Theresienstadt and your forever-grateful, beholden men and women. We also ask of you to remember us with kindness, if one day fate separates us from you.

Auxiliary Service of the Ghetto Watch
Formerly
The Orientation Service

And, to our sorrow, we were separated.

We had to give up this admirable person—away—to an uncertain future. Elegant and sprightly in a close-fitting brown jacket, the yellow-bordered service cap on his full head of brown hair, he no longer came to us in our office.

Whenever there was something to discuss, Mr. Frey would stop by on the way back from his morning meeting with the chief of security, bringing letters and instructions. He never let us stand at attention. He always said, leave that to my boys; old men don't need to. He was a *gentleman* in every sense of the word.

There was only one thing that Frey couldn't do—public speaking. He had an almost childlike fear of it and refused to speak even on official occasions. This deprived us on some occasions of the highlight because we wanted to hear from our commander. He often attended the evening lectures, but he adamantly refused to take a reserved seat. Here, he only wanted to be a listener.

Since his departure, we've had no direct news about him. We heard only that he was working in Birkenau, and that he was doing well.[29]

[...]

* * *

In Theresienstadt all daily activities that are not related to work have to be let go. Private things, which hardly exist—except, perhaps, literary ones—are out of the question. What would these be for us workers anyway? I really don't know. Beyond the things that are essential for survival, we do not own anything. Keeping items for our personal hygiene or small stocks of edibles, or safeguarding the three-day bread ration from mice and thieves, of which the former are the less common, a few pieces of clothing—everything can be stored in one or, at most, two suitcases. There were no closets with locks; there would not be any room for them.

We store things under the bed. What we don't need on a daily basis is kept in a closed hatch in the attic of the house. The bed in which we sleep is our whole world, and it takes great skill to store as much as possible around and keep it away from thieving roommates.

There are no cozy evenings. Every usable space is taken (and what isn't usable, as far as the department of "space management" is concerned?). The casemates are lined up to the door, with 20 to 40 beds pushed against each other, separated only by the central aisle. There is no room for a table. The only seating is a small stool without a backrest or the 20-cm-wide edge of the bed. The electric bulb is weak, giving off dull light, which is not enough to read by.

By day, it is a bit better in the room since it is bright enough by the window to read, at least. It is also possible to put two or three tables together, where jolly skat parties gather in the evening. The Austrians play their beloved *tarok* incessantly, and chess is also played. But most residents of the less-favored *ubikations* can only escape the winter cold by lying down very early in the *kavalec*[30] and then waging a battle with the fleas and bugs that destroy the peace of the night and wear us down. [...]

* * *

The lecture evenings rolled on without any interference from the authorities. Rarely—oh, very rarely—they were interrupted when the technicians wanted a day off to rest. We must not forget that our service is on duty here from the morning roll call at half past seven until the beginning of the lecture. Then the room has to be cleared. The tables come out; the benches, which were stacked during the day, have to be arranged for use by the audience. The stage has to be set up. The room must be swept and cleaned to be ready to receive visitors. It was a big job that had to be done quickly every day, because we had little time.

The audience arrives half an hour early to get good seats, and then waits quite patiently. The room holds only 100 people, and they have to sit close together, very close. But every evening they listened with complete attention. For them, the two hours for performances like *Faust* are too short.

There is a particular group of people who always attend, keep faith with me through thick and thin. I was on my own. None of the gentlemen of the Leisure Time Organization took the time to even once calmly talk through the serious problems [of mounting the lectures] and to give me their views. They allowed me to work, but gave me no support.

This has been painful for me, because I could not understand it. In official statements it was proudly said that we "pull together," but if one is not given the rope one is supposed to pull on, it is quite difficult to do. I must refrain from speaking about the large and complex Leisure Time Organization. I know too little of its internal operation. I only read the weekly program, which gives me an overview of what the various departments are presenting.

The music is outstanding. Berlin could not achieve more than they do here. Even the lighter muse receives its due. The program to read aloud in the sick rooms and for the blind is well-organized. They do achieve a lot, but more could be offered if they allowed a number of groups to work, following my example, which has proven itself. But independent creative activity is not appreciated from above, so mine remains alone as a group.

[...]

* * *

In the following pages I will try to sketch some of the speakers and their presentations in order to provide a faint picture of what I sought to achieve.

[...]

Indisputably, one of the most versatile speakers was Dr. Arthur Kohn, born January 16, 1890. His first lecture was entitled *Early Jewish History*. He described his participation in excavations in Palestine and [talked about] how lucky archaeological discoveries confirmed the information in the Bible. One could follow the traces of Jewish life far, far back. He unlocked [the past] for us and made the Bible come alive, giving its characters flesh and blood.

On some evenings he spoke about the history of music. I will mention in passing that he was the only person in Theresienstadt who could tune a piano. Then came his greatest presentation: *As a Mountain Guide and Ski Instructor in the World War*. I envision Dr. Kohn at the desk, neat, slender, lively, with intelligent eyes behind strong glasses. A soft voice—picturesque language—his lectures flowed.

In his youth, he was among the first avid skiers in Austria to conquer the Alps for sporting purposes. He was at home in their vastness, knew every mountain and its perils.

During the war, he created the ski division of the Alpine Corps, and he was its leader on the [battle] front in the Italian Alps. Modest and unpretentious, almost retiring, he rarely spoke about himself in any of his lectures. He depicted life high up in the snow and ice. Long experience and a strong intuitive sense enabled him to detect the danger of an avalanche in good time. One of his superiors refused to allow an evacuation that he wanted to order [because he sensed an avalanche]. Hundreds paid for the commander's stubbornness with their lives. He described many such scenarios, in which he actively and helpfully intervened.

On his last evening, he described the first trips into the mountains that, as a middle school student, he took with his brother, which led him far into the Austrian lands.

In March we heard that he was gravely ill, and soon thereafter, on April 4, 1944, we had to follow his coffin. A truly good and wonderful man had passed over all too soon. Who is to say where he caught the fatal disease—in his beloved mountains or on the plains? His spirit will live on, and those who knew Arthur Kohn will not forget him.

The rabbis in the ghetto represented every shade of religious opinion, but two were famous and at the forefront. I emphasize that they both towered high above the unusually large number of academics of all fields. They won the hearts of the audience not through erudition alone, although both were singularly learned, but for the way they spoke.

One was very dignified, serene, and possessed of a priestly majesty as he began to speak plainly and simply. One fell immediately under the influence of a wonderful personality who cast an enigmatic spell. This is Dr. Leo Baeck, the 71-year-old rabbi and highly esteemed scholar from Berlin, born on May 23, 1873. But his community [in Berlin] did not like to listen to his sermons, not because of their content, but because his delivery was not suitable for the pulpit.

The first time I heard Dr. Leo Baeck speak, I was astonished by his transformation since Berlin. He had changed completely; he was easy, fluent, and pleasant to listen to. His demeanor was quiet and calm, and he spoke convincingly, without pathos, forcefully, and memorably. This was how we imagined a philosopher to be, at the evening of his life, having gathered the harvest of many decades and generously giving of his wisdom. We rushed to his lectures, which he delivers without the slightest sign of fatigue. He also spoke in Room 38—he made such a deep impression that he had to repeat the Spinoza lecture.

I would say that his "opponent" has a quite different style. Dr. Leopold Neuhaus, [born] January 18, 1879, a rabbi who had spent many years in the East before being called to Frankfurt to take up a teaching post. After the Chief Rabbi left, he became his successor. In autumn 1942 he came from Frankfurt to Theresienstadt in a large transport. He and his wife were put in my building and lived under the same crowded conditions we did. Then he was appointed to the Council of Elders, and they got a first-floor apartment in the Magdeburg barracks (large, well-furnished room, anteroom, and their own kitchen).

Dr. Neuhaus, 65 years old, had a stocky build. His face was framed by a well-groomed beard, and he had expressive eyes that could look at one sharply and energetically. He immediately put himself at the service of Room 38. [...]

His knowledge seems limitless. There is no subject one might seek to explore that he had not studied very deeply and thoroughly. His specialty was the history of Jews and Judaism throughout the world. Dr. Neuhaus speaks about Hasidism with a rousing enthusiasm, and himself becomes like a Hasidic preacher. He vividly brings to life every epoch of the past—its people appear before us as though alive—and challenges us to empathize and share in their world of ideas.

Names unknown to us formed the content of the lectures. We got to know these carriers of the lamp of Juda, about which we had known nothing, whose lives were unknown to us yet were brimming with universal, world-changing ideas. The miracle, however, that was manifested in Dr. Neuhaus was his absolutely phenomenal memory. He knows all the dates of history; he whirs down the longest lists of names with the speed of an express train. Geography is his hobbyhorse. He can cite every reference from every text, by memory. He knows the specialist literature up to the most recent publications. He is as much at home in German literature as in the Talmud, which he had studied in Halberstadt.

He presents all of this easily, almost playfully, without even using a single note. He speaks clearly and succinctly, always in immaculate German, without an accent. Dr. Neuhaus does not seem to need to prepare. It is as though he shakes the topics out of his sleeve. When one discusses an idea with him, he immediately gives it shape and form. He has become our inspirational teacher. We old people never tire of listening to him; his gift to us in these two years has been immeasurable.

When we regard Theresienstadt not just as a ghetto, a prison (which it has never actually been), or even less as a mild form of concentration camp, we owe this forgetting of our condition to Dr. Neuhaus and the other scholars, who, like him, have led us from the lowlands of daily life to the heights of spiritual culture.

A[nother] person of great stature and youthful exuberance works among us: the 76-year-old Geheimrat Professor Dr. Hermann Strauß, of the hospital of the Jewish community in Berlin.

I am not qualified to judge his scientific significance; it has been part of the history of medical knowledge and research for decades. Here in Theresienstadt he teaches courses for doctors in all disciplines. He has taken upon himself the task of training the younger physicians, and not to allow the knowledge of older ones to get rusty. Professor Strauß had been interested in the lecture series from the start, and made himself available. He spoke every month; it was always a pleasure to listen to him. He did not choose medical themes, but instead spoke to us from the rich treasure of his experience. Thus, to name only a few lectures: *Berlin Doctors at the Turn of the Century; Travels in Upper Silesia As Consiliarius; The Egyptian Wonderland; Robert Koch's 100th Birthday; Travel in the Baltic States.* The talks were naturally given without notes, standing, in the easiest and most amusing conversational style. His wealth of memories encompassed two generations, and he had forgotten nothing.

Variatio delectat![31] [Anna Aurědniček] should now be mentioned, one of the intellectual giants of this town—which is certainly not short of them. She quickly won the hearts of people with her charming, amiable, lively, and sparkling disposition. When she sat at the table [on the stage] in her dark dress with white ruffles down the front and a silk scarf around her shoulders and narrated and read, one just had to love this woman.[32]

[...]

* * *

The musician Willi Durra, from Breslau, introduced a completely new note into the series of presentations. I had requested him for the Auxiliary Service of the Ghetto Watch, and he was quickly confirmed. [...]

Durra got to work cheerfully and energetically, and in a short time put together a first-rate choir whose performances quickly won favor in our circle. There were evenings of folk songs featuring solo performance[s]. Kurt Messerschmidt, 28 years old, blond, and very handsome, sang German and Yiddish songs accompanied by a lute. Mrs. Edith Weinbaum presented an evening of Schubert, which concluded with improvised Schubert melodies, played by Alfred Loewy on the harmonium.

The music brought a very welcome change from the monotony of the spoken word and was enthusiastically welcomed. Once we had the Ledeč Quartet as welcome guests in the cramped Room A6; but they took up too much room, and their sound did not unfold, and so we did not repeat this experiment.

Song and chorus in antiphony seemed like a fresh drink from a forest spring and refreshed both the audience and the performers.

[...]

* * *

All the lectures attained a high level.

A former senior civil service engineer, [Robert] Stricker, spoke about his friendship with Popper-Lynkeus,[33] from Vienna, and painted a vivid picture of the man and his work. [...] On the days between Rosh Hashanah and Yom Kippur,[34] weighty lectures were held: Rabbi Dr. Leo Baeck, Rabbi Albert Schön, [and] Rabbi Heinz Meyer. Dr. Leopold Neuhaus spoke about the psalms, and the Durra mixed choir sang them. These evenings were solemn and formed a bridge to the Day of Atonement, on which I twice held overcrowded prayer hours.

Hanukkah on December 21 [1943] began with a celebratory talk by Rabbi Albert Schön, framed by the Durra choir.[35] Two *Fairy Tale Evenings for Adults* were much enjoyed. Jewish fairy tales and some by Andersen were read.

Dr. Kurt Singer from Berlin, the founder and head of the Kulturbund [Culture Association],[36] came here in autumn from his Dutch asylum and took an enthusiastic interest in all artistic endeavors. He held many lectures. For me he spoke [about] *The Aim and Purpose of Music.* His easy, charming conversational tone pleased the audience very much. This animated man, with his white head, wraithlike face, and expressive hands, received hearty applause.

We were deeply shocked when the news spread that he was gravely ill, and a few days later, the end came. A man who could have been a leader, steering the rocking ship with a sure, steady hand, he had to abandon joyful creativity, [and go] down into the darkness that he so hated. He, who so loved the light, the brightness, and joy. He, who had given so much to so many in Berlin through the years—perhaps the last few joyful evenings that we Jews were still allowed to enjoy.

Vale! Every time Verdi's *Requiem* is performed here, it is a funeral celebration for Kurt Singer, and for all the prominent men who died here in Theresienstadt. *Requiescat in pace* rings for each one of them. It is like a soft prayer on wings of music, rising up to every spirit, that has become joined with the infinite.

* * *

The Theresienstadt ghetto is as delicate and sensitive as a voltmeter in some electrical machine. We have no newspaper giving us news from the outside. For a few weeks the Prague *Neue Tag* was put out in various places, and its columns were eagerly read and talked about. After this privilege was rescinded, we relied on packages, which sometimes contained pages from the prohibited newspapers, and this news traveled quickly by word of mouth. But this had a disadvantage: It could not be verified, and lost its original value hour by hour. In addition, there was the "mouth-radio," the dead-certain informants [who said], "I know it from the most reliable source." If one calmly and coolly considered the possibilities, compared them with one's experience in the World War, and assumed that the truth was somewhere in between, then one could get some picture of what was happening outside. We all longed for messages from the outside. The postcards that we receive are—meaning have to be—neutrally written, without any reference to events at home.

We hear about heavy bombing of German cities. Our hearts are heavy; we are deeply sad, despondent. Our homeland, our streets, and our houses were struck, and we knew nothing, experienced nothing. This uncertainty was demoralizing, utter torture. Then a parcel would be delivered to us. Instead of the familiar address, the sender gives a new one—a silent but clear message: bombed out.

We build our knowledge out of many small pieces, and if it forms a mosaic, at least we get a shadowy picture, unclear and out of focus, but at least it is a picture. As evacuees we feel deeply that we are completely closed off from the outside world to which we are so inextricably linked. If the authorities would grant us some relief [from this isolation], it would be easier to carry the burden of our lives on our weakened shoulders.

Since our first days here, we cling to the words *if* and *when*. They encompass our wishes and yearnings, but never provide a satisfactory answer, because only a miracle could lift the veil. And we have lost the ability to believe in miracles. How often it is asked—by those who should know and those who do not—why God let the "chosen people" suffer so much here in Europe. Why does "He" not create a miracle and free us from captivity, let us return to participate in world affairs, free us from the shackles that oppress us so painfully day and night? There is only one answer: The will of God knows no "why"!

And therefore, because we do not know anything definitive; because we are dependent on the *dicitur*, of Julius Caesar's "it is said," we do best when we do not ponder and ruminate, and instead fill every hour of the day with useful work, which leads us to rest in the evening. Then time doesn't pass so slowly; then the weeks and months do not seem endless. One can stretch out every night in his bed, thinking about what he did [that day], and happily say to himself that all of his strength was used for the good of the community. He does not need a frightened *when*. For him the weeks pass too quickly for that. He may look back over a year with satisfaction—it will not be wasted among the 60 [years] of his life.

*   *   *

For those of us who are not at the top, who are only a small cog in the gears of the ghetto and its administration, with little access to the German authorities, there is no other way to get one's orders except through the [written] orders of the day or direct commands issued to the individual.

We came to Theresienstadt as advantaged people.[37] On account of some act—fighting at the front, the Iron Cross first class, merits of an exceptional nature—we enjoyed this advantage. After we had settled in and resigned ourselves to our new circumstances, we felt safe and secure, and this made us feel that we had found our home for the time being.

We lost this cozy sense of security in the autumn of 1943, when, for the first time, the word "transport" sounded in our ears, like a dissonant trumpet blast.[38]

We could not grasp it. We did not believe it. We took it as idle gossip of unemployed do-nothings until one night the horrible rumor became reality, shocking us to the core.

The [German] authorities have the task to regulate the ghetto, to keep it working, to see to it that there is the right ratio between those who are too old to work and those who are working. If room for certain categories can be found in other ghettos, those who are not suitable are removed and replaced by "deserving" people from elsewhere.[39] The German authorities gave the Council of Elders the order to come up with a list of a thousand people to be relocated to Poland. The Council convened immediately, and instructions were decided upon and issued. The transport department and the registry prepared the list on the basis of personnel files. All residents of the ghetto were recorded in painstaking detail in this "registry." Not having the necessary experience in how to organize this, the elderly people were summoned to the second floor of the Magdeburg barracks, where they had to wait in the cold for several hours before they were dealt with. The lists were read later in the various houses in the offices of the house elders. That went faster and was more comfortable for all concerned. This was the basic method of the selection of those to be sent away. I do not know what criteria were applied.

Certain categories, officials, were protected because of course people could not be summoned randomly without endangering the ghetto; there had to be a well-thought-out plan. Ten men of the Orientation Service were protected as a core, and that security certainly stimulated our desire to work and to do our best, in order to be worthy of this privilege.

Day and night, work in the offices continued at a feverish pace. Then, the ghetto watch got the order to transmit the summons to the house elders during the night. The actual summons is a small, two-centimeter-wide strip on colored paper, which is handed out with a sheet of paper detailing the instructions to be followed for the transport. What one is allowed to take along: a suitcase; backpack; a little luggage, meaning bedrolls; hand luggage; food provisions, etc.

The house elders had the painful duty of waking those who had been called during the night to tell them their fate. When the door to the room opened and the light went on, we knew what it meant. All 24 comrades listened, trembling, still half asleep, to the name call. It was reminiscent of the door to the dungeon being opened during the French Revolution; the same thing happened to us.

To sleep was unthinkable. Those who were not affected tried to comfort the others, without success. Everyone clung to one very small possibility—a query to the administration. The next morning, stormy scenes took place in front of their office in the A wing. Hundreds of desperate people wanted to be let in; there was no order. Throngs of people crashed into one another, pushing and shoving. Hell had broken loose.

Terrible commotion in the anteroom, the wooden barrier broke apart, and the mob squeezed in. Any negotiation was quite impossible. Then they began to converge on the members of the Council of Elders: They should help them, liberate them, be their advocates. What did the supplicants not do in order to escape their fate! And the men of the Council of Elders could help only the most urgent cases. They were held accountable by the [German] authorities for every release, and were at risk if too many were released. In those days, a tremendous responsibility rested on the officials; their decisions had to be final. More were summoned than were needed, in order to have a "reserve" to cover all eventualities. The [German] authorities demanded 1,000 men, and they had to be assembled.

On such days, there was a gloomy, stifling mood in the ghetto. Everyone trembled in fear that he might be struck by this fate and be among those selected, or at least relatives and close friends. It seemed as though the hours stole by slowly; the pulse slowed; thoughts could no longer follow their usual paths. We had the deepest sympathy for those who had to go into the unknown, torn from the security of comfort and habit. The packing began in the room as soon as it was light. Many possessions had to be left behind because of the weight restriction. Again and again one went through things and checked and assessed, not wanting to be separated from the little that the ghetto had left one and given one—really just the necessities, no luxuries, nothing superfluous.

And yet—as things were taken out of suitcases and boxes and removed from the wall, it turned out there were too many possessions; [they could] absolutely not be packed and taken. One had to decide, weed out, and leave behind. With the help of comrades who were skilled at it, everything was properly packed, tied up, and labeled. One helped the clumsy elderly men and women and, to the extent possible, tried to give them courage. What was really known that justified despondency? Nothing. We had received neither favorable nor unfavorable news from the East. We had already suffered our biggest shock when we left our homes. Now it was just a rearrangement.

Could Poland not offer more freedom than there was inside the walls of the Theresienstadt fortress? Here, we learned that everything was different from what we had expected. We led our own lives, peaceful and undisturbed. It could not be much different in the new camp or ghetto. Everywhere there is work, that dear consolation. So we told those who were going.

They had to assemble in the courtyard at a specific hour. The large pieces of luggage would be picked up. One could carry the small pieces, if possible, or be helped. All the little groups of people went briskly toward the Aussig barracks, where the *Schleuse* would take place. There, people had to stay for one or two nights on straw sacks in the clean, wood-paneled casemates, until the control was carried out and the train stood ready in Bauschowitz. We men and women of the Orientation Service had passes that enabled us to enter the closely guarded barracks, and we could thus render them this or that last little service. It seemed odd, but everyone was brave and composed, without exception.

The children played in the courtyards, the elderly sat in the warm sun, chatting unconcernedly, as always. Food was plentiful, and the distribution was punctual. The provisions center took care of everything. Those who lacked clothing, blankets, shoes, or something else received them from the distribution center, which maintained a very well-stocked storage area in the barracks.

Generally, on transport days, everything was focused on those who were enlisted on the transport. For example, anyone who did not have a clean bread sack got one. The distribution centers and services worked only for the transport. When the message came that the train was ready, the thousand marched slowly and heavily toward Bauschowitz. The luggage was brought there by vehicles in a shuttle service, as were those who were unable to walk. Nurses and doctors accompanied the transport. When the section of railroad tracks was opened, the long march halted and the boarding took place going out from the Jäger barracks.

This was the procedure used for transports, which sometimes included as many as 2,500 people.[40] There were no small transports of, say, 100.

[...]

The Orientation Service was not much talked about. It did its duty and demonstrated that it could manage, even without a large official structure. The fact that things had gone smoothly day by day in 1943 proved it. The reorganization in September 194[3] had not affected the Service. Nevertheless, it brought profound changes. Dr. Karl Löwenstein was appointed as director of security services—the title of the newly formed authority. He was roughly 50 years old, stocky, energetic, and a Reich German, who regarded the ghetto watch as a military formation and organized it accordingly. Our commander, Kurt Frey, was placed under him. While continuing as head of the ghetto watch, he had to report to the beautifully decorated office every morning and wait in the anteroom until the many conferences were finished and he and his adjutants were let in.

When I think of Mr. Frey in the cramped Room 73 at a narrow table, leading the ghetto watch in an exemplary manner without ever (unfortunately) demanding an improvement, I shake my head. And more went through my mind when my two deputies and I were received in Dr. Löwenstein's private room upstairs in Room 236, to present him with birthday congratulations in the form of an address. It was a beautiful, bright space, with modern furniture, an anteroom, and its own kitchen. A tea table was laid out. There was tea and delicious cake. The most beautiful thing was the view through the window out over the wide landscape. Just half an hour in such surroundings—and Dr. Löwenstein could be very charming and chatted easily—served as a welcome reminder of our own lives, our homes.

Officially, we seldom came into contact with Dr. Löwenstein because we only dealt with Mr. Frey, and even more with his eminently capable, knowledgeable secretary, Ms. Martha Gubot, a clever, simple, amiable lady from Vienna, who helped us as much as she could and expedited many requests.

There were some annoying incidents with comrades, who used and defended the term "comrade" only when it was to their benefit. But woe betide when they did not get their way! Then the loudest proponents for sticking together cast off the thin veneer of their character and turned out to be unrestrained egoists and big nonentities. [...]

Perhaps one can understand Dr. Karl Löwenstein this way. [...] A lawyer by profession, he turned to banking, came here from the Minsk ghetto, and soon became chief of security. Those who knew, characterized him as a man of great energy, who saw himself as the epicenter of power and believed in his mission as the new chief to fight corruption. That was a tremendous undertaking, worthy of the sweat of a noble man.

Dr. Löwenstein possessed all the qualities for such a task, but he had one weakness that undermined his success. He was easily influenced and often lacked the proper reserve. Decisions were made haphazardly, without careful consideration, and left to stand despite being questionable.

As an example of his style of governing—only one time was I made to feel it; we otherwise understood each other very well—I quote the following "edict":

> In my instruction of 5/29/1943, I gave you the task of submitting a systemization plan within 48 hours. You have not done this until now. You will now inform me of the name of the official who should have prepared this plan, so that I can penalize him. The systemization plan is to be put before me by 12 o'clock tomorrow afternoon.
>
> —The Head of Security

I may add that the plan had been submitted to our superior, Mr. Frey, within 24 hours, but he had not passed it on.

His [Dr. Löwenstein's] need for power was great, and necessarily led to opposition in the ghetto. He arranged for uniform jackets to be made for his praetorians—the 450 men of the ghetto watch. In celebration of its two years' existence, a parade was held in the courtyard of Dresdner barracks: a swift march past the chief, the Council of Elders, and a thousand spectators. The new, gray-green uniform jackets with two pockets left and right looked very attractive. One envied the wearer of this new, elegant piece of clothing.

When I called the next day [in his offices] to request such a jacket for my men, I was told that the jackets had been seized by the [German] authorities [...]. I would have been so happy for my people, if they had been granted the light, airy jackets for summer duties.

Dr. Löwenstein put his heart and soul into his work. He felt solely responsible for the security of life in the ghetto, and never took even an hour off. Conferences, visits, meetings, and court hearings followed hard upon one another. He could suddenly pop up anywhere. He demanded that we greet him when he was passing. One had to see him—the watchman who wasn't paying attention was no proper guardian of security. Yet his small figure could be easily overlooked, and in his blue suit and cap, he didn't stand out.

He looked after the Auxiliary Service of the Ghetto Watch as if they were his direct subordinates. When there were special rations, for example lemons or onions, we received a full allocation. But if there was ever any complaint, Mr. Frey quickly smoothed it over with a swift intervention.

In [August 1943] we heard that a fundamental change had been decided on overnight. Security was to be reorganized into three departments:

Criminal Investigation Department, autonomous, under Dr. Ernst Rosenthal
Economic Police under [Robert] Mandler
Ghetto Watch under Captain Weisl

The Jewish elder would be the nominal head of these departments.

Dr. Löwenstein was relieved of his duties at the same time. His opponents had won, and ousted the brave man.[41]

* * *

The Service ran quite smoothly and according to the timetable.

How many arduous evening hours it has taken! How many attempts were made and proposals drawn up and submitted! Erich Narewczewitz from Frankfurt, teacher of mathematics, had been busy for weeks trying to solve this problem: how to schedule the working hours for 46 men, so that each would get lunch and a day off.

The biggest challenge was caused by those on sick leave, usually 8 to 12 each day. The slips of paper with the assignments that had been prepared the night before were given out punctually at the morning roll call. The absentees wreaked havoc with all the arrangements. The bastion required three men; the grocery store, two men; the green spaces were guarded by our seniors, aged 70 to 74. Organizing this was not entirely easy, especially since the guards were also to switch among themselves.

First, we made the daily plan, working with numerals: On the left, the place names, along the top the hours, from 7 to 21, and in the columns the numerals [identifiying the watchmen]. We could thus say exactly where each man stood and what his hours would be. This had one disadvantage—the complicated plan had to be newly written every third day.[42]

To remedy this, I had a strong wooden panel made. Our calligrapher, Walter Sedelmeyer from Berlin, drew squares on it using India ink—750 squares—with a nail in every one. And now we worked with little cards that we hung up in the evening. The crew could copy their tasks on them in the morning, and we could immediately make adjustments for those who were out sick.

In theory, it was an excellent system. Our Narew—which was what we called our part-time helper for the sake of brevity—sat every evening in front of this hanging diagram board with his box of little cards, and worked—reconsidered, made changes, and was never finished. He was hindered by the cussedness of things. A clumsy comrade would touch the board, knocking a few dozen cards off. This was just one of many such examples.

Finally, it became too much for us. Narew, unfortunately, became ill and had to spend a long time in care, so we changed the system. He died after a prostate operation, enduring unimaginable pain manfully. He had wanted to stay alive for the sake of his wife and his seven-year-old son. We left the board hanging and used preprinted time sheets that Lieutenant Colonel Herschan, the old practitioner from Vienna, prepared and filled out.

[Herschan] divided the personnel into three groups, with a group leader who was responsible for the running of the service. Under this military expert, who needed only half an hour to draw up the arrangement, everything went superbly. There was no more confusion or misunderstanding. External operations were

taken over by my deputy, Hugo Weinmann, from Vienna, who did his job energetically, and fortunately shielded me from many a complaint and dealt with
things expeditiously. My comrades really avoided anything that could upset me.
They respected that my head had to be free and clear for the evening events. For
that, I will always be grateful to all of them. It was only because of this strong
support that I was in a position to accomplish the literary work and to gain general recognition for it.

[...]

I had another idealistic impulse, and proposed an idea to my comrades that
I had been mulling over for a long time. We would at some point go our ways
and be cast to the four winds. Should the cord that bound us together here be
broken? Had the years we lived together been in vain; should they leave no
trace? Should men brought together here, for better or for worse, never hear
from each other again? No and no; this went against my sense of what it meant
to be a comrade.

The plan was [to create] a card index containing names and peacetime
addresses; when the comrades were employed again somewhere, they should
remember each other and request them if they were looking for co-workers.
This should be channeled via representatives of the group in Vienna, Prague,
and Berlin. Personal reports would be sent to them, and a monthly news-
letter published by them; thus our cohesion would be maintained. Because
a number of comrades had children who were doing well, they committed
to provide money when needed. These were all comforting thoughts of the
future—if...

Here in the ghetto I wanted to build up an account, initially with 10,000
krone, meant for comrades who had to make large purchases or to pay for a suit
or a winter overcoat. There was enthusiastic support. Every comrade committed
to making a monthly contribution. When our lecture audiences heard about the
idea, they wanted to participate.

Mr. Kurt Frey donated 200 krone as the foundation stone. Now the legal
issues had to be dealt with. The legal department raised no objections. After
prolonged consultation, the finance department approved the establishment of
a savings account. Withdrawals required two signatures on the payment order.
With that, everything was set. I happily accepted the green bankbook. At the
end of the first month, our balance amounted to not quite 10,000 krone. We
had reached our goal. Other departments called me for information so that they
could copy my campaign.

But with the powers that be, it was "with fate O ne'er believe / An eternal bond to weave / Swiftly on Misfortune comes."[43] Our superior, engineer

Otto Zucker, had heard about our new scheme. My basic mistake: I should have brought the idea to him first. But I had not wanted to bother this man who was so enormously in demand and who had always shown me favor and support. So when I negotiated with two departments headed by members of the Council of Elders and decision-making power, I thought that was enough, that I was completely covered. More [than this] I could not tell Mr. Zucker when he summoned me.

A few days later I got the command to close the account, to deposit the monies paid by comrades into their personal accounts, and to transfer the rest to the Leisure Time Organization. *Sic transit!*[44]

And so all that remained of my plan was the card index.

*   *   *

If I wanted to report in more detail about our duties, it would make for monotonous reading. For us, who were concerned only with keeping order, there were no sensational incidents like at the Kripo and the ghetto watch.

Our street patrol ended as soon as it got dark, and the only one on duty was the watchman who carried out the checks at the lectures. In winter, the curfew started at eight o'clock. Then life stopped in Theresienstadt and, consequently, also for us. Every day, every week was like the previous one. Apart from when transports went out, we were sheltered from surprises.

We had to part from very many dear comrades, most recently, to our great regret, Wilhelm Marburg, the creator of the address book, who, despite all our attempts to claim him as an indispensable person, was not released [from the transport].

He was highly service-minded and selfless. His zeal and conscientiousness made him forget the precariousness of his health. He had a consuming ambition to collect the material for the address book, and he did not allow resistance, wherever he found it, to deter him from his goal. He completed this great and important work [the address book]. When he presented it to our boss, he was amazed by the wealth of material, some of which he was totally unfamiliar with.

The biggest task, however, was to keep the address book up-to-date, and this too was resolved. Whenever Wilhelm Marburg was confined to bed for a few days to preserve his health, he took his material with him and continued working. Despite being slightly hard of hearing, nothing could shake his joy in working. If something was wrong with the information, he could not rest until he found the error and corrected it.

When he left, his work stalled, and it now sits unused in the offices. We will not forget its creator, and will always gratefully honor his work.

Another, more powerful entity took away our dear comrade: attorney Max Meyer from Münster. He had been sick for several months with stomach problems, later diagnosed as cancer. During the intervals when he felt better, he would come to work for a couple of hours, until he began to feel weak and had to lie down again.

How pitiful his bed was! He, who had owned his own house in Münster, lay on the floor in a garret. But he did not exchange it for a better one because here he could sleep in the same room with his wife and had the use of a warming oven. This outweighed every discomfort.

How attached Dr. Meyer was to the Service—he had only one fear: that he could be dismissed because of his long absence. Of course we should have done it [dismissed him], since in the Service one was expected to be healthy, not sick. But we did not have the heart to inflict that pain on him. In January, a slight improvement; he came to visit us, drawn and faded. He had to be transferred to the hospital, where, unfortunately, after a few days of excruciating suffering and struggle, he died.

It is really difficult for us, the death of beloved comrades, who had held so fast to the belief that they would survive to be liberated and see their beloved children again. These thoughts are indeed what give all of us the strength to endure, to perform our duty happily, hoping for "the day"! In the long winter hours, when we sat together and spoke of the future, there was one theme: home and what we had left behind; and another: the children.

In Theresienstadt, everyone has to accept the fact that he might die here, that he could also be caught by any one of the many possible [causes of death]. The malnourished body is not capable of defending itself, of resisting, yet the resources to rebuild [the body's strength] cannot be supplied from outside. Every small ailment can—although not necessarily—become life-threatening, and that is the great danger, for those who lack the will to survive.

* * *

December 1943. The last month of the year. Tired, but not despairing, [the year] wound down to the end. The Jew in Theresienstadt no longer calculated, no longer set dates, rejected dreams and visions, and did not want to think about the future. That is left to the old who do not work, who had enough time to measure the time.

Those in the Service dutifully performed their assigned tasks, and could only speculate about the best possible way out. What did we care about the world outside, "...if back in Turkey, far away, the peoples give each other battle"?[45]

We look back and realize with a sigh that [the lectures have given us] beautiful, enjoyable, satisfying hours here. Isn't that something in the ghetto? Should one not note them most gratefully, and not forget them? We should see, not only the misery, despair, and oppression within these walls, but also hold in mind that which is uplifting and encouraging. That way we will remain above it and survive our time in custody.

[...]

We of the lecture series experienced pleasant episodes of contemplation and tranquillity. On October 26, in celebration of the 250th evening, there was Georg Kafka's *Orpheus*. Professor Dr. Emil Utitz spoke the introductory words.

The 300th lecture took place on December 24; it had been arranged as a Hanukkah celebration. I wanted again to make it both serious and festive, as I had last year. Still, this time one did not wish to use the same title: "Year's Finale." Reason: In the ghetto one does not celebrate New Year's Eve. We are Jews, and our New Year's celebration is different. So I chose, with the agreement of Dr. Neuhaus, the title *Hanukkah Finale: A Contemplative Hour*.

The Jewish elder, Dr. Paul Eppstein, Dr. Leopold Neuhaus, Karl Schliesser, Professor Dr. Emil Utitz, [and] Fritz Janowitz spoke upstairs in Room 241. The Durra choir opened and closed the celebration, and the Dr. Henry Cohn Quartet played Beethoven. We felt grateful that the overburdened Dr. Eppstein found the time to speak to us and—a rarity—to stay until the end. It was a worthwhile, memorable evening.

December 31, the last day of the year. The sun shone pale and cheerless, and, as always in these December days, no cover of snow redeemed the gray earth. The temperature was not winter-like. We worked, as always. The shops stayed open and sold diminished stock. People who could not light a fire at home warmed themselves in the café. And in the offices, one wrote and dictated as usual.

In the evening we gave the *Talisman* as a joyful conclusion.[46] A prologue by Gustav Hochstetter and an epilogue by Wilhelm Sterk were added extras. After the happy conclusion, we shook hands and went home.

We did not want to organize a party for the comrades without Commander Kurt Frey, so each [of us] celebrated the end of the year in his own way. After the presentation the men who were especially close to me [and I] still sat together for a while, but we did not have much to say. Our thoughts were far away, and everyone had the same question: What are they doing on the outside now; are they thinking of us as intensively as we think of them; do they have the same longing in their hearts as we do?

No answer. One after the other took his cap and went forth silently into the darkness—toward the New Year, the long-accustomed, familiar working day. [...]

Drawing by Friedrich Lerner, Theresienstadt 1944.

Philipp Manes during the First World War.

Philipp and Gertrud Manes on their balcony in Potsdamer Strasse, August 1939.

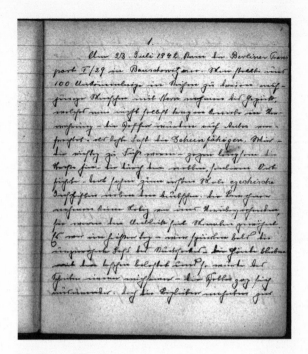

The first page of the Factual Report.

Philipp Manes, drawn by the wife of Willi Durra, 1944.

Drawing by Hermann Löwinger, 1944.

Theresienstadt drawn by Henriette Lehman-Laizner, 1943.

Theresienstadt drawn by Henriette Lehman-Laizner, 1943.

The manuscript of the poem "The Yellow Star".

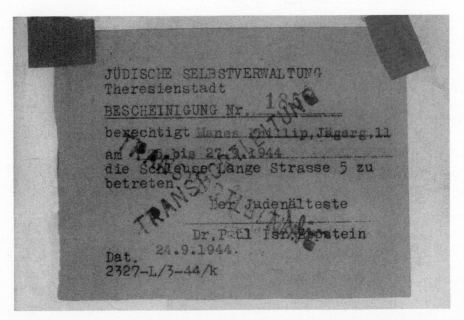

The manuscript of the poem "The Yellow Star".

Authorization for Philipp Manes to enter the Schleuse, signed by Dr. Paul Eppstein.

Theresienstadt, drawn by Hedwig Brahn.

In memory of beautiful Faust evenings in Theresienstadt, drawn by
Etta Veit-Simon, 1944.

Theresienstadt, drawn by Dr. Karl Fleischmann.

Philipp Manes in September 1944, drawn by Arthur Goldschmidt.

Part III

1944

Section I   January–July

What is the difference between today and tomorrow in the ghetto? We may dig so deep, look around us, check, weigh—we do not find it. We hate or we love yesterday as much as today.

The daily routine is always the same. Getting up in the cold, meagerly illuminated room. Washing with ice-cold water. Walking to the barracks at dawn to receive lukewarm coffee and the three slices of bread, spread thinly with margarine, some sugar on top of one of them—one must budget this very important nourishment—then on to work.

At noon, a pause—lunch. The elderly lie down for an hour's nap. Those who do not need sleep to preserve their strength play cards or read in the warm room [of the Auxiliary Service].

It is warm for us day and night. The nearly 70-year-old room orderly, Wilhelm Bauchwitz from Berlin, takes care of this very well by not allowing the stove to go out. And there is always hot water. The afternoon creeps slowly into the evening. The room is prepared for the lecture—this is done with ease.

The visitors mostly arrive three-quarters of an hour early in order to get a good seat, on the benches with backrests. We begin punctually, because we have to end exactly at 7:30 or 8:30, depending on the time of the curfew.

We in the Service stay until nine o'clock, and then we leave the barracks, showing the door guard our permits when he does not know us; otherwise it is not necessary. The day is ended. As noted, every day of the week is the same, nor is Sunday distinguished by anything different.

Only the lectures are different every evening.

So, on the first of January, we visited our commander Captain Weisl at the German House, to wish him and his colleagues, the adjunct Fackenheim and the secretary Mrs. Martha Gubot, luck in the name of the Auxiliary Service of the Ghetto Watch. We expressed hope for further fruitful collaborations [between Manes and Captain Weisl and his staff], and promised to do everything possible to smoothly perform our service.

In the streets was the familiar scene—hasty, hurried people. The elderly sat peacefully in their rooms. People lined up in front of the shops. Spreads for bread (essential ingredient: hot horseradish); bags of substitute condiments; mustard; and garlic salt, a good-tasting powder, were available in the way of food. This shopping usually cost 20 krone. With luck one got tomato paste and soup cubes, in either case, a thoroughly enjoyable and useful contribution to the evening fare.

Most clothing stores were closed for inventory.

[...]

Advertisements in foreign newspapers said: Those who have relatives in Theresienstadt, indicate the exact address, send so-and-so much money, and the addressee will receive a parcel corresponding to the amount paid. A very charitable arrangement and a rich blessing.

I was not among the happy recipients. I was fortunate to receive two parcels every month from my faithful Starnberger friend [Adolf Franck], chosen with love, that gave us all we needed to pull through: Dextropur glucose; foodstuffs such as oats, barley, semolina, flour, sugar, the important saccharin; and, once, a pair of blue wool gloves and warm stockings helped us to survive the winter. How boring and bland would the "extract" soups have been had they not been improved and seasoned by my friend's "nutrient yeast powder," or whatever all the packages are called.

We eagerly awaited each shipment, [...] just as any "allowance" [of extra food] from the authorities was joyfully and gratefully welcomed by us hungry people. But the parcels are the lifesavers for everyone here in the ghetto, and are appreciated commensurately. They will remain an important chapter in the history of Theresienstadt, and God willing, one day we may thank those who gave in person.

On the other hand, the letter post has stopped nearly altogether. In contrast to before [1943], I received no messages for months, except two postcards in April, which had been mailed in February. We could confirm each parcel by preprinted postcard with a few personal words added and, every six weeks, write a postcard.

The Auxiliary Service of the Ghetto Watch began the new year with the firm conviction to be useful in the ghetto so that it would be considered as "indispensable." The shops had gotten used to our people. In the café, the tall comrade Stern commanded his men. Three men worked in the children's home, where preventing stealing and maintaining order was no easy task. Without school and education, the children felt that they had outgrown discipline and behaved with pretensions, as though they were Lords. But more on that in another section, as this subject cannot be dealt with in a couple of sentences.[1]

The post office negotiated with us to take the whole Orientation Service into its large organization because the extremely efficient and knowledgeable Victor Janowitz, who had been appointed its head, knew our performance from our work at the distribution center. We were pleased to undertake this interesting, varied service, and already had decided on Lieutenant Colonel Herschan to be its head so that finally he would have the position he deserved. Then one evening, a small document was placed in my hand, which I did not quite understand at first; I could not grasp it. And yet its significance was so far-reaching.

It read:

To the Auxiliary Service of the Ghetto Watch:
   Pursuant to the decision of the administration, the Auxiliary Service of the Ghetto Guard is disbanded as of February 1.
   A meeting regarding implementation [of the disbanding] will be held on February 1 at 11 o'clock in the Central Secretariat, at which you want to appear.

                                                            The Administration

One will exempt me from describing here what I thought at this moment. The rest is silence.[2]

That morning, we assembled in the office: Captain Weisl, his adjunct Mr. Fackenheim, Dr. Sunsfeld, and Dr. Levy represented the administration. Then engineer Otto Zucker appeared, wanting to be informed about what we had discussed.

I asked for a postponement until the end of the month, but Mr. Zucker firmly rejected any possibility of negotiation. If the administration has made a decision, he said, it should be carried out without haggling and bargaining. Room A6 had to be vacated immediately because it was going to be put to another use. The men of the Auxiliary Service of the Ghetto Watch would be taken on by the Order Service,[3] as long as they were not too old. Colonel Neuberger had agreed to this.

At the behest of the administration, the lecture series would continue to exist, and I would stay on as its head but as a member of the Leisure Time Organization. I would have to contact Dr. [Hans] Mautner about finding a new room.

Bows on all sides. The funeral fourth class was finished.

At roll call the next morning, I shared the information and found that the comrades were truly sad that our circle would be dissolved.

Still, I did not want to separate from the Service that unceremoniously. On February 10, the date we had to vacate Room A6 because renovation was to begin on the next day, I arranged a ceremonial final roll call. Captain Weisl, Mr. Fackenheim, and the block elder, Fritz Janowitz, attended and expressed warm words of appreciation for our work.

Then I took the tablet with the names of the dead down from the wall. Death had so filled it that there was no more room on it.

Books and lists were handed over to the Order Service. Then I remained alone and very reflective in the room we had become so fond of over two harsh winters and had enough time to form my own ideas about the meaning of duty, recognition, and gratitude.

It was really not easy for me to give up my office as the head of the Auxiliary Service of the Ghetto Watch. I had become caught up in it, had given it my all. When I lay awake in bed at night, my thoughts were preoccupied with the Service, its men, and where to find contacts in order to get them new posts if theirs had been canceled. My existence belonged to this office. I was not concerned about anything else—all my physical needs were met—I could concentrate my mind entirely on the Service.

And as the lecture series took shape, and the learning period lay behind me, I was able to delegate some of the work to my deputies, and I could rely on them. So I was able to go about building up the evening events, which I had created, without any support, from nothing.

I devoted myself with honest enthusiasm to the task because—just as during the World War—I was allowed to do work I enjoyed and did not have to sit and be miserable as a clerk in any old camp elsewhere. And now, without warning, discussion, or negotiation—disbanded. Even the gentlemen who sat in the office shook their heads at the fact that we had been dismissed without even a normal period of notice, as would have been customary in civilian life.

The way it was done was not nice, neither fair nor just. We—as well as those we served—should have been heard. [Then] it would have been different. The Moor had done his duty...[4]

Some facts can be reported as follows:

Room A6 remained unused for almost two months. Empty. Only then did the workmen come to make it habitable. The crib that my beautiful cabinet stood on was removed. The wall between the main and back rooms was torn down to create a larger space.

Then the men from Funeral Transportation moved in. Here, they waited day and night to be called to carry their gruesome load on the two-wheeled carts. At first, these vehicles stood at the doors, and the inmates fetching food put their pots on them. In the end, they were stored in the third courtyard, where no food was given out.

How often I later heard it said by reliable authorities that the Auxiliary Service of the Ghetto Watch should have been allowed to go on, that there had been no reason to disband it in this way, that its often-proven dedication [to its work] was missed and its dissolution deplored. The dead cannot be brought back to life. All attempts to save the Service were unsuccessful.

The men were taken over by two formations, the Order Service and the Economics Department. The post office also took a few. We were scattered to the winds, and it is peculiar—[even] in the small Theresienstadt, we do not see each other anymore, since our paths no longer crossed.

[...]

* * *

The swan song to my Service had to be short. What could I say? The facts speak for themselves. We had no veto rights; no clemency appeals would have been successful. On February 10, Room A6 was finally closed, and I was left homeless. I was told to turn to the Leisure Time Organization, of which I had become a member—they had to accommodate me. That was easier, mind you, much easier, said than done.

I refused to settle in their lecture department room because I could not be expected to sit in this unheated, ice-cold cellar. The ladies and gentlemen of the Leisure Time Organization sit so tightly pressed together. They have nothing except their table around which people crowded the whole day. I could not find my place there either. Thus, every man for himself.

In Room 148, the most amiable hospitality was extended to me. I even got a file cabinet. There worked Salo Krämer, member of the Council of Elders and a frequent visitor to the lectures, my patron and supporter; Mr. [ ] Wollner, to whom reported the important "duplication" section[5] and who took care of the paper and boxes, which were difficult for me to procure; Dr. E. Simon, statistician; and Dr. Friediger, chief rabbi from Copenhagen, who was in charge of his compatriots and took care of them.

They cleared off a desk for me and my Secretary Sedelmeyer (in Theresienstadt every person had to have a title, and this small, efficient, and versatile chap absolutely earned this one). Now and again, there was no coal and we froze, sitting [there] with cold hands, but we had a place. After all, I had to be accessible. People wanted to speak to me, the speakers wanted to know dates—in short, an undertaking such as mine would have been impossible without a place to set up shop.

From February 1 I dedicated my energy exclusively to the events, which now operated under the name of:

Leisure Time Organization
Manes Group

At the behest of the administration I would remain independent and continue working within the existing framework, i.e., completely without interference from anyone else. I was extremely grateful for this recognition and the show of confidence, as I could continue to develop my work in peace and security. So I went back to work with courage.

Now I have only two subjects to report on:

1. The lecture series of the Manes Group.
2. What I further saw, heard, and experienced in Theresienstadt.

These two subjects overlap again and again. Their roots go back to the past. Because I could not describe Theresienstadt in all its variety until February 1, 1944, I must make up for this in the following pages. [...] The reader has a right to become thoroughly acquainted with the accomplishments of Theresienstadt.

Now that I have peace and the time I need to do this work, I can devote myself to it without distraction. And still the days go by too quickly. Midday, with a somewhat longer break than before, passes in no time at all, and then it is not long until dinner. At six o'clock I have to be ready for the lecture, for the admittance three-quarters of an hour before the start and the end at 8:30, and already one longs for bed. At 9 P.M., it is mandatory lights out, and then one has to lie down.

It is so nice when, before going to sleep, one has only one thing to think about: the lectures. No further cares—at most, a sudden cancellation, which is not tragic. Nothing can surprise or shock me. A speaker can be easily replaced. [In fact,] I always anticipate such an occurrence, and have a number of men standing by, "ready to start."

It is more difficult when an actor in *Faust* or *Nathan* falls ill. When tickets are sold out, postponing [a performance] is impossible, and consequently it has to be read. And it works. Our faithful Mrs. Anna Steiner from *Nathan* recently canceled at lunchtime because of total hoarseness. I did not have another Daja. Miss Cläre Arnstein readily filled in and, in addition, had to speak [the part of] Recha. Since one did not *act* but *read*, this solution was possible.

Difficulties arise to be overcome. That stayed my motto, along with another that came from Paris: Stay calm in a fire.

The last lecture held in Room A6 was part of a special event. Dr. Leo Löwenstein, the noted chemist and the first chairman of the German Reich Union of Jewish Front Soldiers, celebrated his 65th birthday.[6] His many friends insisted that the day [February 8, 1944] be celebrated. One needed a ticket issued by security to attend the lecture, *The Jewish Soldier over the Millennia*, given by Dr. Löwenstein himself.

We had illustrious guests, Dr. Murmelstein and other gentlemen from the administration and all former group leaders [of the German Reich Union] present here in Theresienstadt. A calligraphic address of congratulations was presented, artistically laid out. It was a very simple, quick, soldierly celebration, in keeping with Dr. Löwenstein's straightforward nature.

Still, I want to proceed in sequence. I [know I tend to] hurry the facts and get ahead of the story. We were talking about January, and there are still all kinds of things to say. The first day of the new year [...] brought a lecture of a unique kind titled *The Newest from Yesterday*. I had selected interesting articles in old magazines and had them read out loud:

I found *Sulamith: A Magazine for the Promotion of Culture and Humanity Among the Israelites*.[7]

An *Ex Libris* said: "Gift of Mrs. Fanny and Mrs. Bertha Oppenheimer, in memory of their son and husband Hermann Oppenheimer, Leipzig, November 1874 (Professor Julius Fürst'sche Library)."

The stamp indicated that the series of books had been owned by the Library of the Higher Institute of Jewish Studies in Berlin. A smaller stamp simply registered: *Ghetto Library*. Browsing through these old books was doubly interesting for us in the ghetto. We can see in them how wonderfully far we'd come.

[...] On January 5, there was a "premiere reading." Wilhelm Sterk, with Georg Roth, read three one-act plays of his that originated here. The Vienna milieu delighted and enchanted us, as if by magic. In honor of the great Berlin painter Julia Wolfthorn-Klein, who celebrated her 80th birthday here on January 8, there was an evening of "Painting." With admirable mental vigor, the artist described her life; Paris was the highlight.

On February 8 we had to finally vacate Room A6 [as described before]. Our material was put in the small room where theater props were stored, and it should be said right away that we got only part of it back. Apparently, it could be put to much better use elsewhere, and people helped themselves to what they liked. I stood there, a poor fool, a king who lacks land [...].[8]

Space was a really difficult and insurmountable problem for the management of the Leisure Time Organization. But not for me. I took it upon myself to find something, no matter where, and...I found it. In the early morning, I went along the long corridor in the left wing and saw that the large Room 109, where the kitchen had been, was empty. There was only a wooden scaffold in the right half, which supported the burnt ceiling.

I learned that the room was not to be repaired until further notice. When? Uncertain. The administration allowed me to use it in the evening, at least for the time being. The windows did not close; it was ice cold inside and out. It did not bother me. I had blankets hung over the windows, set up the stage and straightened it out, set up the benches, had the room swept, and in the evening, the announced Schubert Evening could take place.

Dr. [Margarete] Merzbach spoke about Schubert's life. The terrific singer Eduard Fried sang hymns accompanied by Magister Pick, and at the close, Alfred Loewy improvised Schubert melodies on a small reed organ. The evening was repeated on March 2. This time the soloist was Edith Weinbaum from Berlin.

Up here tickets were not required for admission. The room had the capacity to hold approximately 300 people, and they radiated the necessary warmth. In order to be able to see, they came with stools and folding chairs because there were not enough of my benches. Even when masons moved in a few days later and began to fiddle with lime and sand and buckets, it did not disrupt [us]. The additional scaffolding was welcome and provided more seating.

Professor Utitz delivered the scheduled lectures on the great philosophers without interruption: Descartes, Spinoza, Leibniz, Locke, Hume, Kant, Brentano, Cohen, and Husserl.

Word quickly got around that lectures could be attended without tickets, and the visitors poured in endlessly. It was usually so crowded that a falling apple wouldn't reach the ground—the extremely unclean ground, which was covered with piles of mortar and large quantities of sand; buckets and boxes were in the way. But this did not interfere; one just did not take any notice. Only to fill the evening hours after the day's work—that was the goal.

[The question] always was, Will you still retain the room? Should we write to the administration? I had to gratefully refuse all offers of intervention because my case was represented in a completely first-rate manner by Mr. Salo Krämer, member of the Council of Elders, who did all he could to secure a dignified room for us.

The Leisure Time Organization had the use of Room 46 in the first courtyard. It was narrow and had the capacity for no more than 80 to 100 people. It housed the shoe-repair office, which could still not be moved to its new home. Therefore, I had to try to stay up there in Room 109 as long as possible, so as not to become homeless again. The uncertainty was awful. Even worse was the eternal running around and begging for the allocation of a modest, secure lecture room.

For the grand Accommodation Department, there is only the "sacred" square meter, and its decisions take into account only blueprints, not possibilities and necessity. They were, however, culture-friendly enough to listen to our many requests and to support us. To make things easy, the head of the Leisure Time Organization, [and at the same time Jewish elder] Dr. Paul Eppstein,[9] could have simply decided to assign room number so-and-so to the Leisure Time Organization.

But the way it was handled caused departmental difficulties. The administration argued that the Leisure Time Organization already had enough rooms and did not need another. They would use Room A7, which we had requested, for their own purposes. This room was empty, and so I used it for the lecture series when we became homeless again, and then actually got permission to use it until further notice.

The wide, straight room had excellent acoustics and proved to be very suitable. It held about 200 people, which was the right number. I really did not want more than that because this was as many as we could possibly handle. Issuing tickets, even at this number, required more manpower than we had available. This may suffice to show why I refused to take an even larger room; it would have involved too much administrative work.

On March 16, the last lecture in Room 109, Julius Arnfeld spoke on *Shylock, Nathan, Rabbi Akiba: Three Jewish Personalities*. Then there was a break until March 22 when Professor Emil Utitz inaugurated the new room [Room A7] with a lecture on *Locke and Hume*.

We gave out tickets again, and as always they were sold out in an hour. Now it emerged that the tickets were being hoarded: People bought tickets for all the lectures, but for some reason did not use them, after all. We therefore had to limit issuing tickets to three evenings per person.

*   *   *

This winter brought long periods of frost, a lot of rain, and heavy snowfalls in the middle of March, and with it endless slush. This made getting food extremely arduous and unpleasant. Only the kitchen in the *ubikation* managed to deliver hot meals, as long as there was coal. Then [after it ran out of coal] all brainpower had to be mustered for gathering wood.

The battle for [heating] material began. Nothing was safe, not the benches, stools, or the small wooden tables that we had, with difficulty, made. Everything that could be burned disappeared. One cursed and swore that the thieves must be caught. And when one had nothing at home anymore, one eyed every shelf to determine its suitability for the oven.

[...]

How everything has changed from waking up to going to sleep! How bravely we all accepted our hard fate. It will soon be two years that we have lived in the ghetto. Yet, shouldn't we be grateful that we were allowed a measure of freedom, unlike in any other camp? Shouldn't we therefore be grateful to the German authorities because we really do not feel the power of their command? We have to salute the men in uniform. That goes without saying. We had also required that the Russian civilians do this during the First World War. Otherwise we are free, within the ghetto limits.

The mountains greet us. The trees rustle in the ramparts. We hear the mating calls of the blackbirds in March. They have come through the winter well. We stroll through the streets and the parks, and look longingly at the bushes to see whether they are already showing the first buds.

Now in spring of 1944, in contrast to 1943, everything is still bound by winter; there is not even the smallest sign that spring is approaching.

[...]

We never see the German authorities. They deal only with a few officials of the Council of Elders. We see the gentlemen only if they appear in Magdeburg for a visitation or a meeting.

Otherwise, we know nothing of their supervisory activities. Any direct contact [with them] is prohibited. A request can only be made through the Jewish elder. And that is how it should be.

We Jews tend not only toward sharp criticism; we are even more addicted to complaining. Everybody thinks injustice is done to him three times a day and that he must assert his rights. There is an official complaint body that accepts both oral and written applications if there are grounds for them, and they are submitted by name. This body has hours of work every day, sifting, examining, negotiating, mediating, and interceding.

The German authorities would be flooded with documents if their dispatch would be allowed. It is much better that we wash our dirty laundry alone.

[...]

How business is conducted between the two authorities, we do not know; we get no insights into their relations. Therefore I cannot say anything more about it, and must confine myself to these indications.

* * *

I am writing these factual reports in the month of March 1944 in the cramped office of the block elder who, in his eagerness to help and despite the crowding of his room—21 square meters with five desks in it—still has given me a place [to work]. It is warm there—except on some days—but I can sit and write undisturbed. The continual comings and goings do not bother me, and neither do the court hearings that take place two afternoons a week and afford quite interesting insights into the lives and doings of the high and low. The postal censor, who works on every even day of the month, can deal with a long line in half an hour. He is endlessly patient with people who do not want to understand what they are allowed to write and what not. In addition, the typewriter clacks, the two ordinance officers get their orders, the clerks are in demand to impart information that can only be obtained elsewhere.

The imperturbable and calm Fritz Janowitz governs, enthroned at his desk. His work can be absolutely described as governance because there are a hundred decisions to be made every day, and many of them are not easy. To give some idea of what this man is in charge of, the barracks, which house about 600 people, and the approximately 1,400 people working in the offices are all under his auspices.

An example: The blackout rules in Theresienstadt are very strict. The authorities imposed rules that absolutely have to be followed, and there are severe penalties for noncompliance. The barracks have approximately 3,000 windows to the outside. These are checked by the Order Service every evening and by frequent nightly patrols to make sure they are closed tightly.

For the first complaint: a summons [to appear] before the block elder and a warning. Second complaint: the same with a serious warning and threat of punishment. Third complaint: arrest for 24 hours.

I would have to fill many pages to *perhaps* present a picture of the block elder's many functions, to show what he is expected to accomplish. The block elder of one barracks was sentenced to eight days' arrest because the courtyard had not been kept clean.

Consider that currently 4,800 people fetch their food three times a day. The mud in the three courtyards cannot be removed, despite all the laying of slag. Cleaning crews are at work during the day to remove paper and other refuse.

The stairs are silted but cannot stay dry because of the frequent traffic—equal to about 15,000 people a day.

Spotless cleanliness is nevertheless demanded. There is no excuse. Poor beleaguered block elder—thou shalt be amiable, courteous to everyone, and are denied the right to show a temper. You have to adapt to new situations every minute, officiate now in Czech, now in German, should know all the prominent people and officers by name and position. [...]

*   *   *

April 4, 1944. In the early morning, I went to pick up coffee at the Hannover barracks with my jug sewn in a woolen cloth. An icy wind blew; icicles hung from the edges of the roofs. Even our dear brave singer [a bird] went on strike up there at the ridge of the roof.

The sun shone radiantly. Our beloved, distant mountain had still not discarded its white robe, and the entire snow-covered mountain chain looked spectacular when the sun shone upon it. Winter does not want to retreat. It nestles in the valley and does not relax its icy grip.

We wait so eagerly for warmth. There is hardly any coal, only "sluiced" wood, which is used only for heating food. The slightly ill have to stay in bed. The healthy, however, who come home from work tired and would be happy to read for an hour, have to go to bed, too.

The windows do not close. Windows to the outside exist only partly, if at all. This makes for good ventilation day and night. Otherwise, one could not stand it because some of the elderly residents timidly avoid fresh air in the room, and at night, when there is a need for constant air circulation, allow it only reluctantly. Well, the beds are very close to the windows, and it is horribly cold for those who have to sleep there if one does not own enough blankets and *ducheten*.[10]

A notice at the warming kitchens says: "Open only when coal is available." It would be bad if this charitable institution fails. The same principle applies to heating the offices. Thus, one will understand the hot desire for warmth this year and the midday search for signs of spring. Nothing stirs in the soil. The garden of the Youth Home L417 usually sends the first welcome messengers. The spear of the lily leaves and primrose appear very early. Today, I looked for them in vain. There are no buds ready to burst open on the bushes. Over there, the park is gloomy, black; the chestnut tree, dead. The same thing in the garden of Hohenelbe. In the afternoon there was a heavy, brief pummeling of snow, the likes of which we had never experienced, even in December. So spring cannot make its entry, and filled with longing, we wait for it in vain.

[...]

* * *

The Department of Criminal Investigation: Room BV/112, second floor. A small, dark vestibule, then the large office. Since the founding of the office, at the table by the window, the small, nimble Mr. [Hans] Bass has reigned, who keeps the files on all entries and exits. He would be a living *chronique scandaleuse* [chronicle of scandal] if he would ever talk about his experiences.

There are two typewriters and tables, at which officials write reports and messages; cabinets, bulletin boards, prisoner lists, enlarged town maps. On the left are two more rooms. Investigating magistrate Dr. Alfred Weissenberg works in the smaller one. [...] On the right is a larger room, with a plaque on the door: "Director." Here works Dr. Ernst Rosenthal, the chief of the police. This is the structure of an organization that, unfortunately for Theresienstadt, turned out to be necessary in order to stop rampant crime and, to the extent possible, to prevent it, and to cut off its sources.

One knows perfectly well that in a community of 45,000 people, there are plenty of asocial elements. They do not want to be part of the necessary strict order. They cannot adjust to having to sacrifice their own interests in favor of the interests of the general public. These *outsiders*, who are unfortunately large in number, were out to use violence to obtain what the authorities cannot and do not give them because they have to keep to a budget.

These antisocial elements unite in the ghetto and build a network of supply points that appear wherever profit and addiction to cigarettes beckon. If the German authorities had decided to repeal the ban on smoking, criminality would have fallen by two-thirds. Smokers do anything for cigarettes, most believing that it is their right. Everything has been taken from them, so they are now entitled to take as well. Thus, in the ghetto the only gold standard is the cigarette. Indeed, the cost is often prison because it is contraband, but this doesn't seem to bother dealers and clients. The trade continues.

[...]

Now, I seek to venture into territory that for me so far has remained hermetically sealed, and yet it cannot go unmentioned. It is the sexual question. My age clears me from suspicion of sensationalism. I have not been concerned with the problem in these two years. It did not exist for us, like so many issues here in the ghetto that are not up for discussion because they are just not thought about. But even so, they are still present, as has been revealed to me today in a conversation with a female detective.

She has a fourteen-year-old daughter. Due to a prolonged illness she was placed in a youth home and ought to have remained there. The girl fought vigorously against it, although the food there was more plentiful and better than at her mother's. Reason? All the girls [there] had boyfriends, and she wanted no part of it. The goings-on of girls who were not much older than herself were abhorrent to her, and she did not want to have any association with them. So, I got a flash of insight into what is happening in the sphere of youth that gave me a lot to think about.

The fact is that for several years, these adolescents have been without any schooling. Anyone can imagine the dangers of such a situation. To occupy the young generation without instruction is difficult. And yet, they are eager to learn. In our house, there is a seven-year-old boy from Frankfurt who plays a lot with the Czech children. Now he speaks the language that is so hard to learn fluently. He has truly learned it playing.

The strong lads and lasses are put to work in gardens and fields at an early age, from four to eight hours, depending on how old they are. They are mostly separated from each other, but in their free time they still come together. Is it surprising then that love affairs develop? The young people are well fed, have no worries, do not yet focus on the future, and only live from day to day. Such affairs cannot be prevented by any supervision.

If we look at the growing youth, the lasses in lederhosen, with loose, well-groomed hair falling gently around their shoulders, and the smart, brisk lads, who look so cheerfully and confidently at the world, then one must wonder why, in fact, so little happens. In the morning, a crew of 50 girls with shovels over their shoulders march, singing, through the streets out to the fields to work. It is a pleasure to see these youths marching by, the guarantors of the future.

[...]

* * *

Bright, light days! In the early morning, the sun already shines. Not into our room, but over there, on the wall of the barracks, it already seems to be calling us to awaken. *Lift yourselves up from the earth, you sleepers, out of your rest.* When we go out into the arcades of the courtyards, it is still cold, sheer icy, but the sky shines so blue, the white clouds float by with a slight pink still showing. The blackbird calls out, but no longer sings her long love song. It seems she is already building her nest.

The swallows, those lively harbingers of spring, entered the stable over there a few days ago and moved into their ancestral quarters. In twos, they fly in and out, perhaps wanting to create order, to clean, ventilate, and make preparations for a comfortable "sitting room."

Even in Magdeburg, these trusting little creatures can be found, although still, not many; but in the toilet of the third courtyard, at the top of the ceiling lamp shade, the nest sticks are thick and bulky. Even in the overpopulated corridors of the barracks, they have taken possession of places they like. With loud calls they whir in and out, surely speaking about the nest, happy to have rediscovered an old spot. Oh, if we could understand the language of the birds, what would the swallows tell us about their extensive travels, about the countries and seas over which they have flown?! *Now, for a few months, you are our welcome guests. And when in the autumn you again turn to the south, will we also be released from our detention?*

In this late spring—even the chestnut trees are reluctant to unfold—it is really warm only at lunchtime, so that one can happily discard the trusty, over-used winter overcoat. But soon the first evil, the first of many plagues, arrives: the dust on the streets. When the heavy tractors rattle by, it whirls up high into the air. Fleeing is useless; one cannot get out of the way and has to swallow it. There was a flusher truck, but it is still "asleep" for the winter in the bottomless magazines of the builder's yard.

The bastion lures the elderly to the sun, in the dust-free air. From above you can see down into the deep, wide trenches of the ramparts. Like illuminated ribbons, the youth crews, working in rows, till the soil and immediately plant lettuce. Every square meter is used and planted, as long as the ghetto still has free land available. With great zeal, our magnificent youths engage in this healthy activity that firms the body and makes it healthy—the curative effect of air and sun.

Even behind the Magdeburg barracks, at the gate where heretofore parts of huts were stored lengthwise and "sluiced" (now they are completely gone), the fallow land in front of the beautiful, short avenue of trees is being dug up and raked, probably to be prepared for lawns.

Except the herd of sheep from the stable is no longer there. We no longer see the slopes climbing up to the ramparts, and, sadly, no longer enjoy seeing the two very pretty blond Czech girls with hanging braids and trousers, guarding their animals with a rod. It was truly a charming sight, the maidens with their animals moving along, shown in silhouette against the sky.

The faithful watchdog is still there. The fat, gorged sparrows are noisy, at their usual volume. A couple of blackbirds eagerly inspect their territory, over which they are the sole rulers. All sorts of things are being built on the square. The old folks are sitting in the sun on their flimsy little chairs; the very brave lie on the sprouting lawns. At the very minimum, their optimism will result in a persistent runny nose. But so what? We in the ghetto receive the spring with jubilation and fervent gratitude, and every sign affects us as though it were a message from on high. That we have not been forgotten rings in our ear; the sounds of the birds singing and the sun's rays melt even the most hardened heart of the elderly, and they learn to hope again.

[...]

April 17, 1944. Through the long night the tractors rattled and clanged through the Jägergasse. They hauled the cargo of incoming railroad trains, furniture from Prague, into the courtyards of the barracks, where it was crammed into temporary storage. Our sleep was disturbed not only by the noise and floodlights (the occasional nightly howls of the sirens do not affect us; we have become indifferent to them), but by something even more terrible: our pests, the bugs and fleas, had been lured out of their winter quarters and pounced on us tired sleepers. Enough of this inferno. I use an hour after eating and sleeping to pay my first visit of the year to the bastion.

One climbs across the railroad tracks on improvised steps to the top of the walls, and sees the plateau, dominated by the plane tree that already has red buds sticking out, in contrast to the shrubs around it, where only a hint of green can be seen. The playground is off limits; it is being renovated.

One is now allowed to walk on and occupy the other walls, in contrast to the past years when entry was strictly prohibited, which caused us guardsmen frequent disagreements with visitors. Now, the old and the young (rather carelessly) already lie down on blankets and enjoy deliverance from the bonds of winter. The children start to take off their winter clothes, so that they can run and jump unhindered. There, on the right, the ten-year-olds try to form a soccer team, and are as eager and spirited as the older ones.

Couples everywhere lie closely snuggled together and look out over the wide landscape.

The sun is still veiled. The mountains are visible only as contours.

[...]

Toward Bauschowitz, where the Elbe takes many twists and turns, stands the Georg Mountain, sloped on all sides and looking like a pot, the legendary holy mountain of the Czechs, who call it Řip. Starting from here, the original father Čech is said to have taken possession of the country. Everything around is still bare, except the mighty weeping willows before the Sokolowna, which stand like bright specks of color against the white houses, wide and high.

Groups of youths work on the outer walls, leveling, loosening, and breaking up the soil for sowing. There a lively squad arrives with shovels and timber grills. Large areas have already been cultivated and wait for the first warm rain, which is now very necessary. The sun really dries out, and sowing here requires moisture that the soil itself does not provide. On the other hand, the ramparts on the right, through which the narrow flood channel flows, are partly filled with water, which makes work impossible.

But nothing in Theresienstadt is not ultimately useful. And so the youths discovered a new, wonderful "playground." They drag along boards and boldly navigate on the water, laughing, exclaiming, shrieking, and shouting. It is a true pleasure to watch this from overhead. Last year, a ditch was dug for cultivation at the Jäger barracks. Premium vegetables were harvested there in season. Now those beds are clean and empty, except for the lettuce that is now beginning to grow. The sick sit outside and enjoy the sun, and a chess match is being played, surrounded by onlookers.

A steady stream of visitors of all ages flows up and down. Those who can squeeze half an hour from their lunch breaks take in the quiet beauty of the square, enjoying the view of the mountains. Even this short amount of time is enough to clear the lungs of dust and to fill the soul with new willingness to work. On sunny days like this, one can completely forget the notion of the ghetto, feel at peace with the world, and draw hope and confidence up there on top.

[...]

* * *

Under the fresh impression of the 400th lecture evening, I want to report: April 19, Professor Dr. E. Utitz, *Philosophers of the Present*. It was the last in a series of six lectures.

The friends of the [Manes] circle insisted on pleasing me with a substantial and nutritious gift. Alfred Stettenheim, [Arthur] Koralek, and Dr. [Hella] Fuchs joined forces to put together a table of presents that bore witness to the joy of giving, which is not the norm in Theresienstadt. Two slices of bread and half a loaf of bread, onions, garlic, conserves, butter, a real cake, and a garnish of spring greens and lettuce.

Two of the gifts touched me deeply. One lady had scrimped and saved from her lunch in order to bring me a whole *buchtel*. Another lady gave half a *buchtel*.

To contribute from a scarce meal in order to pay a debt of gratitude is a great feat in Theresienstadt.

When I entered the room at ten minutes to seven, it was [already] over-crowded. I was greeted with vigorous applause and shouts. I had to shake out-stretched hands all around and accept congratulations.

Actually, I did not want to give a speech, but I had to at least say thank you. I said that I was always the one receiving gifts because I had been able to work, undisturbed, in a milieu that matched my abilities, serving only the arts and the needs of the ghetto inmates. For nearly two years, this had kept me healthy and fresh. The loyalty of the audience had encouraged and sustained me, and only in such circumstances could I have been creative and effective. Therefore, all thanks to the listeners, who had been with us all the way, to the friends of the Manes Group. Again, there was warm applause in the room, which gave way to silence, as we listened to the prologue by Wilhelm Sterk from Vienna, who had chosen as a theme, *About Culture!*

Four hundred times have people sharing the same values come together in the evening hours, which are usually so dreary and lacking in content, for the last 18 months. Whether the events were serious or amusing, they wanted to widen the scope of their gaze and their hearts' receptiveness, and to keep their minds sharp. Not just to learn or to repeat what they have learned, but to refresh their minds. I had almost said "to soak them," the way a languishing animal is led to the well to recover after a drought. Nowhere else could you ever find such an institution, one that gives those who attend it the opportunity to educate their minds, their intellects, their emotions as well as to nurture their knowledge. The Manes Group is, after all, no adult-education college or night school. It is too universal to be compared to a teacher's popular pulpit; its scope extends from the depths of rabbinic wisdom and the heights of philosophy to the civilized contemporary songs of the *Überbrettl*. Just as I said a moment ago, these evenings develop the hearts and the minds of the listeners.

And now to the close of the talk:

Four hundred evenings spent in jest and in seriousness have a meaningful influence on the spiritual atmosphere. There can be no doubt that they have contributed mightily to the culture (in the sense of higher and deeper education) of the listeners. Their impact on our minds—of this, I am certain—is certainly so great that none of us, whether he be a listener or a speaker, will forget these evenings. Their echo will still be heard; their culture will continue to be felt when we, with the help of God, have long been freed from the confines of Theresienstadt.

After these beautiful and penetrating words, the aged Alfred Stettenheim dedicated some verses to me.

Then, finally, it was time for Professor Dr. Emil Utitz to begin the last in the series of his philosophical lectures, covering Husserl, the great philosopher from Freiburg. After his rich lecture explaining phenomenology, the evening ended; it has been an unforgettable experience for me.

* * *

April of 1944 nears its end. It still blows cold from the mountains; the sun still does not warm, one cannot sit outdoors but freezes in the room. I ogle the chestnut tree in the small park in the morning when I get my coffee, to see if the brown hulls are still closed, not heralding spring. The bushes in front of the bakery have made no progress with their green tops. The gardeners dig around and level the encrusted earth, which has for years served as a yard and is solid underfoot, to create a green belt around Theresienstadt. It will be a sight for sore eyes when the seeded lawn rises.

The shrouded mountains look unreal cloaked in their robe [of snow]. The trees around the parade ground with their broom-like branches, so ugly and grotesque in their baldness, say that it is still winter. But the square itself, where in winter the big tent for the packaging production stood, will be granted a new life. The large square will become a garden. Extensive beds have already been prepared, filled with nutritive soil, brought in on carts drawn by oxen, moving strenuously.

In the corner in front of the café, a nice open pavilion, simple in form, has been built. Daily concerts will take place in it. In the wide avenues in front of the church a promenade is being envisaged for the residents. In the spring many will enjoy listening to what so far only a few could hear in the café or in the concert hall of the town hall.

This generous gift was announced at the beginning of April, and still more: the dreadful planks that closed off so many streets were taken down, as was the barbed wire used for the same purpose. Even the barriers in front of the commandant's beautiful, modern house were removed. Now the square, with its mixture of buildings dating back to the time of Joseph II and of his later descendants, finally came into its own, offering an unobstructed view. Now everything is open and free; there is nothing visible to remind one of captivity. Only the magnificent church remains closed, not open even to non-Jews who want to kneel and pray.

When one looked into the rooms, there were green branches in makeshift vases everywhere. Creative hands had planted proper little miniature Japanese gardens in sardine tins—still lifes. Small wildflowers were brought in from the fields, where they had been clinging to the soil, unseen. These works of art looked charming when displayed between the windows. One often saw clusters of blooming violets, and their fine fragrance was truly the herald of spring.

April 24, 1944, was a wonderfully warm, sunny day that made one feel happy. The chestnut trees were visibly unfolding, and overnight became pale green, overtaking their "comrades," the other species, who were still afraid to show their buds. The next day, it was rainy, cold, and windy—April weather.

In Theresienstadt work progressed at a feverish pace in all the courtyards. By decree of the [German] authorities, a comprehensive beautification drive[11] was under way. Only when it had been pulled off, and everything accomplished, would the improvement be seen.

In [...] all the courtyards, sections of adjacent walls had been demolished to link previously separate areas. It did not look nice, just improvised. Many of the houses and walls looked dilapidated. This is all being repaired, patched, plastered, smoothed, and beautified. Skilled and unskilled bricklayers were busy, working arduously to plaster the walls. The holes in the floor were filled in, and the awful damage was repaired at last. The arcades of the barracks were "yellowed," which means that they were freshly painted in light yellow using a spraying apparatus. The dirt was terrible. It was tracked into all the offices, to the despair of the cleaning crews, who had already had enough to do cleaning the arcades. These valiant women had to work very hard these days; they were not allowed a break, even at night.

To return to the almost mythical spring, on this day, April 27, I noted again its absence. It was cold even in the sun because of the sharp north wind blowing in front of the barracks, where the workers lay out paths to make us elderly people comfortable. We wondered if benches would also be put there so that we would no longer need to rest on the ledges of the garbage pit.

Feverish creation everywhere—only nature held back, unwilling [to arrive], perhaps, because people were fighting each other all over the world.

[...]

And if the siren wakes us in the night, we are frightened at first, but then it is like a glad sigh of relief. What do we care about the airplanes? We do not need to hide in a cellar. For us, the thunderous planes over Theresienstadt are dream apparitions in the dark night. If we cannot fall asleep, our thoughts were with the pilots, and we see them struggle to defend themselves against the hostile, incoming aircraft. As we had in Berlin, we see the bright fireworks of the anti-aircraft ammunition and the sky illuminated by flashes. Where will the attack take place? How many human lives will pay for these nighttime hours? What will be destroyed, turned into rubble?

[...]

*   *   *

In the month of April, the general beautification[12] affected even the orders of the day—they were now illustrated. At the top was a [picture] of Theresienstadt, and there were pretty little pen drawings in each section.

Under "menu," there was a [drawing of a] cook attending to a cauldron. We received an overview of the weekly menu and could regulate our appetites accordingly.

Another type of announcement proclaimed:

The following roads and squares are to be renamed...
The residents of Theresienstadt will be given the opportunity to participate in a competition to name them.
Eight prizes will be awarded:

    I. Prize: two tins of sardines in oil; one loaf of bread
   II. Prize: ½ kilogram of flour; ¼ kilogram of sugar [ ]
  III. Prize: 20 decagrams of quark; 10 decagrams of sugar; 15 decagrams of marmalade

Five consolation prizes: two leisure time tickets each.[13]

[...]

*   *   *

On April 19, 1944, all offices received the following notice from the administration:

The following designations will be used in the future:

    Ghetto Watch = Community Guard
    Guard and Order Service = Security and Order Service
    Ghetto Court = Court
    Ghetto Library = Central Library
    Ghetto Theresienstadt = Jewish Settlement Area of Theresienstadt

These sweeping changes were conveyed to us without comment, and we had to try to make sense of them on our own. The [underlying] condition of our territory had not changed. The construction work had made progress all around. It was being carried out intensively, and people were passionate about it. The fruit of this labor belonged to everyone, after all, securing and preserving their lives.

* * *

May 1 was an official holiday, even in Theresienstadt. The post office was closed, but that was the only outward sign. On the other hand, spring still had not set in. It is freezing cold. Vegetation does not make progress. Mrs. Sun is unable to make any impression on the icy wind. The winter of our discontent weighs heavily, hanging over us in a dreadful way, and we can hardly bear it.

* * *

Can I end this section without mentioning the fact that on May 3, that which we so eagerly awaited [milder weather] arrived during the night? It was a clear night; the stars and the half moon shone brightly. For the first time, it [the weather] was so pleasant that we could stand on the [open landing] of our house, which one otherwise passes by so quickly. All around us was silence, and a soft breeze wafted over the rooftops. The clock of the Genie barracks chimed; otherwise, nothing else stirred in this broad courtyard that was so busy during the day.

The air was mild, soft, caressing. Schumann's *Moonlit Night*, so familiar, sounded within me, and I felt as if I were listening to a very soft, sweet voice from far away. The moon rose over the house, and our courtyard was suddenly bright. Only the walls below me and the barns were deep black. Light clouds softened the illumination. It seemed as if the moon traveled with an army of stars.

How could I return, after such a wonderful experience, to the crowded room full of people? I dreaded it. After such an experience one does not want to be in the grim reality. Still, it has to be. The night is very short for those of us who worked. It passes by so quickly; as soon as we lie down, sleep takes us in its loving, strong, healing arms. One more deep breath and then: go inside. The morning woke us with bright sunshine. There had been a light rain, and the streets were free of dust.

At 7 A.M., I went to go get coffee over in Hannover. On the way, the small park to the right looked proud, resplendent after this first warm night. What must the earth have done; by what effort had the mighty chestnut tree made its

small, tender leaves—which had hung limply on their stems, looking frozen—
stand up and grow in the morning hours? Now it was a magnificent tree wearing a new gown of green, and would soon display its "candles" of white, held
up high.

The park is a mass of shining green, hiding the ugliness that is otherwise visible through the bare branches. The bushes in front of the bakery, dressed in yellow, white, and green, are, in their luminous power, competing with the rippling,
shimmering curtain of leaves on the slightly swaying trunks of the white birches.
How the eyes drink in the colors after the long, hard, burdensome winter!

[...]

A few figures:

Up to April 15, 128,327 people passed through the ghetto.
Transported away: 60,937 people
Died: 30,879 people
On April 15, 1944, there were 36,183 inmates in the ghetto.

At lunchtime on May 11 came the bitter truth: three transports, totaling 7,500 people, were ordered to leave the ghetto. What I attempted to describe earlier is now,
after a break of half a year, again going to be carried out—to the fullest extent.

The lectures are canceled as of May 12. I felt sorry for Gustav Hochstetter,
in whose honor that evening was to be held—his 71st birthday. He had wanted
to present a selection of his best creations and was happily looking forward to it.
But the plan was axed for two reasons: Gustav Hochstetter became very ill and
had to be taken to the hospital. Then, all the lectures were canceled. We hope
that a belated celebration will be possible.

And now eight difficult, painful days lay before us. We had waited with such
longing for May, had greeted it with such heartfelt joy. It still gives us no warmth
but, instead, transports to unknown destinations.

*   *   *

[...]

Now, the whispered and uncertain rumors spreading by word of mouth
solidified into the bitter, deeply distressing truth. Seven thousand five hundred
people have to leave Theresienstadt, as they say, in order to be relocated to
camp Birkenau in Upper Silesia. The authorities want and need to reduce the
number of residents in the summer. For reasons of hygiene alone—which are
irrefutable—among others.

The administrative procedure was the same for all transports that had been carried out so far. Certain categories of people were exempt: senior officials [of the Jewish self-administration], as long as they were not designated to hold the same position in the new place; severely disabled war veterans; those who were highly decorated; and the prominent.[14]

The registry and the transport department made the lists according to specific requirements of the [German] authorities. The call-ups under the new transport number were issued until the evening, and then again in the early-morning hours. The rules were listed on a half sheet of paper; a very narrow (1 cm), long strip contained the summons. People called up last had just a few hours in which to pack. The majority had one or two days.

In order to have the necessary reserves for this transport, more than 12,000 people were called up between May 15 and 18. The 7,500 were not negotiable.

The departures took place on three days with a gap of two between each.[15]

All the inhabitants of the Hamburg barracks were cleared out, and it was designated as a collection center. Those who had been called up had to report there at specified times with their luggage, which was delivered on a wagon by younger helpers. No one else could enter the barracks. From the barracks, they moved in formation toward the gates.

Boys and girls, aged 8 to 12, wearing armbands stamped with their identification, accompanied each group. These youngsters took to the work enthusiastically, dedicating themselves with frantic eagerness to their new task: to help. They pulled carts and wagons; they hauled light and heavy luggage; they helped the disabled; they acted as couriers. One saw them until late at night, always cheerful and chattering happily, helping those who had been called up to get over the worst.

It was a great joy for us to see how these young people, who were growing up here without regular schooling, were proving themselves. They knew how to lend a hand and did not know fatigue. When the *Aktion* was over, a roll call for the young was held at the bastion. Dr. Paul Eppstein spoke to them and extended his thanks.

Last year, I had asked the young poet Georg Kafka to write an epic on the theme of the transports. Every time, he was evasive in his reply. In the end, he said that he was not able at the time to concentrate: He was involved in preparing the transports and did not yet feel that he had enough distance. Instead, his puppet play about the Golem came into being.

Now, things had gotten very close to Kafka. His mother—his father had died in March—was called up for the transport. Her son immediately volunteered to accompany his beloved mother into the distant unknown. It was a very painful parting for me. I had gotten so much from this very promising, straightforward, and humble person.

But he was not the only one. The list of those I would like to commemorate who were taken by the "Poland transport," as it was known during those one and a half years of uncertainty, is too long.

At that time, everything was different—harder on the soul, more agonizing and grueling, than it is today. Even just the march on foot toward Bauschowitz with heavy luggage: everybody wanted to take as much as possible, the most valuable items: the washbowl, cooking pots, and hulking objects that took up a lot of space and could not easily be accommodated.

Those who were unable to walk were driven—it looked so terrible, the truck with its human freight. But for the elderly people, who could not carry anything and could barely drag their tired bodies, the way to the station was a *via dolorosa*. Today, the train cars stop in front of the barracks. The young helpers load the luggage, and then the provisions—bread, meat paste, margarine, and sugar— were distributed.

All aboard? With a hiss and a whistle, the locomotive pulled out, and the train traveled slowly past the bastion; the chestnut trees by the burial ground rustled a soft farewell. Then the train passed through the gate. Farewell, Theresienstadt.

[...]

* * *

This time [ ] people were called up from my *ubikation*. Among them were my wife's three companions, who had come with us to Theresienstadt and had shared our joys and sadness. [...] All three had set out with only one goal; it was the hope that kept them going: to be reunited with their children. They had not thought that they, the widows, could be sent away.

That's why the call-up in the early morning hit them even harder. But they accepted this latest trial without complaint, even though they had barely recovered from long illnesses. Our small room turned into an encampment. Possessions (how much one accumulates in two years, despite the lack of room!) had to be looked over and sorted out. The weight limit for the luggage was 50 kg, plus hand luggage, as much as one could carry.

Now Julius Weiler took charge of the operation. He was a lean, sinewy 61-year-old man, born in Hessen. He was unique; there was no one like him in Theresienstadt. We live in the same room. He sleeps on the right, in the top row; I sleep on the left, below. His loud voice can be heard everywhere, but one enjoys listening to him because he is always amusing. When the 19 men in the room engage in conversation, Julius Weiler—trained butcher, soldier in the world war, much traveled—will contribute a personal experience, no matter what topics are spoken of.

If army days and training are the subject of conversation, for example, he will say: "There was a sergeant, Karl Schubert, and we trained him," and then there follows a long, funny story about how they did it. To properly describe this vigorous, virile man, with his talent for telling stories and his quick-witted turn of mind, is beyond me.

So Julius Weiler, who could do everything, was in his element. He rolled his sleeves up and packed. The women had only to indicate what to include and he securely tied everything up so that nothing would be lost. If the luggage is stacked up in the courtyard, it needs to be able to withstand a few knocks or the owner will never see it again. He tirelessly helped in all the rooms, sacrificed his customary afternoon nap, and lent a helping hand whenever—and wherever—someone's strength failed.

Finally, it was done. Those who were being transported were allowed to rest and wait for the call to line up. The time dragged by—a quarter of an hour at a time. The request to write to the children far away, if it was possible from here, was repeated again and again.[16] One spoke about the two long, hard winters that had been endured together as comrades; the way people had supported and cared for each other during days of sickness, taking all the work upon themselves. When parcels were happily received, how proud they had been to share in the blessing. Here, in this awful passageway, there was an exemplary community spirit. And the tears flowed. The women cried their hearts out and held each other in an embrace.

The women accepted the painful fate of becoming wandering Jews.

The call rings out loud and clear over the courtyard: departure. Downstairs, checking the names, the young people take the bags and baskets, suitcases and backpacks. The train proceeds slowly to the gates opposite the [Hamburg] barracks, comes to a stop, and waits for passengers to board.

The streets are full of people. Small groups approach from all sides, all with the same destination. Those who were spending the night in the barracks [awaiting their own transport] gazed from the windows.

My wife's three companions had the luck to be assigned a downstairs room. We could stay in contact with them, take them hot drinks, or perform a last act of kindness, bringing a forgotten towel, a pot, the walking stick. In the barracks itself everything is taken care of. Fresh sacks of sawdust are ready; the kitchen delivers its usual meals. The preparations and final arrangements are made quickly and without annoying formalities. By contrast, the process of raising objections to being transported is difficult.

The [German] authorities had opened an office in my Room A7 for eight days to receive objections and to accept the completed forms there. Cases were assessed three ways: refusal, decision, cases of doubt, to be left to the discretion of the administration.[17] Every applicant believed that he had a right to avoid the transport. I read so many destinies on these pages [of appeals] that it would take a thousand pages to write them all down.

Only those with high numbers had a chance to be dismissed from the barracks as surplus to the requirement. And since [...] a large number had to be called up, there remained a chance of a favorable decision.[18] And so, after two days, we had the joy of seeing a young family from our house again.

It sometimes happened, however, that the bedrolls and large luggage that had been loaded were lost. In these cases, the administration provided suitable replacements.

It was admirable, the way all the offices on these days worked on just a few hours of sleep. Everything was done to make the evacuee's journey easy. Also, the German authorities were perfectly humane and acted only as facilitators. Their boss did not allow himself to rest at night, in order to be able to watch over everything and to ensure the smooth flow of the transports.[19]

The last train is dispatched. The sentries withdraw, except for a few. The huge barracks feel lonely and abandoned. The next day the disinfection crew move in, and the rooms are gassed. Then slowly the barracks fills up again, serving its old purpose until further notice.

The events of the Leisure Time Organization had been discontinued during the [...] days of the transport.

And now, normal life resumes; the day goes by for each one of us in our manifold jobs. It [normal life] yokes us, keeps us tethered in its grasp, and does not allow us contemplation. That is the consolation that Theresienstadt gives— absorbing activity that keeps all gloomy thoughts away. Only at night, before going to sleep, do our thoughts go out into the distance, with a goodnight wish to our loved ones, who are, hopefully, [doing] well in their new homes. After all, God's sunlight reaches everywhere.

*　*　*

An unusual month, this May, whose delights we got to taste only for two days.
[...]
In the courtyard of our *ubikation* a diligent woman laid out three flower beds in the unused corner entrance and planted them with spinach. In the beginning of May, the tips showed but dared not leave the protected soil. More than that, and the spinach would be eaten by sparrows, which have survived

the winter much better than we did. They are fat, unlike us, and eager for a varied diet.

On May 23, the thermometer read one degree centigrade at 7 A.M., and by noon, cold winds prevented the weather from improving. Only our dear blackbird does not care about the weather and the wind. She perches on her branch and whistles her variations loudly and clearly from up above.

Before the day dawned, this small, exalted creature is already singing, although it really has more to do than to make music so early. For a little black head with a yellow beak peeks curiously out of the nest and waits for his mother to bring his morning feeding. Papa seems content to amuse himself in his own way and to leave the work to his wife (which is said to happen sometimes with people in Theresienstadt).

The trees and shrubs are an exquisite bright green, but today, on May 26, it is still not possible to sit, dreaming, and enjoy the pleasant warmth of the sun. The expert farmers among us laud and praise a cool May, which normally means a good harvest. As far as the eye can see, everyone is cultivating any suitable plot. Youngsters of all ages are employed everywhere to do the plantings. Over on the outer ramparts, which is totally exposed to the sun, the beds down at the base thrive, already showing lush growth.

[...]

All this bloom and growth is not for our benefit.[20] The cherries and apples do not ripen for us in this sun-drenched hill country; we do not harvest vegetables from the enormous beds.

We receive none of the earth's blessings, which are made possible by the devoted, hard work to which most of us are not accustomed and have never before practiced. We are excluded from harvesting. No fresh vegetables or fruit refresh our parched tongues and decaying bodies, which have used up the last fat and energy reserves and [depleted] the life-sustaining vitamins a long time ago.

This spring we once got a little fresh spinach, but no more of Mother Nature's abundance nurtured us. We made do with the monotonous fare that was served up through the entire winter. When there is thin soup for lunch (32 decagrams of potato and a small amount of unrecognizable sauce) and, in the evenings, one potato, how can the working man be satisfied?! Even the delicious white *buchtel* baked with good flour and served for lunch cannot fill us up.

[...]

However, as noted several times, the parcels help provide us with what we need for survival. At this moment, the grocery store has that spicy spread, good mustard, which is forbidden to me, and otherwise only bags filled with every possible *ersatz* foodstuff. My last purchase cost 26 krone: honey flavor, caraway, paprika, herbs, garlic powder (8 krone for a large bag), etc.

On May 1, a movement known as Town Beautification had started in Theresienstadt, and it was now in high gear. The [German] authorities had ordered it. There was a date set for its completion, and now all forces are deployed in a frenzy of activity. Our town will be cleaned—externally: the building facades, streets, and squares, and also internally: the interiors of the *ubikations* from the cellars to the roofs—to improve their appearance.

It began, as I already mentioned, with the digging up of all the public areas, and then the laying of beds, creating lawns, paving the paths with slag and gravel to make them passable. The large "L" streets were freshly graveled and covered with yellow sand. Powerful steamrollers accomplished good work everywhere. Even the seldom-used roadway around the sheep stall, one of the few places to take a peaceful walk, which could not be navigated in bad weather, was paved. The open stables on either side, which served as a storage area for all sorts of junk, were removed. The old railroad cars, which were used as a repository for bones, were moved away to perform their less-than-fragrant duty elsewhere.

Saplings were planted around the barracks that housed the laundry collection and distribution center and the shoe repository, and beds of greenery were put down in the wide entryways. Benches were also placed there.

A great effort was under way everywhere. In the [houses of the] courtyards, with their colorful muddle and clutter of rooms, things are cleared away and cleaned, particularly in the mornings, when the laundry flutters cheerfully on the clotheslines that reach up to the first floor. Every block elder does his best to ensure that he will be noticed during the upcoming inspection, and praised.

One day, massive hanging scaffolds were brought here from Prague. Our good, gray Magdeburg barracks were to be rejuvenated. On the swaying scaffolds workmen were busy with brushes and water, sweeping away the dirt of many decades. Then the electric spraying machine was put to use, and its rays of color produced a bright new dressing for the walls. When passing the two gates, we had to take care not to be "rejuvenated" as well.

Dashing through the long corridors, you could almost believe yourself to be in the beloved homeland, just before Easter. Everything that is not nailed down is in front of the *ubikations*, awaiting a thorough cleaning. Inside, men and women alternately brush, scrub, and rinse the winter dirt away with hoses.

Oh, if only one could have at the same time torn down the wooden beds everywhere and burned them! What use are chlorine, petroleum, and Lysol? None, absolutely none. The pests arrive at midnight, and their raids continue until dawn brings them to a halt.

The windows are washed, those that have panes. Not all of them do. Empty cavities yawn in the second outer wing. Glass is used only for urgent purposes and therefore was generally not available. The *ubikations* do not fall into this category.

So, the building elder requested that the windows in my room be washed. A long debate ensued. Who was willing to do the cleaning? There were more excuses than inmates. Finally, one man says, "If each of you gives me a teaspoon of sugar, I'll do it." Naturally, someone protests. Do Jews have any unity, coordination, or feeling for community and the common good? Again, there is a long discussion. Finally, the dissenter gives in, after his antisocial attitude is pointed out to him.

The same problem recurs: washing down the room. Also, only for pay. Each inmate has to take turns doing the daily sweeping, and it looks like it. Everyone is responsible for keeping the space under his own bed clean. Yes, there are plenty of problems with living in such crowded conditions.

Now back to the barracks. The office spaces are also thoroughly cleaned, whitewashed, and painted, which is quickly done with the spray equipment—in two days everything is finished. This is no small feat considering that there are so many rooms spread over the two floors. Those responsible put all their energy into getting this job done. Even the totally inaccessible office of the administration, where hundreds waited every day to be admitted to the heads of the departments, is a dim anteroom, cupboards, capable of accommodating at most 20 people crowded together. Now it has become wide and roomy, and when it's painted, it will be really worthy of the "administration." Finally!

The hardworking men who—much to the envy of all the children—go clambering up the scaffolding or slide down from the roof on ropes moved to the second courtyard, cleaning, spraying, and laying bricks there as well. When everything is finished, what will become of us?

Is the town beautification being done for us, is so much beauty being created for Jews? Is Theresienstadt being planted, dug, and built as though we are to have a beloved home here—forever? Will others harvest what Jewish labor, Jewish sweat, and worn, calloused Jewish hands have created? After it is all completed, will we have to vacate Theresienstadt—our home that we have already begun to love just a little bit—and settle in Birkenau, an actual camp, not a town like we have here? We discuss these questions passionately in the evenings, and none of us know any answers.

Meanwhile, on Whitsuntide,[21] May 28, 1944, sun and warmth broke through. It was a double holiday because the celebration of Shavuot[22] fell on the same date. For the first time, one could go without an overcoat. It is finally, finally spring.

Would it be meaningful on a day such as this to look back on the long succession of Whitsuntides marching past in a long column, and smile and bow? Could I implore them to cast off their shadowy nature and appear before me clearly? That excursion to Buckow with comrades from the club, with that unforgettable night in the courtyard of the barn. The repetition the next year with my dearest friend Adolf Franck. The three marvelous days in Lugano, Lake Como, and Milan. Whitsuntide in Interlaken. Whitsuntide in Munich. Whitsuntide in Holland. *Retreat behind your concealing veil, you messengers of the past; I'll wander with you through all the beauties of this world. And after my meal, when I take my customary walk under the magnificent linden trees in front of the stables, come back to me, so that I can pretend that I am wandering through the Alps.*

These images are around me, and quietly reflecting on them embellishes my day. Lunch for the double celebration: potato soup, *buchtel* without cream, and in the evening: coffee.

After the endless winter that only slipped away at the end of May, one cannot quite take in all the blooming and greenery. One looks shyly up at the trees, wondering "Is it real?" One stands in amazement before the profusion of the laburnum; the green of its leaves can barely be seen because it spreads its golden, glowing clusters of flowers so lavishly. Four weeks late, the hawthorn wraps itself in its robe emblazoned with snowy blossoms.

And the chestnut trees, which have unfolded so slowly and looked frozen for many days, caught up and are now overflowing with their white and pink candle-like "pyramids" as never before. The most beautiful trees are in the courtyards of the Sudeten barracks, where we are not allowed to go. But their mighty crowns tower over the walls and greet the columns of young workers when they pass by. They, who lived there at one time, had felt safe and secure in its big, bright rooms.

A double row of young linden trees line Seestraße, where the houses of the prominent are, with wide, bright corridors, and high rooms housing only a few residents, iron beds, tables, chairs, and a bit of comfort. These houses of the prominent are unusually well-kept, and sparkle with cleanliness. The stone floors shine like mirrors, as do the windows. In short, a house couldn't have looked much better back home, even with all the resources that were available there.

I visited Professor Utitz, who lives with his wife, a nurse, in a beautiful, light, second-floor room at Number 26. It looks out onto the garden next to the Sudeten barracks with its tall, old trees, and in clear weather one can see the Kegel Mountains in the distance. If one were sick, one could quickly recover in a place like this. In such an environment, being ill for a few days would be a pleasure, a comforting rest. When I think about my dark corner, where I can read only at midday and at no other time; when I think about the noise made by the constantly bickering old people and the coughing of the two who can't shake off their fever (which is between 37.5 and 38 degrees Celsius) and were found to have tuberculosis, it is enough to make even the most peaceful man indignant and ask, "Why not me; I am also worthy."

Yesterday, May 29 1944, at six o'clock, there was a memorial service in the beautiful, dignified new cinema hall for the deceased *Justizrat* Dr. Julius Magnus, born in 1867. We have a "Legal Association" to which all the lawyers in the ghetto belong, which holds lectures and offers courses. At the service, Rabbis Dr. Baeck and Dr. Neumann recalled all the things the deceased had done for the legal profession and for Jewry. One should have done something for this man who was isolated while he was alive, lodged him in a house for the prominent, and given him a caretaker. It didn't happen. Now one wails about the famous man known and treasured by the whole world.

[I met him as follows.] After one lecture in March, I was introduced to an elderly gentleman, who offered to lecture in my circle. He did not look the part. He had a wild beard in which pieces of food were stuck; an old, shabby overcoat, also speckled with flecks of food; and dirty hands. He was an unusual sight, even in the ghetto. Was this a famous man? I did not want to believe it. But as I spoke with him, I knew that a spiritual hero stood before me. We agreed on a lecture program with the following subjects:

1. *Heine's Religion*
2. *From the History of the Jews:*
   a. *Berlin*
   b. *The Old Austria*
   c. *Frankfurt am Main*
   d. *West Germany*
   e. *Scandinavia*
3. *Migration and Culture* (two nights)
4. *The Inheritance of Law and Rights*
5. *Great Jewish Statesmen*
6. *Esther in Art and Literature* (two nights)

Out of all of these lectures, he gave only the first one, and in it he demonstrated a spirited liveliness and an unerring memory. He knew all the poems by heart, and he spoke with a brilliant command of his theme for one and a half hours. He came to us every evening for several weeks.

He was supposed to have begun the *From the History of the Jews* lectures but had to cancel because of hoarseness. We hoped for a speedy recovery, and he did, too, because he was immensely pleased to be giving the lectures; he talked to me often about his far-reaching plans. Again and again, he expressed his appreciation and enjoyment of what had been accomplished in Rooms A6 and A7. He said his heart was in it; he wanted to be my most devoted collaborator.

I wanted to know, what title should I give him? Doctor, he said, nothing else. I'm proud only of my honorary doctorates from Heidelberg and Frankfurt. To you, I'm Doctor Magnus.

At the last lectures, he mostly fell asleep after just a short time. It was awful for us to see his physical deterioration from week to week. Then came the final stage—transferred to the infirmary in the Hamburg barracks. I visited him every other day. He did well there and received good nursing and medical care. One day he was feeling especially good and hoped to be able to give his lecture soon. I had to describe my program to him in detail, to report on the speakers, the visitors, and whether Room A7 was finally be renovated.

But my next visit revealed the destruction that the onset of pneumonia had wrought. The sick man lay there with his eyes closed. There was a smile on his face as I spoke to him, but he had difficulty opening his eyes.

"Ah, Mr. Manes, what is new with you?"

"I am studying *Urfaust*."

"Ah, *Urfaust*, Miss von Göchhausen, Erich Schmidt. I would like to give a lecture on that. Beautiful, beautiful, *Urfaust*—fine."[23]

I took his hot hand and pressed it, again awestruck. The next day, May 15, Dr. Magnus passed over to the other side, to that realm of the great spirits, of the shades of the men whose lives had inspired him and whose herald he had become.

[...]

* * *

On the second day of Shavuot, *Maskir*[24] in all the prayer halls, the festival of the dead. In my own way, I commemorated my beloved parents and the many people who had died here. I had to visit the library, which had moved to new rooms in the Dresdener barracks, and did my business.

The new lecture hall was next door. The delicate Mrs. Käthe von Giżycki sat at the grand piano and played Schubert. I sat there very quietly, the only audience, and listened to *Impromptus*, masterfully played on the good instrument.

How often my daughter—far away—had played it for us! And now Schubert's solemn music stirred memories and opened barely healed wounds, and at the same time, comforted and soothed. After that, Gideon Klein played Brahms. This was my personal celebration of the dead.

After that, I went alone to the memorial at the columbarium and prayed the oldest prayer for the dead as our fathers had done.

* * *

Shortly before lunchtime, I walked down the main street and heard music—a march—being played on a piano. I was astonished. It was not coming from the pavilion in the town chapel nor from one of the houses. What was going on? I saw a cluster of people rolling from side to side in the middle of a wagon that was being pulled by merry boys. There was a grand piano in it, accompanied by musicians, who were moving the precious instrument themselves, guarding their treasure against damage. One of them had opened the top and was hammering out a lively march as he walked. So, to the quiet jubilation of the passersby, they pulled it to Magdeburg and disappeared into the dark gateway.

The beginning of June is not very summer-like. There are two hot days, followed by a period of cool, overcast days. The bright young green of the trees has already turned more somber. The laburnum shows only the faded remains of its golden splendor. The "candles" on the chestnut trees have burned out, and the trees stand like a solemn wall. Soon, [however,] the linden trees will bloom.

Bunches of colorful, fresh flowers are brought home and displayed in many windows. Also pots, real flowerpots with forget-me-nots, pansies, and—oh, more down to earth—parsley and chives. The beds in the courtyards are carefully maintained, and the young vegetable plants are developing splendidly. The first lettuce is, to the gardener's satisfaction, nearly ready to harvest.

I should now explain why I had to vacate the very adequate Room A7 so suddenly. The guilty party was Lisbon, the capital of Portugal. It happened like this: A resourceful exporter of sardines had advertised in newspapers all over the world that he would send two tins of sardines to every address in Theresienstadt as often as they wanted, if one [the person placing the order] paid a certain amount in U.S. dollars. Apparently, there was an agreement with Germany that all shipments to camps would be tax-free. As compensation, Germany would be allowed to send the same kind of shipments to prison camps abroad, in exchange for payment in German marks.

In a very short time, approximately 30,000 shipments of sardines had been received, addressed to the Jewish elder of Theresienstadt, followed by the individual recipient's name. The post office didn't quite know what to do with this unexpected blessing. First, they had to eliminate the names of those who had been taken away in transports, and then the heirs of deceased persons had to be identified, which was painstaking, detailed work. Those who had been called up for a transport could grant a power of attorney to someone else, who could then pick up the packages.

[...]

My room was filled up with long tables. Approximately 12 officials moved in and received the people who felt they had a claim. It will take weeks to carry out this difficult process. And it is never-ending. As soon as one shipment of donated gifts is sorted out, there will be others right behind it, and the entire process will begin anew.[25]

The cool weather prompted me to make an excursion to the builders' yard at the edge of town. A selfish purpose drove me there. I wanted [to visit] the cardboard-packaging department.[26] For the past year and a half, the head of the department had been donating all kinds of cardboard waste to me, which I used for tickets. Previously, I gave them out for each lecture. They could be small and need not be impressive. But the theater tickets ought to look good. They were cut into the size of 8 by 12 [cm], with a border, and the text written decently. Now in the new room I needed 300 for every reading, and obtaining that many was not easy.

[...] Today, too, after not coming for a long time, it [the wait] was not in vain. I got what I needed and could begin writing out the tickets for the next readings of *Faust*.

This time I allowed myself a little time to really look around at the expansive space. It [the time spent] was worthwhile, because here was the center of engineering, of workshop-like production; the essential [manufacturing] operations are concentrated here. To get to know all this manifold activity was not only necessary in a factual report [such as this one]—it was also satisfying to see such extensive activity. It showed Jews [working] in the kinds of occupations that they wouldn't previously have been allowed to do or that no one would have thought them capable of.

It unequivocally and clearly demonstrates that without Christian masters and foremen, the Jew manages to work just as well as those who have followed a trade for many generations. No matter where they work, be it at a machine, at a lathe, the anvil, or the forge, they can do the job. Just to give one example, the utility furniture that was made in the joinery here would be the pride of any large urban workshop.

The cardboard-packaging department is located at the end of an oblong compound. Ramparts surrounded the entrance, and enough space was found to put in a lovely vegetable garden that promises a rich harvest. Small sheds to each side house the atelier of Professor [Rudolf] Saudek, the sculptor from Berlin, and small ceramics workshops.

Professor Saudek puts his heart and soul into his work, happy to be able to continue doing his beloved art. He designs small ceramic items, creating figures out of his imagination, such as a larger-than-life bust of Schopenhauer, and is now at work carving the figure of the Bamberg Horseman from the cathedral out of a block of sandstone. We chat about old times, when he was studying in Berlin, and then taught and worked there. Like me, he knows the artists of our time and can certainly tell me many things about them that I did not know.

In such a unique setting, one forgets the time and place. I feel as if I was back in one of the many Berlin ateliers I had visited in 1906 to get reproduction rights from the artists for the New Photographic Society. I was a most welcome visitor then. Here, too, I am warmly greeted and can observe the master at work and watch a young woman with gifted hands form a vase from the red clay. That even the art of the sculptor has found a home in Theresienstadt, where such fine examples are made, is truly a source of great joy.

Books that had been worn out through overuse are being restored in the bookbinding department. Logbooks, books, portfolios, and other office supplies are also produced here. Boxes for card indices and beautiful folders for special occasions are made here as well. One celebrates the birthdays of men who deserve recognition by presenting them with bound speeches or compilations. Painters got together to produce a portfolio of drawings of Theresienstadt, and it is here that they give it a beautiful cover.

Sitting at long tables, the women do mass production. Jigsaw puzzles are made out of cardboard, cut into individual pieces, and then inserted into each other. In the autumn there is always a rush of large orders that have to be delivered by a deadline, and that means drudgery. [But] the women like working in this clean environment; they receive special allowances and larger portions of food every other day. During the lunch break, they sit outside in the sun, lie on the woodpiles, and enjoy the view of gardens surrounded by tall trees.

We want to go on with our visit and see first the production which combines many departments. All tests and analysis that have to do with food are performed in the chemical engineering laboratory.

The departments are grouped together organically: locksmiths and forging, welding, mechanical milling and turnery; a repair shop for wheelchairs for the war-disabled; carriage repair for transport; new construction for transport equipment; woodworking assembly for such things as doors, windows, frames, scaffolding, chairs, benches, stools, etc.; cooperage and carpentry; the department for producing high-quality furniture; the working group for young people who can perfect their skills and apply their knowledge here.

The rooms are all the same elongated shape of the casemates. Into whichever one I glance, there is activity everywhere. The men in blue overalls are masters of their professions. Here, they stand at the forge and make the iron glow. There, they study drawings in order to realize them in the available materials and consult with their colleagues about how to make everything.

A large transport trolley has been built on a frame of wood and iron, and stands there nearly finished, needing only to be painted to be ready to begin its daily work. It is a special vehicle designed for a specific purpose, and requires no small degree of skilled labor.

At the joinery it is most encouraging to see young people who are actively engaged putting great energy into their work. An exhibition last year showed how much imagination, skill, and talent the ghetto's young people had! They had all created such exceptional things using [only] primitive tools and materials, strikingly dispelling the myth that Jews have never been good craftsmen. When one sees how the young have mastered the equipment, controlling the levers, turning the wood, assembling the pieces, one is convinced that a generation is growing up here that will survive to accomplish great things.

The second section of the builders' yard goes by the name of "Technical Workshop." It houses the glazier's workshop, painting, varnishing, oven repair, receptacle soldering, and all repair and maintenance work for tableware, furniture, and other household effects.

This sober listing should give an inkling of what the ghetto needs to function as an operation.

We are, of necessity, forced to be satisfied here with the minimum compared to what we had when we were free. We gave up privacy. Once, we had taken those things for granted, and now we have become like soldiers again, living under strict rules. Only now do we know the value of a quiet room to which we could retreat whenever we pleased, according to our mood and needs. This is only one of the negative things about Theresienstadt. But the positive is and remains the freedom we enjoy inside the ghetto, a thought that perhaps never occurs to those who do not know about the strict regulations in other camps.

Work ennobles. I recognize this more than ever as I leave this place [the builders' yard] that fosters dedication and creativity. I am certain that no one who works there would want to change places with an office worker.

Intermezzo sinfonico

It is seldom possible for me to visit a competing event.[27] My presence here in the evenings is absolutely necessary. [...]

I was happy when one morning someone brought me a ticket for a piano recital by Mrs. Renée Gärtner-Geiringer in the town hall at 6:15. I would be able to attend because this evening's reading was scheduled for eight o'clock.

The beautiful hall was crowded. The artist is greeted with lively applause. César Franck—*Praeludium:* a powerful, heavy, solid, dramatic, raging work. It was rebellious, accusing, heralding fate; it held no tenderness, only force and violence. One listened, shaken, to the wrath of this overture to a drama that we ourselves were feeling.

Interval. One must allow oneself a moment of silence in preparation for another world, another, more serene, sky.

Johann Sebastian Bach: *Italian Concert.* What unique, beautiful clarity! We could almost see the lovely Italian scenery, hear the babbling of the springs, the fluttering of the wind, and the rustling of the trees. We could see festively dressed people walking through a colorful meadow on their way to a nearby grove to lounge and enjoy the sunny day. One apprehended all this in the music. In this sober room Bach's divine music vividly conjured up the land of our erstwhile yearning: Italy.

[...] Beethoven: *Sonate op. 90.* It is one of the bright, generous, and light pieces. One who was not a connoisseur would think it a piece by Schubert. The song-like melodies were exquisite and lingered in the ear. One beat time to it, wanted to sing along and join the happiness. Then the runs bubble up, and one remains behind—and all too quickly the mirth and merriment roll away.

[...] The delicate woman remained seated at the grand piano, her fingers gliding over the keys as though exploring them. Silver rays of moonlight shone through the wide-open windows. And then, as if directed by some invisible hand: *Adagio sostenuto*, the opening notes of "Moonlight Sonata." [...]

It was dead silent in the hall; the audience was completely spellbound by the music. They had experienced it as a revelation, as an invitation to a different, better world. Then, the rustle of the applause; it disturbed me. I would have preferred to walk out silently and go to the nearby park to savor and revel in the wonder of this hour. Thanks. Thanks for the precious gift of this hour, which we were all fortunate to receive.

* * *

Our regular listeners remained true to Room A7. Over time, a community had formed whose members, with a few blind people among them, visited almost every evening. It was seldom that the room was not full, although in a third of it one could only stand because we had not been able to get enough benches, not to mention chairs for the first row. Chairs are a first-class luxury in Theresienstadt. I have been trying unsuccessfully for weeks to get at least a half dozen, but they are given only to the offices. Instead, enormous sofas from the café were brought in. They took up a lot of room, and the insects that made themselves at home, even here, easily slipped into the crevices. Despite the [efforts of the] cleaning crew, they remained the victors.

Strangely enough, being liberated from my duties with the Orientation Service did not gain me any more free time. On the contrary, I was now completely devoted to making the preparations for the evenings, and they made even more demands on my time. I had to spend many hours in the library researching material for the program and to read relevant books. I had to write drafts and deal with the lecturers and actors. I sometimes had to go on many errands to arrive at a *single* destination, and it took up all my time. As the host and the MC, I had to be there every evening; I could [rarely] go to another event, which I very much regretted. There was just so much to hear. The Czech events, especially the stage plays, were also of a high quality, which made it painful for me to always have to stay away.

[…]

Dr. Karl Fleischmann is a strange but instantly fascinating personality. He stands at the helm of health care, works in the town hall, and is unbelievably busy. He cares for approximately 10,000 elderly people, which is no small undertaking considering the scarcity of resources that are available to him. Additionally, his free time—and there is not much of it—is devoted to the arts.

Dr. Fleischmann, a son of Bohemia, grew up in the homeland of Stifter.[28] He is a connoisseur of that vast mountain range, which the poet took such pleasure in describing. His interests are diverse. He is a first-class painter, has a boundless knowledge of literature, and he is a poet who writes his verses in the strange, and yet so soft and melodious, language of his homeland, which unfortunately I do not understand. […] On an evening that he called *A Painter Experiences Theresienstadt*, he showed large charcoal sketches, impressions, and scenes from the life in our town. Heavy and bulky, drawn with rough, broad strokes, they recalled the visions of Goya and the style of Käthe Kollwitz. His figures had splendid movement. With limited resources, he created pictures with penetrating impact.

On another evening he spoke about his painting excursions to Corsica. We got to know the island's mountains and its people, who even today live by the laws of vendetta. He told us about the time he had escaped becoming caught up in one such confrontation, only by chance. The morning after, he was told what had happened during the night. His companions in the compartment of the train, who had been cumbersome in cleaning and loading their revolvers, had challenged the people of the village to a veritable battle, in which there had been dead and wounded. Nevertheless, he described the countryside as magnificent, a painter's paradise of color.

Speaking of painting, another lecture addressed the three great Jewish masters: Israëls, Liebermann, and Chagall. And Dr. Fleischmann certainly could not be accused of one-sidedness, because his next topic was *The Idea of Social Medicine*.

When I invited Dr. Fleischmann to speak in our circle, things proceeded in an unusual way. He wanted to refuse, protesting that he had not mastered enough German. This was false modesty. Of course, one could tell that he was not a Reich German, but the slightly unfamiliar sound or the occasional struggle to find the suitable expression only increased the appeal of his lectures. A written copy of his novella, *Landscape Portrayed in the Spirit of Stifter*, showed that he had a complete mastery of German. If Dr. Fleischmann can one day totally devote himself to his poetry and painting, we can expect much that is beautiful from him.

[...]

This is some spring! It does not want to turn into summer.

The mornings are cold, and it rains almost every hour. What the last two years had too little of, this one has in abundance. "All to the good," say the pious. "At least we are spared the evil, sickness-spreading dust, and it cannot torture us." It is just too bad that because of the weather, we cannot enjoy any of the improvements of our newly beautified town.

Summer will officially begin in a few days. We are entering the second half of the year. It arrives subtly, barely noticeably at first, and then will proceed rapidly into August, and then, trembling, we shall see autumn coming. We are unutterably frightened of it because our weakened bodies—unable to store up strength from our monotonous diet—will not withstand another cold period. Unless we receive a different kind of nourishment, we shall not make it to 1945. The young might, but not us old ones, who are nearing the end of our seventh decade.

How the German authorities went about the transformation of Theresienstadt; how grievances that had existed for two years were quickly remedied; how the old soldiers' town, which was entirely geared to the military, took on a new guise will be described in the following pages.

Where to begin? It is quite difficult to know where to start. I think we should first thank the offices and their heads who carried out the great work. The German authorities issued the order, requested proposals and plans, decided what work should be done, and set the pace. That means mobilizing the workforce, from engineers to excavators, to draftsmen in the engineering departments, to the crowning of all work, the coming of the cleaning crew. It is easy to write this. How many nights—not to mention days—it takes to turn the plans into reality can be imagined only by someone closely involved in the planning and creation, who has been part of all this himself.

[...] If such a task had been undertaken back home, all the necessary tools and resources would have been available. All it would have taken was a phone call, and any missing tools or supplies would be delivered. Admittedly, some things were sent from Prague, because even the most skillful worker is powerless without the right materials, but in the end, the prerequisite for fast work and success was lacking: trained, skilled craftsmen. Nevertheless, we in the ghetto managed; Jews of every class and age worked on the project. This earned them their first renown, and proved that when called into action the Jew tackles the job wholeheartedly and simply says "order carried out."

To the observant onlooker, this is a major event. For hundreds of years the Jews were, with few exceptions, tradesmen, scientists, doctors, writers, engineers, and inventors. A Jewish craftsman or heavy laborer was the exception. That inevitably changed when the Jews in Berlin were ordered to work—when the employment office on the Fontane Promenade registered all Jews of both sexes in their file index and called them up for work.

I knew many young Jews who proved themselves as railway workers. I knew lawyers, mature men who were assigned to do hard labor in the factories, and died after two years of willing deployment. They were accustomed to working at desks, and this work was such a physical strain that after a while they could no longer withstand it. On top of that, they had to get up at 4:30 A.M. in the winter and travel the long way to the factory, without enough food and worrying about the future. All this, taken together, had to undermine even the strongest constitution. Yet the majority pulled through. If at a later date, Siemens and Borsig,[29] the great enterprises of the East, and the small businesses in the urban centers are asked what the Jewish sections had accomplished, the answer can only be "more than we expected." In terms of diligence, dedication, punctuality, and conscientiousness, they were in every way the equals of their Christian colleagues.

It was the same gratifying picture in Theresienstadt. Everything appeared as if by magic. Let's begin our tour—it will be long, but not boring—at the Bauschowitz gate.

Let us remember that the railway lines here were laid by Jews. They demolished and flattened the protective casemates, which seemed to have been built to last an eternity. Now one sees a wall of green turf that veils what was here before. It was a huge amount of labor that required strong hands and firm backs. The result is that the trains now go into the town and can be unloaded there. The road embankment, once an ocean of sewage not to be traversed in rainy weather without getting stuck in the mud, is now paved with small stones, macadamized, and turned into a promenade that is popular in the evenings.

The German authorities gave a great gift to the ghetto. They made the mighty moat between the walls—about 15 meters deep—available to us. In the spring, there was a call to cultivate it, and whoever wanted one was given a strip of land. Thus, a colony of allotments developed, where industrious activity takes place after office hours. In a few weeks, land that had been fallow for 200 years became green. The poles of the tomato plants rise in the air like spears, as do the canes for the peas. The lettuce grows in the good soil, some of which had to be brought in by wheelbarrow. The planters harvest spinach, giving them a welcome and much-needed supplement to their diet. Outside of the gates, agriculture works only for the benefit of the German authorities. But here the newly allocated land is harvested only by Jewish planters.

Directly opposite the bridge in the outermost casemates are the two halls where funerals take place. From the beginning, I was disgusted and sickened by the crudeness and disorder there, by the lack of dignity in this sacred place of mourning. No office, no hand had intervened to give a dignified appearance to the site where we bid the very painful farewells to our dead. In the summer, only the two mighty chestnut trees hid the old gray walls and the entrance to the dark corridor leading to the barracks where the dead are put in coffins.

Now the consecrated site finally has the appropriate appearance. The sloping road is evened out; strips of grass are put around the walls; and the balustrades of the lower right wall were fitted with flower boxes. The heavy doors, in their terrible black, that close both vaults no longer inspire dread and fear. Ornamentation was applied to them with wooden strips [reminiscent of mighty candelabra on an altar], and this softened their terrible aspect. One felt that behind them must be peace.

Only now does the mighty elder bush unfold its broad, white luminous umbels, and their sweet scent radiates far. Below it, the cultivated beds spread out, covering the entire ground. Our young cultivate this part, which will produce a bountiful harvest and has already done so for the last two summers. Part of it was delivered to Prague and fetched good prices in this receptive market. In the ghetto we see the flowering and growing, the fruit ripen on the trees.

The tempting red cherries are a testament to the rich blessings of this hallowed stretch of land, which is so fertile. Still we harvest it only for others.

*   *   *

The great park, still closed off two years ago, now takes up a rectangle stretching from the main street to the rear gateway. Mighty chestnut trees form a dense roof of foliage. The grass seed that was sown has grown; the paths are marked off with wire. The space finally lives up to its name: It is a park. The second, upper end is reserved for the children. There are sandpits in a circular area that give the little ones a place to play in clean sand. There are plenty of new benches with cement bases and seats and backrests made of wooden strips.

And now we want to enter the children's hall. This is another new miracle in this peculiar town [...] The front part is divided into two halls made entirely of glass. In between them is an open square with a large wading pool.

We start the tour [of the children's hall] in the left wing. Toward the back there is a warming kitchen equipped with abundant tableware, with a spotless modern oven and a sink with a rotating faucet. There is a separate dining room for 50 young guests. The stools painted in bright colors and the low tables are reminiscent of home. The washroom is arranged sensibly. The sinks are placed at different heights, doors too were to their heights. Children of all ages were able to reach the handles. Everything was easy to clean and user friendly.

To the children's delight, there is a big playroom in the second wing, with rocking horses, play tables, and colored stools. In the back there is a changing area for the babies and for nursing mothers. But the prettiest area is still the open-air wing; it is reminiscent of the [house of the] seven dwarves. It has very low beds with green wooden frames, 12 in all, with blue pillows, sheets, and blankets, lined up neatly and protected from high winds by the glass walls. Only the sun was allowed in.

This whole facility—the front was colorfully decorated with a frieze of animal images by Jo Spier—could be a model house at an exhibition on hygiene.

The designers deserve to be sincerely congratulated for this achievement. They have shown great skill and a real love for the task that they so brilliantly carried out.

There is a big playground behind the house. Large-scale sandboxes with benches to sit on, wooden seesaws—to the delight of the older children—as well as gymnastic equipment, benches, and a beautiful meadow where one can lie down. The mothers, who are always worried about doing the right things for their children, are able to breathe a sigh of relief. Here, they find everything that is appropriate for recreation and beneficial to health.

In the end, one may say that a children's paradise has been created, for which we all have to be very thankful.

The construction of the parade ground in front of the church is completed. The lawns have grown well and have already been mowed once. The paths are covered with yellow sand. On two of the wide ones that were planned to be used as promenades while music is playing, there are benches for the elderly. Unfortunately, they rarely get to use them because one still cannot sit outdoors, even when the sun is shining. The cold continues. We have passed the middle of June and are still cold, and need to take out the warm sweater again.

The square with its beautiful buildings—a pity that some modern ones had been built that destroyed the architectural unity—and a profusion of beautiful trees that envelop it like a shining silken band, look quite grand. The perfectly situated church with its distinctive, dignified architecture is the central building on the square. What a pity that it is not open to us!

God is in every place where the devout gather together. If they had not been relegated to cramped attics, which are not very conducive to prayer, one could assemble the community in the large church. I wish that the heavy entrance gates would open and the organ would come to life in service to God and music.

*　*　*

In Theresienstadt one should not look back, not allow oneself to relive one's time here. A town that perpetually—almost daily—increased in population, on some days by 1,000, cannot be judged by our normal standards. A settlement has been created from empty, vacant barracks and buildings that at times had to maintain 56,000 people.

It has been an enormous undertaking for the administration to ensure—in a state of captivity—that this number of people is adequately fed every day and has a place to sleep at night. It remains so to this day. They always have to begin anew. The transports take away trained men and women who need to be replaced immediately. None of the work can suffer any interruption; lives depend on it.

Now all efforts have to be dedicated to the town beautification. A pace is demanded that is difficult to sustain, yet it is being sustained. No matter if the typewriters in the offices clatter until after midnight or the blueprints are being drafted in the drafting rooms, or the discussions among the leading men of the administration last until the early hours of the morning, the German authorities, now known officially as the Department, set the deadlines, and everyone is ambitious to meet them.[30]

There is only one endeavor and one goal: to document, through the work in Theresienstadt, the Jewish aptitude for construction work and for creating an organized society. It is the duty of all workers, of every age, to help with this. That this effort is successful is shown by every description in this report.

* * *

June is a time of the inspections. We learn this only through the directives of the house elder, who goes from room to room in the evening and announces that by eight o'clock the next morning, the rooms must be immaculately swept and cleaned and the beds aired. The walls (used for hanging clothes) must be covered, and the windows cleaned. Suitcases, shoes, and dishes must be stowed away out of sight.

The work begins at 5 A.M. The large courtyard is swept, and the toilets are cleaned out and washed. The work must be finished by noon. Then the administration commission will come and inspect every section of the house.

There were even rewards for the houses that met all the demands. The house elder (I would not want to be one, not even for a mountain of gold—it is the fastest way to end up in the cemetery) now has only one goal: to be among those honored when the dignitaries assemble and to receive a distinction. It is his only reward for the endless hours of toil and labor, the unspeakable aggravation that every day brings.

Except one should never imagine that the inspection will actually take place at the appointed time; there are sure to be at least two cancellations. But we of course have to be ready every time. Oh well, the exercise is good for us, and frequent cleaning doesn't hurt in the men's quarters. So much dirt is tracked in from the road every day that a single cleaning does not get rid of it all; keeping things clean is a Herculean task.

Sokolowna!

It is located far away—that is, by Theresienstadt standards; in Berlin one would say it was next door—on the avenue that leads to the plain. To the right and left of the entrance are the yellow agricultural buildings with their farmyards. A team of oxen is just leaving the left yard, pulling a load of straw. They are well-nourished, heavy animals, secured in their yokes, driven by a teenager, barely more than a boy, who calls out to them in Czech.

The Sokolowna is the largest, most modern of the few buildings that were built in the fort. Sokol is the gymnastics club, to which the building [Sokolowna] had been dedicated.

The cinema hall inside will be restored in the near future. Wide front steps with plant pots on the landings lead up to the large entrance hall leading to the theater and lecture hall, which accommodates 250 people.

Upon entering the hall, one stops short: This was not expected. There is beautiful seating made from stained brown wood with folding seats. Two colors dominate the room, light blue and dark blue. The stage, hung with dark cloths, is deep and high. The spacious room with its impressive windows that let in the light works most splendidly and greets the visitor with a festive atmosphere.

The whole beautiful building has been placed at our disposal and, following inspection by the [German] authorities, should begin to serve its multiple purposes: worship, lectures, and theater.

[...]

The area around the building deserves a mention. The approach is wide enough for cars to drive up. The road is barricaded by a high railing and concealed by three mighty, broad weeping willows that span almost the entire front. They are magnificent specimens—one wants to sit under the cover of their branches with a volume of Stifter one morning and read, read.

There are beds of roses to the left and right of the building. The right wall is concealed by birch trees whose leaves are still pale green. The back of the building faces a wall of the redoubt, on which a real grapevine grows. Young trees have also been planted there. In a short while, the flower bed, which is approximately 20 meters long, will be in full bloom.

In just a short amount of time, this very neglected building—it was for a long time a convalescent home, for which the broad terrace at the front made it particularly suitable—was turned into a little jewel box, earning the chief architect accolades and the gratitude of all the residents of the settlement every time they will visit.

Some more factual information. There are three halls: the cinema, with about 450 seats; the theater and lecture hall, with 250 seats; and the hall of worship, with 370 seats. The second floor houses a reference library and a reading room. Sixty visitors can sit at tables (but not borrow the material) and read selections from the extensive collection. The music department has its own chamber in the building. There are five small rehearsal rooms. The stage directors work out of two rooms that have been set aside for them. The entire building is put to good use by the Leisure Time Organization, which has always suffered from a shortage of space. You had only to have seen the office spaces when people crowded around the officers' desks in the mornings, to appreciate the joy with which this building has been welcomed.

This building complex is dedicated entirely to culture, and by Theresienstadt standards that is quite something—a house in which all the arts are at home, and no official suddenly appears to commandeer the room.

*   *   *

The work of the town beautification in the days before June 23 takes on a momentum that we haven't experienced before. The streets have never been swept so clean; entire crews have been deployed to put the main street, especially, into tip-top shape. It is indeed our avenue of pomp and glory; it is beautiful on a clear day when the mountain seems so close that the light green of the deciduous forest can be clearly distinguished from the dark fir forest. Up high, the bare areas near the summit, where the snow held fast for so long, can be seen. A particular effort was made to spruce up the Seestraße. The windows of the houses are fitted with flower boxes planted with hanging petunias. The mirror-like windows were hung with white curtains. The shops being used for accommodation also have beautiful curtains or were painted white. Light-colored sand covers the carefully raked paths. All the houses had to be cleaned and washed, the courtyards spotless, and the ash cans [lined up] dead straight. Every inhabited space has to reflect comfort; nothing should be left hanging around to get in the way.

Why this campaign of tidying up and cleaning? Supposedly, a commission from neutral countries is coming to inspect the ghetto. According to another rumor, they would be high-ranking men from Berlin.[31]

Say what you will, this massive and necessary cleaning operation cannot be praised highly enough, no matter what the reason for it is. After all, we know from our experience in the military what a to-do there was when an inspection was announced. Regardless of whether it was the barracks, or we who were inspected, we had to get down and work. It did us no harm.

In any event, we in Theresienstadt benefit from the mystery visit. There is more to eat. For lunch we get a thick slice of salami and a whole fresh rutabaga cut into thin slices, which tasted very good raw, sprinkled with sugar. In the evening there was a potato and a *bosniakel*, a large roll made from strong-tasting rye flour; it is a welcome change. Moreover, the bread we are getting is excellent. It is no longer moldy, as it was in 1942, but dry and well-kept, and it tastes good.

As in Germany, the ration [of certain foods] is reduced somewhat: The hard laborers receive only 500 grams of "S-bread"; everyone else receives 375 grams of "N-bread." The ration of potatoes boiled in their skins is around [320–350] grams per portion, which is carefully weighed. So everyone received their entitlement, and the endless disagreements about weight reduction are silenced.[32]

There is an innovation in the distribution of the midday meal that represents a great gift to the unmarried. A new dining area has been set up in the new barracks to the right of the BV-Magdeburg barracks. New, white tables and benches seating [ ] people have been set up. The hot food is brought to one's table, and one can eat in peace at—just imagine!—a clean table. This is an enormous advance in the nutrition problem. The food lines are shorter, and the process is made easier. One can be sincerely grateful for this pleasant and practical setup.

   [...]

∗   ∗   ∗

Room 107 is a large office of the "internal administration." There are about 15 desks, covered with piles of paper. There are only narrow aisles in which to move between the tables, and a wider one leading to the boss's office, which can be accessed only by appointment. And in this space, I am supposed to present lectures that will be attended by 200 or more visitors! From merely a technical point of view, it is impossible.

It wasn't only the head of the department who refused this unreasonable demand. Nor did I take this preposterous suggestion seriously. I went to the Leisure Time Organization, to which I reported, and complained.

They told me to go to 7 Rathausgasse-Q307. There is a loft vacant with a stage, and it would be assigned to me. But the house elder was difficult; I had to be very careful and promise to come to terms with him. So, caution, great caution!

In my life, rich in incident, I have never been so pleasantly disappointed as here in building Q307. The house elder, Mr. Pollak, a thin, gray-haired man about 50 years of age, received me very affably, and when he heard what I wanted from him, he expressed great joy. His loft, which was formerly used as a theater and for religious worship, stood vacant, and he most eagerly wished to see it occupied.[33]

I took a look around and saw how suitable it was. It had the capacity for an audience of 250, or 300 if necessary. This served my needs, and I said that I was pleased to accept the hospitality of the house. Mr. Pollak offered me every support, and we parted as good friends.

The house has only one floor. It is not a strenuous climb to the loft. There is a narrow, winding staircase leading up to it, but we are in Theresienstadt and need to take what we can get. The space is high and airy. Heavy beams separate the loft from the roof space. We put up a ceiling to enclose the space. Toward the road the roof slanted. We concealed this with burlap.

The stage is approximately 75 cm high, four by three meters wide, and open at the rear. We created the necessary neutral background using blankets and curtains. There are plenty of benches.[34] [...] I was once again freed from worries, especially since I had been told that I could use the stage until late autumn. So I moved in and began the season on May 23 with a lecture by Dr. Karl Sterzer: *Humor in a Lawyer's Practice.*

The room is so large that I no longer needed to issue tickets and was spared the laborious task of writing and handing them out, which was a big relief for my colleagues. Now, we needed tickets only for the theater performances. Our visitors were happy not to have to go through the cumbersome process, and told me so repeatedly.

Faust was completely different on this roomy stage. The actors were not crowded together on the short bench. They could "act" a little, which heightened the effect. But even the most virtuous cannot live in peace "if it doesn't please the beloved police."[35] Someone alerted the [German] authorities in writing that if the room were filled to capacity, it would pose a serious risk in the event of a fire: The narrow stairs made a quick exit impossible, with potentially catastrophic results.

Inspection—visit from the experts. [Creating extra space by] breaking through to the two neighboring houses was refused. Our audience size was limited to 150; a fire watchman must always be there when the room is in use. Two filled buckets and a fire-beater to be ready at all times, and we have to take extreme caution with the lights.

Word had got around that one could attend a performance by the Manes Group without a ticket, in contrast to the Leisure Time Organization events, for which advance tickets are almost always required. A necessary measure in view of the limited capacity of all the rooms and the rush of listeners, especially in bad weather when the bastion is not an appealing destination. Publicity for my events is restricted, and they are unknown to the general public [in the ghetto]. So all I have is an audience that appears on a regular basis and forms a community. Now we have lost this freedom.

I give out number tickets at the doors to keep a tally and am not that strict about the exact count. Twenty-five people more or less do not matter. If, however, on "big nights," there are 100 people over my upper limit of 175 who want entry, the fireman has to carry out his duties, put his hard hat on, and block the entrance. But they do not yield, thinking that I will eventually give in and not send away such old, faithful listeners. But I have to remain firm. I have been given written orders and am responsible for upholding them.

So there are unpleasant fights every night, which is extremely aggravating to me because I recognize the impossibility of remedying the situation. I distribute a maximum of 175 tickets for each lecture, which means the huge job of writing them out and distributing them. It is an arduous task, given that I have such a small staff, and some of them are often absent due to illnesses. I can't change it. People have to depend on their good luck [to get a ticket] to get in.

One regular visitor, who is connected to the buildings department, is committed to improving the space and has put himself at my disposal. The walls are to be painted white, and a row of benches is to replace the planks we had for seats. If this can be done, I will be extremely happy: seats with backs! A cleaning crew also comes once a week, and the disinfestation people spray insecticide—can one ask for more in Theresienstadt? Only connections make it possible to achieve one's goals rapidly!

According to astronomy, we are now in summer, yet this so capricious phenomenon visits us only for a short while. For two or three days it is warm, and the sun shines. For an hour we can sit on the new benches that are generously placed virtually everywhere, and enjoy the sweetness of being idle.

We can officially do this. It says in a communiqué dated June 24:

> The Council of Elders would like to thank all residents, in particular, for their service in the last few weeks in carrying out the work of the town beautification. In acknowledgment of this work, there will be a holiday from 1 P.M. on June 24 and on the 25th.
>
> The Council of Elders expects that all residents will continue to cooperate in the town beautification with the same understanding and the same willingness.

* * *

Another gift was given to us, which is highly gratifying—we are allowed to send a postcard every month. To go from every three months to every month is really something, and we are optimistic enough to count on a further increase.

And now to a recent, major innovation, with significance for the well-being of the visitors, the likes of which we had never dreamed of. Last winter, a new hut was built next to the Magdeburg barracks, [...] which housed the laundry operation for a short time. It has now been remodeled as a canteen or restaurant or dining hall. There are [ ] snow-white tables, decorated with pots of flowering plants, and matching benches. On Saturday and Sunday they are covered with colorful tablecloths for a festive look.

The space accommodates 1,000 people. Food is given out by nine experienced women from two open counters. The canteen has its own white stoneware, a flat dish with two sections, for potatoes, either peeled or pureed, and vegetables or salad. We already had pickles, green salad, and red turnips. An army of waitresses—each wears a number—brings the soup in these dishes and the second course at the same time.

The food is delivered from the kitchen of the Magdeburg barracks, and those portions are said to be a little bit larger than the ones we are getting now. We eat at white tables, and only those who live here can imagine what it means in Theresienstadt to have tables and benches.

I have never yet eaten at a table. We were happy to be able to put a square wooden board on our bench that offered a place to put the dishes. Plates were equally unknown. One feels exalted in this light, wide room, being served by young women who smile and do not sullenly dip their ladles into the barrels. Everything is clean, and this is already a huge plus compared to the food distribution at counters, where every gust of wind blows sand from the courtyard into the narrow lockers where the open vats stood. Nothing can be done to prevent it, short of a continuous damping down, and they do not have any people for that. So the sand and dust remain a garnish. That, fortunately, is no longer the case over there [in the new canteen]. And there is yet another welcome benefit—the potatoes are served peeled. What would the floors look like if the clumsy men had to peel them at the tables?! Of all the facilities that the [preparation for the] inspection has brought us, the canteen is perhaps the nicest. Its creators, Dr. Merzbach and Karl Schliesser, deserve sincere thanks from all visitors.

Let us go back once again for a short time to the Rathausgasse 7—but not during the day. That is when the loft serves as a laundry and drying room for its many residents, and it is quite heavily used. In the evening, the linens and clothes disappear, much to the displeasure of the women, who feel threatened in their domain. Still, in summer drying is very quick, and what is hung up in the early morning is definitely ready to be taken down by the afternoon.

In one respect the cool weather is better for using the loft as a theater space. When the sun beats down on the roof tiles all day, the heat builds up under the roof, and because it has no place to escape, the room becomes as hot as a baking oven. This has a paralyzing effect on the speakers and the listeners, and makes for an unpleasant experience. As was also the case in A7 because there was no window in the thick walls of that room. One must stoically accept this heat (which one would like at other times).

[...] Every presentation of *Faust* is sold out, and I have to turn a lot of people away. They beg, "I'll make myself very small. I brought my own chair. I will be happy to stand if I have to." But I am not permitted to exceed the maximum even slightly with the fire watchman and the police at my throat. Only when young people come—the pretty Czech girls and boys who want to hear *Faust* for the first time in their lives—then do I not say no. That I cannot bring myself to do.

[...]

✳   ✳   ✳

[...] With the onset of warm weather the young people, especially the children, divest themselves of their winter clothing. At first, the boys went around in breeches and braved the rain, storms, and cold. Then the girls followed suit. But when it got really warm, and they risked nothing more than a bad runny nose (like half of Theresienstadt has all year-round anyway), they shed just about all inhibiting articles of clothing.

The streets offer sights like those we used to see in Norderney or Westerland.[36] All the women—age has nothing to do with it—love to walk around in slacks. The boys wear their trousers like the swimming trunks of blessed memory, which means shorter than short. Socks, so scarce and terribly expensive, are not worn in summer. The clothing is made of light material and is extremely colorful—multicolored kerchiefs, bright blouses—and one also sees that most beautiful adornment, loose, flowing hair.

Again and again, I note how wonderfully svelte the girls of this beautiful land of Bohemia are; how noble, open, and enchanting are their faces; how blooming and alive their eyes. When they are in their airy costume, five or six walking with linked arms along the road, one spontaneously stands still and lets them pass, delighted by the sight.

These girls are self-aware, self-assured, and proud. You should see them in the morning at the 5:30 A.M. roll call in the Magdeburg barracks, when some 200 of them report in groups as cleaning crews. Carrying buckets and brooms, they march cheerfully to the difficult and demanding job of cleaning. One feels that this is an optimistic race that does not allow itself to be discouraged, even here in Theresienstadt.

The same is observed in the younger generation, from 8 to 14 years. They are just as pretty and carefree, wear even fewer clothes, and enjoy this life that, without school and the pressure of studying, gives so much to them.

Gardens and cultivations are their domain, where they play out their days, and grow, hopefully into a forward-looking, productive, courageous generation. And if one peers into one of the not-too-common baby carriages, one sees rosy, strong babies who thrive in Theresienstadt and are indistinguishable from other children of the same age. They, too, hold our hoped-for promise for the future.

It is not only the female youngsters that must be looked at again and again, but also the male youths of every age group. In Berlin, it never occurred to me that there are so many truly handsome youths. One finds ten-year-olds with Roman features, blue-eyed, blond lads who might have been born in the Teutoburg forest and are lithe and lissome, high-spirited and lively in everything they do.[37] [...]

After the lecture ends at around 9 P.M., I walk up to the bastion if I want to get a little air. There, the town beautification has been generous. The narrow, unnavigable path upwards has been transformed into wide comfortable stairs, and the ramparts [have been] seeded with grass. A terrace that the lads had decorated earlier with flower beds and a small rock garden has now become a jewel of a square, with benches around. To the right is a staircase leading to the roof of the Jäger barracks, which has been designated a sunbathing area; signs indicating that have been put up accordingly. Then one crosses the bridge, now protected, at long last, by a safe, solid wood railing, to the large square. Also to the right, a wooden lattice stretches across and closes off the deep moat.

[...]

The elevation with the tall old trees that conceal the fortress is still clear, but soon it too will stand lonely and quiet. Soon it will be 10 P.M. The ghetto watchman has sent home the last visitor long ago. We are so glad that this summer we are allowed to stay up for so long; we do not have to go home by nine o'clock and can enjoy the evening. However, ten o'clock is the absolute limit. There are no exceptions; the streets must be completely empty, and anyone who is still out must reckon with a penalty.

* * *

It is not easy to set up the monthly program. First I must ascertain on which days my actors are busy with the Leisure Time Organization. [...] Thirty evenings are available to me; eight to ten of them are for readings. The twenty remaining are dedicated to lectures. Scheduling them is a huge headache.

Scholars, engineers, doctors, graphologists, professors of history, journalists, actors, musicians, collectors, poets, playwrights, and officers all wish to speak. They come to me and ask if a certain lecture or a series would be welcome, and most are deeply hurt if I have to decline.

There are two reasons for declining. The lecturer cannot speak freely, but must read. Unfortunately I quite often have had a bad experience with this type of lecturer. This way of lecturing is boring and soporific. One cannot follow a voice that is a monotone for an hour and a half; it's a struggle to not fall asleep (at 7:30 in the evening none of us is energetic anymore), and eventually we know only one thing: We want the man to finish. But he doesn't and instead clings to his "script," with many more pages to go.

Very rarely—but they do exist—we have readers who are true artists. They read aloud so cleverly, covering the pages with their hands, looking at the audience, and pausing at the right times. Their theme is compelling, and therefore the audience really enjoys listening to them.

But woe betide the professor of history who picks up his barely legible manuscript, stutters, and studies his script, and gives us only facts and figures. After half an hour, listeners flee the room, and the speaker ponders the lack of discipline on the part of the public. Such tedious readers have no idea how boring they are and want to give a lecture every month. They are men of repute, who surely had much to offer their students in their classes, but they are not right for Theresienstadt. But they cannot see this, and instead are angry with me.

Then I have men of stature, distinction, and quality, to whom it is always edifying and a joy to listen. Listeners throng to their lectures. I could let them speak twice a week, and my room would be full.

The last group are men who have not yet lectured for me but have heard about the circle and offer their services. Or, friends bring to my attention this or that scholar, thinking that he would be a gain. I confer with him and gladly put him on.

But how many [desirable speakers] do I have to gently put off until the next month because this one is fully booked? There are long faces. One had expected to be able to speak right away and does not want to wait. To such men I say simply and plainly, well then, no go! I must, after all, draw the line somewhere. One must not put things together higgledy-piggledy, but must provide some cohesion.

According to one elevated gentleman, I am too emphatically "German." To another, I am not Jewish enough for the ghetto. In reply, I need only to remind them of Dr. Neuhaus's ten lectures on the Bible or his six lectures, *Teachers, Heralds of Judaism,* and to note the other Jewish topics.

By July 1, [1944] I have organized 463 lecture evenings. Of those, [ ][38] had Jewish themes. One cannot say about me that I am too "westward" oriented, that I favor the "Germanic" spirit. No, it isn't like that. I have often enough, and especially in my own presentations, stressed my background, and why I am so unfamiliar with the academic study of Judaism.[39]

It was only in Theresienstadt, through contact with men from the Zionist movement, with rabbis, and with the head of the Jewish section of the library, who lent me relevant books, so that I got to know the past and the great intellectual and spiritual development of Judaism.

[...]

The worst evil in Theresienstadt is that any man or woman who holds a post never has any time. In any office, it is almost impossible to schedule a meeting with the appropriate man. If he is there, he is in a meeting, but he is usually out on official business. So, it takes a lot of time, patience, and determination to get to see the head of an office.

Dealing with the officials themselves is easier if they know you, but in any case you have to wait. If, however, one wants to get one of the many permits that are necessary for every transaction in Theresienstadt (the easiest being death and burial), then... *lasciate* ...

For instance, my shoes once needed a minor repair, just a few stitches to reconnect the upper leather to the sole. To get this done, I needed a little coupon. I climbed up to the Labor Exchange and waited for half an hour until I got to the head of the line. Smiling, the lady told me, "Come back in ten days. Permits and coupons will be issued then. Until then, there is too much of a backlog in the repair shop." If one urgently needs a summer jacket, one must get authorization from the finance office for a supplement to the point-card. With this in hand, you go up, once again, to Room 247. (This overcrowded room is so jam-packed with tables that there is barely room for the petitioner. The poor people working here have it bad enough in the truly appalling air, and if they are impatient, I completely understand.)

Here, I am informed that an investigator will be assigned to examine my belongings to see whether I really am in need. This can take four weeks. Then, I get the authorization and, in a happy mood, go to the store. They are full of regrets for my bad luck—summer things are sold out, and no one can say when new ones will arrive. So I walk around on hot days, which fortunately are rare, in a heavy winter jacket.

[...]

The beginning of July 1944. It is very warm during the day and cool at night. It rains every day, and in weather like this, the gardens and fields promise a rich harvest. The cherry trees hang heavy with their small red fruit. Is it that surprising that during the midday break, workers from the Süd barracks go to the nearby plantations and pluck the "forbidden fruit"? Over and over again, it is impressed upon people—do not rob the trees.

This time a number of young people thought they were not being observed and began to feast on the trees. Then, as if he had grown up from the soil, a German official of the Department appeared among the frightened people and took their names—for punishment. Then he called over some women who were not involved, and gave them a few pounds of cherries, saying, "Take these for your children."

*   *   *

The warmer it gets, the shorter and scantier become the pants of the female sex. Their legs are exposed to the uppermost limit. The bathing suits—they are no more than this—are tight and taut; their arms are bare. Not only do they go to the fields like this in the morning, laughing and singing, but they also dress this way for the "spa concert." When maestro Carlo Taube raises his baton, listeners crowd around the kiosk [...].

Meanwhile the benches have been painted green. The roses grow profusely, and the lower ones are beginning to bloom. Whoever sits here watching the people wander to and fro can [appreciate the rich variety of human life] and wonder to himself where the older and younger girls find the time and the means to appear so well groomed. I have to make the point again: I have never before seen so many really beautiful, strikingly attractive people of both sexes in such a small space. I would even say that with their hair not dressed and set, but left natural, the girls look even prettier and fresher. How powerfully they stride, rakes over their shoulders, chewing a last piece of bread, joyful and happy as they go to their difficult work. For me they are witnesses to a better future.

They will make it. And we old ones may, as a punishment for our sins and misguided lives (why weren't we better Jews?), see that land only in our souls, so far, yet so near, but we may not enter it. Our wandering through the desert will not last for 40 years.

*   *   *

We know very little about our government and its administration. We only feel the end results in the form of the unbroken current that guides and shapes our lives. It is a given that every day at the appointed hour we receive our meals, that we pick up our bread ration and the margarine and sugar exactly every three days. We count on it that soap, wash powder, marmalade, and toilet paper are available at regular intervals, as are the authorizations to hand in laundry, to get shoes repaired and clothes mended. We need no reminders; it all runs automatically week after week. Once or twice, at most, the bread distribution had to be delayed by one day because the delivery had not arrived from out of town.

Besides, certainly all the work put into these activities is directed toward satisfying the needs of the ghetto inmates. As the ghetto has to create everything for itself to sustain life, the division of labor is incredibly diverse and ramified. Administration, which includes management, scheduling, allocation, regulation, and supervision, is one large group, and the number of offices is unknown to me. The other one: implementation, equals work. Then, over the whole, because each one is subject to them: justice and the police.

Our life is guided and guaranteed in two parts. Everyone must enlist in one of them. Every person is recorded and categorized in the file index at the Labor Exchange. A doctor determines the level of fitness to work. Whoever is not fit for labor must at least perform house service. There is no age limit for that.

The ghetto has the *right* to the strength of every individual. Anyone who tries to duck this must be held in contempt, because he—a morally defective and asocial anachronism—is an idler and allows the State to feed him as though he were a parasite. That should not and cannot be.

Those over 70, when they fail physically, are excused. On the other hand, I know men and women who are also far beyond this Biblical age and still perform extraordinarily well. Their will keeps them healthy. Work drives away moodiness, hunger, and pain.

The blessing of work is experienced afresh every day by anyone—if they haven't known it before.

You, Ghetto, working productively day and night: In this century, which began with emancipation and release from the ghetto, a period of liberation was brought to an end with an even more cramped and oppressive ghettoization. You will remain for all time a shining, glorious chapter in the history of the European Jews.

[...]

The weather, thank heaven, remains summer-like. At last, we got some longed-for warmth and could experience the pleasure of sitting outdoors on comfortable benches under the shadow of trees. Who would have thought that the lonely path behind the sheep stables would be graveled, with benches inviting rest, and that Steinlagerplatz would boast neat barracks and flower beds? A nice piece of news is going around about the street-naming competition. The path behind the Kavalier barracks, bordered by high ramparts and only a few meters wide, will be named Bölsche Weg [Way]. Why Bölsche? He wrote the famous book, *The Love Life in Nature*.

Since July 7, 1944, the redoubts as far as the Neue Tor [New Gate] have been made available for walking and rest. Before this, it was woe to anyone who so much as started up the bank leading upwards! The sentry invariably chased him down. One so wanted to have the freedom to look out from above [from the redoubts] into freedom, to see the mountains, the wide fields, the Eger, which carries its waves to the fortress and in which one could bathe! One would like to bathe! Yes, a bath. I have not had one in the two years since I have been here. We are happy enough with the shower that we are allowed from time to time. One hundred men per hour get a shower in the central baths, a few minutes of letting the streams of hot water flow over the naked body, stopping to wash, and then more hot water to rinse it [the soap] off. One dries off quickly and gets dressed. The labor office distributes the bath cards. One gets on average one a month, and undergoes this necessary procedure with great pleasure.

[...]

If someone rushes through the streets of the ghetto toward the same destination every day, he will never enjoy the pleasures of exploration, as I so often have. I don't just see the beautiful young people, of both sexes and all ages, again and again, or the many people striding along purposefully and blindly, or the carts with their heavy loads pulled by human strength. No, I find so much [more] that is well worth writing down.

An aquarium landscape has been built in a shop window to the right of the Dresdner barracks. It takes up the whole height and width. There are artificial plants on the bottom, colorful sand, and stones. Cardboard fish hang motionless, as if waiting for prey. The "tank" seems to be filled with water. When one gets nearer, one realizes that the effect is created with transparent cellophane: a splendid achievement by an unknown handicraft enthusiast.

[...]

The displays in our shop windows are always arranged according to modern principles of effective advertising. There are too many beautiful things that are, oh, not available inside.[40] Mostly it is, "Sold out, no longer available."

In ten shop windows can be seen ten different vividly re-created scenes from fairy tales and children's literature, very colorful and designed with lots of imagination and artistry. Since there are only Czech motifs, the German youth cannot participate in the competition to interpret these ten pictures, called *Who Knows? A Competition for Children up to [ ] Years.*

In another row of shop windows next to the Deutsches House (oh, my dear Kurt Frey, if you could now see your creation again, your roar would be heard for miles) are excellent caricatures of the Gerron cabaret.[41] Next door, there are large graphic posters preaching cleanliness, room ventilation, and other forms of hygiene. Then [in the next window] you can see beautiful figurines, vases, jugs, and plates from the ceramic workshop, more proof of will for good craftsmanship.

Life in the ghetto is diverse and colorful, not gray, oppressive, and difficult. Whether you are satisfied with your lot or forever complaining depends on whether you can accept and comprehend [the ghetto], and on how skillful and nimble you are, and what you make of your days and its events. All this is decisive and molds the whole!

* * *

Again, I had to pay my last respects to a dear comrade: Max Beres. More and more, the last of the Auxiliary Service of the Ghetto Watch melts away. We have been torn apart, scattered around the ghetto, and seldom see each other.

Now, in the summertime, the last act of mourning has lost much of its gruesomeness. The two guards in front of the massive wings of the barracks gates, the broad, sprawling chestnut trees, stand, dark green, their fruits already big. Their rapid growth signals the approach of autumn. It is mid-July—how much longer will [we be able to enjoy fresh] air, sun, and warmth?

A welcome improvement has been made to the [funeral] hall itself—large electric lamps have replaced the previous dim ones. The coffins themselves are undecorated and plain, made of rough-hewn planks. Where there are joins, you can see the dead. When they are carried out, parts of the coffin flex and move; the lids are on loosely. Now [the coffins] are covered with a black pall.

The rabbi no longer delivers an address. I do not know why. The consoling words of our good speakers did the mourners a lot of good. The chasan sings the usual prayer in Hebrew, and then the rabbi states the names of the dead and says a short prayer. Then they clear a path through the crowd for the pallbearers; four men carry the coffin on their shoulders and bring it out to the wagon.

There is finally a decent transport wagon dedicated specifically to this purpose. It is a two-tiered carriage that is painted black, with 24 compartments that hold the coffins more securely. The sides are hung with a movable black curtain that has a bright white Star of David on it, and there is also a Star of David on the rear wall. No longer are the dead carried in the open, flat, dirty wagon borrowed from transporting goods as necessary for this solemn trip. No more shaking and rumbling along, with the coffins stacked up high, often four on top of the other, and held together with a thick rope, tottering back and forth. Rubber wheels provide a smooth and quiet ride. Slowly, it sets in motion. We accompany it for a few meters to the barrier, and then it rolls on alone to its destination. For a long while, we can still see the Star of David on the black background. It is a comforting farewell. Then a curve in the road carries it away from our view.

*   *   *

The loft in the pretty house Q307, where we conduct our enterprise every evening, is a raw, ugly space; the walls at the front slant; there are bare bricks on the right and left and heavy beams on the open ceiling; to the side are unusable anterooms, where all kinds of junk are kept. The benches are shoddy, low, and uncomfortable, made from rough planks. I admire my listeners for having the patience to sit in such bad seats every evening, standing up with back pains after an hour and a half.

A young man unknown to me until then took pity on me. He introduced himself as Arnold Munter, a roofer, builder, and scaffolder by trade, who had been entrusted with the renovation of the town, specifically of the building facades. A Berliner of the best kind, a lad whom one can't help but like because he doesn't just talk—he acts, quickly and efficiently. He disapproved of the room and decided to beautify it on his own, without help from the authorities or any public notices and permits.

The work began. He got some comrades to deliver mortar and sand. In two free afternoons the walls were plastered, smoothed, and whitewashed. Then I procured some old and new bed covers. We covered the ceiling and the sloping roof with these cloth strips. The ugly anteroom on the left was edged [around the doorway] with wooden slats that were covered with tautly stretched cloth strips [to conceal it]. In a few days the ugly, dark loft was transformed into a pleasant, bright theater.

A large opening in the roof allowed air to circulate and reduced the heat that accumulated during the day so that in the evening the temperature was bearable. Now the area behind the stage would also be beautified. The gray curtains were sprayed with red paint by this jack-of-all-trades. It contrasted nicely with the yellow flounces along the border. This good backdrop would now dignify the actor.

He also wants to tackle the problem of the benches and find a satisfactory solution. This knowledgeable, skilled Jewish craftsman works nearly all afternoon with obvious joy, and helps me to decorate the room in such a way that visitors forget that they are in a loft, and believe that they find themselves in a beautiful auditorium.

* * *

It is difficult for the organizer of evening lectures not to show off and mention the fruits of his labor individually by name. Every single one is dear to his heart, especially since there have been hardly any misconceived or poor ones. I have to say that I was so careful about selecting the speakers that only once in the long series of nearly 500 evenings did I miss the mark completely—with a speaker who promised a lot and failed miserably to deliver. Naturally, not all 200 visitors are happy with every lecture; certain topics may not interest them. But the speaker is always such that it is good to listen to him, and boredom and its consequence—an uncontrollable urge to sleep—does not occur.

Some visitors are steadfast and come to every lecture, e.g., the two blind listeners or the well-known [Jakob] Bibo, 76 years old, formerly a clothing manufacturer in Berlin; the Dominican Father Neustadt, about whom more should be said; the subtle critic Wilhelm Sterk and his wife; a number of elderly ladies, including the dignified, delicate, Viennese Mrs. *Hofrätin* Moser, the illustrator Mrs. Lehmann-Laizner—who knows [all these] people and can names all the names? Yet, they all stick with me through thick and thin.

The following also deserve a special mention: Mr. Salo Krämer, from Prague, member of the Council of Elders, who, with his wife and secretary, Hoffmann, rarely missed a lecture. He was, and is, always there for me, active on my behalf among both the elevated and the lowly, and he often proved his worth at the most critical times. [Mr. Arthur] Koralek performed a variety of small jobs for me, above all, on the room issue. He was friends with the heads of all the offices and was able to make many things happen that would have failed without his intervention. To these two gentlemen I offer my warmest and sincerest gratitude. If I had titles to bestow, I would award them with the honorary status of "protector." Since, unfortunately, I have no such titles or decorations to offer, I must leave my appreciation to these pages.

* * *

July 13, the birthday of my beloved wife who is ill and in pain, so bravely borne, that has lasted for months. She is in the hospital, under the supervision of Dr. Salus, an excellent specialist in internal medicine, in a ground-floor room, with iron beds (nine in total), white bedding, a narrow, double shelf at the head

of [each] bed, and nothing else. There is only room for foodstuffs and necessary crockery. On admission, anything that is not essential is handed back. No
bedding, linen, clothing—only what the patient is wearing and one change—is
allowed. Nurses in white gowns attend to the sick day and night. Doctors visit
twice a day, when the medicine is prescribed and when it is distributed in the
afternoon. Meals are brought to the bed and vary according to the case. There is
the light diet and the convalescent diet, [and] various diets, ordered by the doctor. There is white bread for diarrhea sufferers.

Still, there is definitely not enough food for recovery, despite pleas from
the doctors or other officials. The ghetto has too little to be able to give larger
rations, and the demand is so great. If we only received the fresh vegetables that
Jewish labor has produced from the soil, then we would be able to help the sick.
But all the diseases we all suffer from are caused by deficiencies: It would take the
entire crop to treat them, and then it would suffice only for a few days. Just figure
it out: what it means to provide for 36,000 people. A lot of fresh vegetables come
in here [into the ghetto], but the children get them, and that is just as well.

It is too bad that doctors are unable to intervene as they should, because
how can one heal when there is a fundamental vitamin deficiency? Most diseases
[in the ghetto] resulting from such a deficiency cannot be cured; they can only
be mitigated, not remedied. Neuralgia, sciatica, and gastric reduction arising
from low weight, sometimes as low as 70 to 72 pounds. No fat surrounds the
thin muscles; the arms and legs—horribly thin—the body is skeletal, emaciated.
The appetite, even cravings, are present, but when the food comes, my wife, the
patient, doesn't want to eat and has to be coaxed, even though she is fully aware
that she must eat in order not to perish.

She should have been hospitalized a long time ago, but she didn't want to go.
She believed that she would be healed in the warmth of the coming spring. [But]
her discomfort increased, and the better weather did not help. The loyal women in
her room had all been sent to Birkenau, and so she spent the whole day alone. The
one companion who remained in the room, Mrs. Berta Weiler, had to work from
eight to ten hours in the Süd barracks,[42] and only returned late in the afternoon.

What finally sent her to the hospital was a serious case of apparent poison-
ing. Someone had given my wife a portion of ersatz spinach made of leaves that
had been gathered in the meadow, cooked, and seasoned. This longed-for fresh
vegetable tasted wonderful, and we both ate a huge amount of it. On the next
day, her whole body was covered with dark, red hives—terrible itching—her
eyes swelled up and remained that way for a few days, and the rash did not disappear. Severe pain in her legs returned, and it was difficult to lie down both day

and night. Her condition was lamentable. When there was no improvement, my wife agreed to be transferred to the hospital.

There, everything possible is being done: X-rays of the organs, a stool examination, all types of pain remedies, and she is under constant medical supervision. She was admitted on July [ ], and now a very slow recovery begins. May she have a speedy and complete recovery. She has earned it; for one and a half years she has devoted all her strength to being a totally dedicated caregiver in the ghetto.

✳   ✳   ✳

[…]

Professor Dr. Klausner, from Prague, repeated, in a more extended version, his lecture: *About Other Animals That I Have Learned to Love*.[43] A fanatical animal-lover, he told us about his dog Lux, which he bought as a biting, caged terror that could not be tamed. It was love at first sight. From this extraordinary animal's cleverness, we learned wonderful things: Man and animal completely understood each other. He told us about monkeys, snakes, the aquarium and terrarium, parrots, and many other animals. But the best thing was when Professor Klausner showed the animals that he had caught here and nursed through the winter—a lizard, which tamely climbed up his chest and shoulder, and a large toad that jumped onto his hand when it was called.

No less interesting were the evenings given by Dr. Fritz Heymann from Düsseldorf. He was a mason, had worked for many months in the coal cellar, and is now working in the transport department. He was an adventurer like his uncle,[44] the Chevalier von Geldern, whose life and deeds, along with those of other adventurers, he had written about in a long book.

He, himself, had spent many years in Spain and Portugal, investigating the Maranos.[45] Then, as a member of the Spanish military staff, he participated in the crusade against the Rifkabylen[46] and was the first German to set foot in the legendary city of Chaouen, which had not been entered for 300 years, since the inhabitants and their king, King Boabdil,[47] along with Jews loyal to him, fled to the inaccessible solitude of the Atlas Mountains. Heymann stayed there for a long time and befriended the Jews, who had formed an impressive community, and was able to gather much information about its history and life. His mother was born a von Geldern and was related to Heine's mother, so he had a heritage that had propelled him into the wide, wild world.

The lectures held by Professor Max Brahn were of great interest. *Geheimrat* Strauß introduced the 70-year-old scholar, who had been active in the Nietzsche

Archive[48] for years and had published the works of Schopenhauer at the Insel Press. A man of superior knowledge, who not only was a medical doctor and a scientist, but also was for many years an arbitrator and a commissioner of the Reich responsible for determining wages in heavy industry.

On three evenings he spoke about Schopenhauer's life and philosophy, on two about Nietzsche, naturally, without notes, and above all, he was clear and so comprehensible to us laymen that a new world of knowledge opened for us.

Dr. Leopold Neuhaus held a lecture cycle on the "Kehilla."[49] The subjects were as follows:

1. *The Jewish Community and Its Formation*
2. *The Synagogue: Building and Furnishings*
3. *The Jewish Cemetery and Its Facilities*
4. *Schools of the Jewish Community and Other Institutions*
5. *The Religious Life of the Community and Its Representatives*
6. *The Mission of the Jewish Community*

Despite the beautiful weather, these evenings were always well-attended by an extremely interested audience that learned many new things and took a good deal of Jewish knowledge away with them.

It is amazing how at home this man is in all fields of human knowledge, how he knows anything and everything, can reel off the important historical dates of every epoch, cite passages in the Talmud by chapter and verse, and, in general, is a master of the most esoteric subjects. He is the model living scholar; he knows how to carve up his tremendously complex subjects into bite-sized pieces so that the audience finds the seemingly dry history to have an excellent taste.

His speech is rich with imagery, fluent. He quickly develops his theme without faltering. There is no stumbling, no pausing while he gathers his thoughts, no confused "oh's." He is an artist of the spoken word who never tires us out because he is always compelling. And above all, he is willing to serve the cause and to donate tirelessly from his vast treasure trove of knowledge.

Cyrano de Bergerac[50] German by Ludwig Fulda!

After the *Talisman*, I had a burning desire to put on a reading of *Cyrano*. I already had a fiery youthful speaker in Dr. Běhal and a pretty Roxane in Frau Deutsch. But the book was not to be had. For months on end I assailed dear Friedmann, the director of the library: Couldn't he possibly still help me with *Cyrano*? He only shrugged his shoulders, until one day, beaming, he handed me two copies of *Cyrano;* one even had a handwritten dedication by Fulda.

[…]

Over 200 people have heard the play, and they proclaim around the ghetto that this magnificent performance is worthy of its predecessors. The actors' performances become better honed with each reading, and are if anything livelier and more sparkling and engrossing. The demand is so great that I have to add two more readings in order not to disappoint too many people. The participants put their souls into it and are pleased with its remarkable success. Now I will not rehearse anything new for a while. I want to relax a bit in the last month of summer and not work so intensively anymore.

It is not easy to deal with actors. Even here in Theresienstadt they are extremely nervous, sensitive, easily offended, irritable, and quickly become quarrelsome. They feel so confident that they are indispensable that they put aside all good manners, which actually ought to be second nature. They have no respect for age, and they do whatever they feel like doing, without self-restraint. For me, this is unpleasant and distressing because other than breaking off with them, there is nothing I can do.

*   *   *

July: this month is also drawing to its end. It brought many cold mornings, cool days, and few opportunities [for me] to enjoy the new perk—use of the upper part of the redoubts, with their beautiful, grassy, open spaces. People stroll up and down there every evening. One is happy to be in the clean, dust-free air, to enjoy the view over river and mountain, and to wander on the soft grass. It is a bit of freedom that has been given to us here.[51]

In the open spaces, the lawn has developed luxuriantly. The parade ground offers a sight that has not been seen in its almost 200-year history. It has been stripped of its formality and has become a green, ornamental square. There are long flower beds in the center filled with colorful flowers and low, red rosebushes that bloom gloriously and delight the eye.

During the day, the four rows of benches—each of which seats 20—are densely populated by the elderly, who hold on to their places fiercely. When a concert is announced, one must abandon all hope of getting a seat. But what else should the old be doing? After the endless winter, they are happy to be allowed to enjoy air, light, and sun. Here, they sit comfortably, always finding someone to talk to, meeting people they know, and hearing from "reliable" sources the latest news about the latest goings-on in our town. There is indeed much to report on because our administration makes sure that there is variety in our daily operations, if only in the form of a less-than-pleasant directive from the housing department ordering relocation because a house is needed for some urgent purpose.

[...]

* * *

Chance brought me into contact with a man who, during our conversation, said that he had served [as a soldier] here in Theresienstadt. I asked him for a description of what the town looked like then, and I am happy to pass along what he told me.[52]

[...] The residents of Theresienstadt were Czech, and they colonized the streets, where a bustling life unfolded, albeit entirely focused on the needs of a garrison of about 6,000 soldiers. There were between 5,000 and 6,000 civilians, and they lived only within the fortress [i.e., inside the walls of the town].

There were eight Jewish families here. [Among them:]

Max Neufeld—Quartermaster of the 9th Army Corps (*Armeelieferant*)
Kornfeld I—Grocery
Steindler—Leather[53]
Goldberger—Clockmaker and banker to the soldiers
Kornfeld II—General store

The commander of the garrison was Field Marshal Lieutenant Moritz Edler von Steinsberg, a Jew who had fought in the campaign of 1866.[54] Taussig, a Jew, was the top medical officer, holding the rank of captain. There was another Jew named Taussig who was the officer in charge of the mess hall and the rations storehouse. There was also Steiner, the Jewish superintendent of the 29th infantry division. The garrison itself was recruited from the Germans in Bohemia.

The inhabitants of Theresienstadt were tradesmen, such as butchers, bakers, and shoemakers, etc. They rented to officers and volunteers who were on one-year assignments.[55] But their main source of income came from bars, which almost every house had, where women were available. The good hotels were the City of Prague and Salazschno, and there were also some lesser ones. Theresienstadt was, you might say, entirely dedicated to soldiers and to love. The officers' casino was in the beautiful house that today is home to the SS. All the officers stationed here temporarily lived in the Genie barracks.

The hospital was housed in the Kavalier and Hohenelbe barracks. In the rear wing was a large section for mentally ill convicts. They brought all the prisoners from Bohemia to the "Little Fortress." We do not go into this area, which is in front of the ghetto. We know that, even today, criminals are brought there to serve their sentences.[56]

Quite a few of the ghetto inmates had been here at other times, as soldiers, salesmen, or spa guests from the neighboring [town of] Teplitz. Captain Klaber, formerly of the Ghetto Watch, served here as a cadet. Where the Süd barracks are today, there was a sprawling parade ground that stretched as far as the Bauschowitz border.

The Theresienstadt of those times is depicted as a cozy garrison that never saw war raging around its walls. Even during the times of its builder, Kaiser Joseph II, the fortress was never stormed. Built as a bulwark against Prussia and Saxony, it remained undisturbed by military operations. Even in 1866, it was a peaceful oasis to which the war wounded were brought.

Later, it was a museum piece, a rare and very well-preserved example of the builder's art in the realm of defense in former times. The parapets and redoubts were untouched and the wide moats unused. Later, orchards were planted, which shows that one did not like to leave the flat areas fallow. Cultivating the flat areas was the preserve of the Jews, who were permitted to engage in a most intensive production of vegetables here and to demonstrate what they were capable of in this area.

*   *   *

In front of the Bauschowitz gate, at the edge of the deep ravelin on the other side of which is the central mortuary, there is a neat and very modern villa with a front garden and a long back garden that is lined with trees. The Aryan supervisor of agriculture lived in this house. This property became vacant in April and was made available to the ghetto.

The administration decided to make the entire complex into a children's home where they could rest and recuperate for extended periods after they had recovered from contagious diseases but still needed medical care and supervision. Since the house was accessible only from the front—on three sides the ground falls away steeply—it was easy to control the entrance. The director of the house, Dr. Ernst Podvineč, is an amiable man, tall and slim, with kind eyes behind his glasses.

I was invited to a children's performance [at the villa] that began at four o'clock. It was a very funny play, depicting the fight against dirt and germs in five scenes. Robert Koch even appeared in one of the scenes wearing a white coat. German and Czech were spoken; folk songs were sung; an 11-year-old girl played a harlequin, ensuring cheerfulness. This noble play was written by Dr. Karl Driml and reworked and directed by Dr. Podvineč.

The stage had been set up in the courtyard, and the audience gathered in front of it. The youngsters sat on the ground or climbed onto the branches of the mighty, laden walnut tree. The fence, the fountain, and even the roof of a low shed were also covered with girls and boys of all ages; it was a charming sight. How their eyes gleamed, how intently they followed the exciting play—in which the devil appeared! Among the children there were faces that were as pretty as pictures. One eight-year-old blonde would have won any beauty contest. Such a play keeps the children busy for many weeks, their minds stimulated and their ambitions awoken. I observe again and again that the Czechs are livelier than the Germans, and their German sounds particularly nice on stage.

After the play, which lasted about an hour, Dr. Podvineč showed me around the garden and house. In the garden each child has his own wooden platform on which to lie down under the trees. The remaining space is planted with vegetables. There is such an abundant harvest that the children receive vegetables to eat almost every day. The house itself is a jewel box. Downstairs are the rooms of the 22 girls, above those for the 22 boys. There are three bedrooms on each floor, each [painted] in a different bright color. In the blue room, everything is blue—the beds, curtains, and chairs. A shelf is divided into eight cubbyholes in which the children put their toys and small items. Each one is covered by a curtain of blue fabric, which is embroidered with scenes from fairy tales. The whole thing looks like a picture book.

Clothes, laundry, and tableware are kept in compartments in the corridor. A shower room makes it possible for the children to wash thoroughly every day; the toilet is a model of how toilets should always look. Oh, if the adults would take this as an example, the state of health in Theresienstadt would be much improved. All the rooms are meticulously clean, with plenty of air and light. The pantry is abundantly filled. The administration takes wonderful care of the children, and when they are released after a stay of two to three months, they return to life as healthy, robust people.

One cannot be grateful enough for the dedication of the doctors and nurses. They are completely devoted to this beautiful mission, to preserve valuable humanity, and that is the most beautiful work that we can undertake here in Theresienstadt. For the rest of their lives, the children will look back on this home with love and gratitude.

[...]

✱   ✱   ✱

Today, July 23, is a day of melancholy remembrance for my wife and me. Twenty-four months—two years—ago, we entered the ghetto. How quickly these years have passed, filled with the great events happening outside and with the small ones in here!

Where have the days gone? Is it really true that we have been living confined here for two years—it would be a sin to say imprisoned? We are removed from the national community, virtually cut off from almost all connections, and possess only what we acquire here. Our whole being had to transform, to be put together anew; yet, we still exist and still breathe the air of today's cool, cloudy, summer day. I mustn't complain. The lectures have allowed me to spend every day working, and I have had the privilege of developing them the way I envisioned, according to my will.

We do not suffer from hunger, thanks to the parcels that our friends send us every month, which provide us with reserves of strength [...]. The main thing is that the stomach and bowel have become accustomed to the diet and function normally. All the rest is child's play, a minor matter.

How important are things—such as housing, roommates, rations, injustice as opposed to protection—for someone who has equipped himself with the best means for preserving health: equanimity, and a certain nonchalance? One learns this by standing in line. Fortunate are those who are not ruffled by anything and can tame their temper. They can cope with anything in Theresienstadt, even a house elder.

[...]

One thing that we must not forget on this second anniversary is the enormous difference between that July day and this one today—how many freedoms we have won, how many bonds have been broken, how many invisible walls have been cleared away, how much have we been allowed to improve living standards inside the ghetto!

We rarely see the German authorities and have nothing to do with them unless someone grossly breaches the decreed rules. But those are exceptional cases. Otherwise, the official form of communication is the written word; only those in administration have to report [to the Germans] in person or by telephone. There is no roll call or any other spoken address on the part of the German authorities. The only orders we receive are the orders of the day, and we get the circulars that the house elders read aloud in every room, which everyone must sign. The orders of the day are posted everywhere, so, "I didn't know" is no excuse.

The rumor mill in Theresienstadt works splendidly. Within an hour every piece of news has made the rounds to all ghetto inmates. And thanks to the ghetto's exemplary organization, we receive the rare letters and the frequent parcels quickly and without loss.

[...] As ghetto inmates we certainly feel that we are incarcerated but nevertheless upstanding human beings who live under just one restriction—that we have had to give up our personal freedom.[57]

For anyone who has been able to live and work for two years in peace and quiet (as it might be said of my own situation), life has not been bleak, bitter, or empty because he has embraced the time happily and filled it constructively. My retrospection isn't and shouldn't be thought of as a lament. I have no cause. Good fortune has—as it did back then in 1915—allowed me to find my way and to pursue my wishes and desires to the best of my abilities.[58] I could bring my ideas to life. I was able to give thousands of happy and pleasurable hours to others. I have achieved my goal and can exit the stage when my time arrives knowing that my duty has been fulfilled.

* * *

Again, I have an obituary to write. On July 25 at 2:30 A.M. in the hospital in the Hohenelbe barracks, Gustav Hochstetter, I/71–9099, fell gently asleep in the 72nd year of his life. I had met him at my evenings. We spoke at length, and I knew that I had gained a dear colleague. Professor, as he liked to be called—it was a Belgian award—Gustav Hochstetter had a leading position as an editor and a multifaceted contributor at the *Lustigen Blätter*[59] in Berlin. He was a man who had everything—wit, humor, satire, and rhyme. He rode the Pegasus in all its gaits, never lost the reins, and always remained an elegant rider.

He had earned a lot of money in life with his pen. He acquired a magnificent estate in Saarow-Pieskow that he still loved with all his heart. Only a few weeks ago, he wrote a poem in my album in which he invited my wife and me there, describing which of three precious sets of dishes he would serve us with.

He did not rest in Theresienstadt. He recorded everything that happened, day and night, in countless poems that always showed the masterful hand of the old practitioner. He wrote witty prologues for my lectures and was happy to have the assignment. He was the most proud when the whole evening belonged to him, and he could recite his own creations.

[...]

I had visited him again on Tuesday and had found him very weak. When I spoke to him, he opened his eyes, which were still the old bright blue, and answered my questions, while I stroked the arms that had been pricked all over by injections, but I could understand only a few words. The nurse had thought that he would meet his end during the night. Death makes no allowances. It came at half past two and closed the eyes of this precious, gracious person, leading him, imperceptibly, to a better beyond.

On Thursday, July 27, the simple farewell ceremony was held at half past eight, attended by six people. His coffin was in the room for non-Jews; it had been draped with a black cloth and placed on the catafalque. Gustav Hochstetter was a Protestant; hence, this sequestration.

A crucifix was placed on the coffin. Dr. Goldschmidt said a short prayer, followed by the Lord's Prayer, and then a blessing. I stepped up to the coffin and said words of farewell, gratitude, and remembrance.

We left the room in silence and walked out into the warm, smiling July day. Below, on the ravelin, about 50 young people were digging in the field, in order to gain a new area for cultivation. And two hours later an emptied, bloodless body was given over to the flames. A small pile of ashes was all that remained of this successful, happy life. He entrusted the manuscripts that he had written here to me, and I hope that I will be able to hand them over to his wife one day.[60]

Children's Hospital, Q317/19

After having visited the wonderful [children's] convalescent home, I was invited also to visit the large children's hospital. It is located behind the Magdeburg barracks, on the corner, not far from the moats. The rear facade looks out over the brewery with its large courtyard. In between and subdivided into beds are the richly appointed gardens that belong in part to the house's caregivers and the patients. This is again a big plus because it means desirable food supplements. The director, Dr. Hans Schaffa, 37 years old, was born in Nikolsburg, Sudetenland. There are six rooms on the ground floor and seven on the first floor. Four additional rooms have been made usable in the neighboring building.

The ancillary rooms, such as the bathrooms, toilets, storerooms, the kitchen, laundry cellar, ironing, sewing, and the accommodations of the doctors, the house elder, and the nurses, are ample. In the garden there are beds and chairs[61] that allow one to be outside in any weather.

The hospital can accommodate 106 patients. Eighty percent have mild cases of tuberculosis; the rest have internal diseases. Children up to age 15 can spend up to one year here. The aim is that with a long stay and the especially good care, the illness will be completely healed, and the children can be discharged in full health.

[...]

A walk through the rooms where afternoon tea is being eaten convinces one that the children are content. The youngest are in cots and are in the process of being scrubbed by the nurses, one at a time, in a bath. There is squealing and laughter and cheerfulness. The children take the hands of the visitors trustingly. One wants to pick up the sweet little ones and kiss them, but that is, unfortunately, not allowed.

Next door, things are quite different. The ten-year-olds lie in bed and keep themselves busy. Two of them even play chess. Again, I find that the liveliest, most beautiful children are those born here in Bohemia, but there is also a Frisian[62] lass with very big, black eyes who can be considered a beauty. Every room, with its white beds and variety of occupants, creates a different picture. One's preconception of the patient with tuberculosis is nowhere to be found; a boarding school or a hostel would not look any different. Most of the patients are in the garden in this wonderful, warm weather, lively and content, lying down, reading, and talking to each other. They stand at the fence and talk to their mothers, who slip little treats to them. Visiting hours are strictly enforced.

Without strict rules, it would not be possible to care so excellently for over 100 children—and children are the most challenging patients. The nursing staff consists of 30 people; three doctors look after the children. They work under the most difficult conditions and surely save valuable lives, strengthening them to face life's struggles.

We may be happy that altruism in the ghetto brings forth such beautiful blooms. A visit such as this makes a deep impression that raises one above all the burdens and oppressions that the day inflicts upon, oh, so many.

* * *

Here, amid the bustle and the spirited life pulsing through this home, which on the outside gives no indication that it is a place of illness—a holiday camp could not look any different—my long-cherished but unfulfilled wish is granted: I am permitted to speak to children. Exuberant boys and girls of all ages are assembled outside. I tell them about [the city of] Bremen, leading them through the marsh to [the port of] Bremerhaven and visiting the ship *Columbus*. One cannot hold their attention for more than a half hour. For that length of time they sit as quiet as mice, listening intently. When I ask if I should come again, they respond with a resounding, "Yes!"

* * *

Our canteen now has customers and personnel. Both parties do their duty. The one is appreciative and grateful to get its meals this way, that is, apart from the perennially dissatisfied and the grumblers. The other endeavors to serve the food as quickly as it is dispensed at the counter. The token is cut off the ration card at the entrance, and there are cardboard tickets for soup and the second course. If there is *buchtel* or *bosniakel*, they are also handed out here. But everything proceeds quickly; one sits down at the table, and a large pitcher of fresh water appears immediately—you bring your own cups. The young woman comes, takes the tickets, and soon brings the dishes of food.

Anyone who can afford it crumbles bread into the rather thin soup, which is mainly chopped vegetable leaves floating around [in broth]. If you eat up your one-third daily ration in the morning and the evening, you cannot afford the luxury of a slice at lunchtime. One does not get very full. Even the lucky ones who have extra food—I belonged to this group for 15 days—could happily consume the same quantity again.

Food is scarce at the end of July, as it is everywhere before the harvest. Soup extracts are no longer available, and barley and noodles must be saved because the sick need them. So you eat baked goods, which really should be reserved for the evening meal. A printed menu reads: caraway roll (fairly large) with hash (meaning a thick sauce containing pieces of meat into which one crumbles bread); a cup of coffee with that. Or, soup with pearl barley—which by our standards counts as plentiful. But when coffee is the only thing listed on the menu board in the evening, it means that a day of fasting is assured.

The bread ration is not enough to get by without the nightly thick and rather tasty semolina soup. One is resigned to being only half full. The doctors struggle in vain against the consequence of this grim reality, and against vitamin deficiencies. But we hope that the situation will improve soon. Our hunger will be alleviated when there are fresh, new potatoes, which will bring a change to the extreme monotony of our diet.

Do not speak about it and do not think about it has to be the watchword for everyone who wants to survive. I know from my own experience that hunger can be mentally overcome. I don't know hunger. My stomach is accustomed to the three meals a day; hunger announces itself only when its object approaches.

✳　✳　✳

July 31 was to be a big day in the dining hall, as it is officially called. After a long period of leaner and leaner meals, lo and behold, there were potatoes again, fresh, new potatoes. We received a good portion, served peeled with sweet and sour vegetables. Vegetable soup beforehand. It was a wonderful meal, and one felt satisfied.

But in the evening there was only coffee—it is too little for those who have run out of bread, who ate it all up without dividing it into portions and now beg all over the place for a slice that they promise to replace. One must remain firm and, despite one's hunger, must not cut oneself slices [of bread]. It is a precious and expensive commodity.

Section II　August–October

August has come, but it has not, as hoped, brought settled weather. Sometimes it's cool, other times hot, during the day. It rains a lot, and the notorious Kessel winds howl. But because the ground is moist, it doesn't churn up the wicked dust that causes persistent eye infections. One tries to use a sprinkler truck to settle the dust, but that does not do much good when the sun is strong. On the other hand, the girls go around with less on, and their shorts have become still shorter through frequent washing, and so one sees that the young, especially the Czechs, are really well-nourished. At the sports grounds of the bastion, one can observe, with heartfelt and sincere joy, that the bodies of the young have been strengthened more here in Theresienstadt than they would have been in a big city. Here, exercise is a natural impulse. The homes see to it that their occupants form sports teams and train regularly. They work seriously every evening; all age groups participate with love and devotion. Something is truly accomplished, and that is a source of great joy.

The only unfortunate thing is that twilight is already noticeably earlier, and even though the summer weather allows us to stay outside longer, it cannot be denied that by 9:30 it is really dark. Because of this, on August 2, permission to be outside until this time was revoked. The lights must be turned off, and that then means lying in bed, by 9:30. Since the day is long enough—usually we get up before 6 A.M.—one is happy to rest, if not necessarily to sleep. It takes a long time for such a large house to settle down and until the wooden clogs no longer clatter on the stone floor.

People sleep outside wherever possible in sheltered spaces in the courtyard, and when it doesn't rain, escaping from the pests [bedbugs] is a good thing. But when it begins to rain, there are really funny moments, worthy of the pen of a draftsman who is capable of capturing the comic proceedings.

Around six o'clock in the morning, there is a flurry of activity. The court-yards and the entrances have to be swept for the daytime work. Carts pick up the throngs, and soon the courtyard assumes its normal face. The early risers appear, with their cups of steaming coffee. The day begins.

Sokolowna is now called Community House. It is, in fact, a house that belongs to the general public, and it will now be fully utilized.

High summer! Over on the ramparts, the gardens, so carefully maintained by those who laid them out, are splendid. The weeping willows in front of the house majestically spread their dense, green, billowing veils. The terrace—bleak and empty on my last visit—now resembles a sophisticated health resort. Colorful open umbrellas cover the tables. The flower boxes are resplendent with their cloaks of sumptuous petunias in dazzling colors.

Behind the house a huge yellow field almost blinds the eye, so dazzling is the yellow of the [ ] that stretches out like a single surface. The wall of the ramparts is green with grapevines from which hang thick bunches of grapes. To sit there quietly, with a good book for company, makes a wonderful special occasion.

The large concert hall, which is also used for worship—the [ ] is closed off by the black velvet curtains that cover the broad stage—is filled up to the last free space. The visitors sit at rough tables, on chairs and stools, and listen to music for an hour from three to four o'clock. Mrs. Gärtner-Geiringer performed Beethoven, Bach, and Handel with her usual mastery. On another day at the same hour, the whole Durra choir sang, excellently rehearsed and led by its conductor, Wilhelm Durra.

One is in another world, forgetting everything that goes on around one and listening, deeply moved by music that one so often studied in one's own home, knew every bar of, and loved. That we may now be allowed to linger in this grand, beautiful place, where otherwise the squad of young Czechs does gymnastics, that so beautiful a house would be made available to us, is a blessing, which cannot to be praised highly enough.

Recently [I] had something to do [here] in the morning, and Beethoven's *Violin Concerto* sounded in my ears. In the anteroom-cloakroom, Professor

Fröhlich practiced, accompanied by Mrs. von Giżycki. I sat down on the stone steps and forgot time and place. That, too, was a special occasion.

[...]

* * *

And now, the 500th lecture evening. Rabbi Dr. Leo Baeck, who had promised me a lecture for several months, could not say no to this significant date, and so, to my great pleasure, I secured the worthiest speaker we have in this ghetto—in which there is an abundance of good orators.

The admission tickets, very delicately drawn by Etta Veit Simon and stone printed by Eduard Schrimsky in a 13.5- by 4.5-cm format, were admired and sought after. [However] it was a difficult week for me because hundreds of people wanted tickets. But for this evening, I was allowed, in a very liberal gesture, to admit only 225 visitors. I had to consider old friends and benefactors first, to think of prominent artists, and not to forget the regular visitors. Everyone got only one ticket, the inseparable wife had to do without this time. Many people became angry with me because I could not accommodate them, but that did not help. Bearing in mind that the normal admission count was 150, I really had gone as far as I could.

The experience taught me that for every distribution of tickets, 10% are not used, and this happened now. So the feared overbooking was avoided, and at the last minute I could still admit a few insistent ones without tickets.

As prelude, there was a repeat performance at the children's home on Südstrasse for my circle of the comic *Battle of the Germs*. In wonderful weather we sat under the shade of the walnut tree and again enjoyed the lively children's performance and also the beauty of so many young spectators.

Then came the evening itself. On the wall behind the stage was a signboard—the number 500 within a laurel wreath. On the lecture table were two magnificent, colorful bouquets, donated to me. The day before I had already received many small and larger gifts.

The Leisure Time Organization sent Rabbi Weiner. Mr. Moritz Henschel had no word of acknowledgment for his collaborator, not even a thank-you for the excellent graphic presentation of the statistical work by Mr. Karl Herrmann and his draftsman Mr. Bähr.

I welcomed the listeners, gave a short overview of the founding of the lecture series, on September 21, 1942, and what had been achieved since. I read statistics that provided a picture of these two years. Then I remembered the many deceased actors and speakers, and the audience rose from their seats.

Then I invited Dr. Baeck to rise to give his lecture, *Epochs of life*. Dr. Baeck spoke standing up with captivating warmth and generosity. For over an hour he held us under the spell of his words; a life blossomed before us, the life we all share, and gave us the motto, "one does not become old if one does not forget one's childhood." The skill with which Dr. Baeck developed this theme and wove it together gave us a rare experience.

The audience listened with bated breath to the 71-year-old speaker, whose youthful exuberance corroborated and demonstrated his theme. The appreciative applause did not want to end. A stenographer recorded the speech.

And now an epilogue. On the next day I met Dr. Baeck on the redoubt. He came to me and thanked *me* for the beautiful evening. That was for me unforgettable, a beautiful and poignant testament of the humility and modesty of this great Jewish philosopher.

Five hundred evenings are behind me. I missed only a very few because of illness. I look back on this period happily. It gave me a life that accorded with my wishes and desires, a chance to be creative and to achieve things to the extent of my abilities, and an inner satisfaction that fully reconciled me to the fate that had brought us to Theresienstadt. I feel most grateful for the loyalty of the many listeners who so often shake my hand and thank me for what I give them in these evenings. Isn't that the best reward? Do I still need acknowledgment from above? No.

That they still come despite the heat and mugginess of the hot attic is the most convincing affirmation—my path is the right one. If I remain healthy, I want to continue, regardless of what goes on around me. I do not listen to what others say to me every day. I do not take my lead from the actors, who only want to get roles for themselves with their suggestions. I set up the program so that I can answer for it artistically, and do not allow myself to be influenced by anybody. I will keep it this way until that day when the outside world calls to us, "Come back to your life. Come back to freedom." May God give me the strength to reach that moment.

* * *

Mid-month, a moment for me to take another look around Theresienstadt to see what has changed, what remains, what is new. The days are summery and hot, and one cannot lie on the redoubt without a sunshade, which makes a colorful picture all day long. An observer must believe himself to be in a bathing resort for the middle classes. The wide expanse is densely occupied. The children, under the direction of the teachers, form play circles and will be looked after during the day. The littlest ones are dressed in small swimming trunks, or even less.

But the adults also expose their bodies to the sun if possible, although the doctor warns about too much of it. My wife and I can sit only in the shade. Many of the young trees here still have no crown of foliage, and so one must go to the slope, to the old, powerful elm and lime trees and take refuge under their cool protection. Every inmate is most thankful for the freedom of the redoubt, which means a bit of physical health for all of us. This cannot be valued highly enough because it breaks the chains that have cramped us for two long years.

At the sheep stable are the three new barracks, for the laundry and for shoes, with a colorful flower bed in front. Where an ugly railway car once stood—the collection point for bones—there is now a rock garden, built in the middle of a green strip of meadow. The numerous benches that invite one to rest under the high trees are always occupied. The path that led right round had been repaved for vehicles. The organizational hand of the administration is noticeable everywhere, taking the appropriate actions and making improvements for the town beautification.

Everywhere on the heights of the redoubt, people of all ages sun themselves. The children lie in their baby carriages, in the restorative air and sun, without covering. There are prams of all shapes and sizes, made of all manner of material—the ones the joinery builds for the infants are particularly pretty and easy to steer. The children are pretty as a picture, usually blond, with rosy cheeks and heads of curly hair. They stretch out their little arms, seeking to be lifted, as if they want to urge every passerby to "Look at me. This is how one is cared for and nourished in the ghetto." The happy mothers proudly show off their little ones and swap stories of their experiences. The important dads are "in service." They can only get a day off once a week to treat themselves to such a wonderful, sunny day.

The ghetto makes huge demands on those who are fit for work; it must make them because during the harvest season everyone who is healthy must help out. This valley is blessed with fertility. Everything that is planted thrives, promising a tenfold yield. The heads of cauliflower in the cauliflower fields are huge, and the tomato vines can barely hold the fruit they offer up. Even potted plants raised on windowsills bear large fruit, and these can be found in every courtyard, yielding so much ripening fruit that it must be protected with barbed wire. We only see the loaded carts that carry the harvest away from the fields.

Those who work outside receive a certain quantity. The garden allotments begin to yield their harvest. And now the bartering begins. People make offers: bread, margarine, sugar, or an extra article of clothing. This market is always ready, and both sides negotiate the prices depending on the offer. There is never a lack of demand, but those who can buy or exchange are in the minority.

Unfortunately, I have not yet succeeded in acquiring from the rich harvest the fresh vegetables we desperately need. So far, we have made do with dried vegetables sent by friends, some of which, like red cabbage, taste fresh. But it is too little. How many meals can one make from the contents of a care package that arrives once a month? Still, we are sincerely grateful for that little bit.

The signposts at the street corners have been well-looked-after by those responsible for them. They are completely decorated with petunias. Also, the flower beds on the town hall square are planted with low red rosebushes and splendid colorful flowers. The lawn—who could have dreamed it the previous year?—has come on well, but then, it is watered daily. All over the grounds, flower beds please the eye, offering a respite, and the many benches invite one to stay awhile.

Since the redoubts have been opened, the bastion has been depopulated; now it belongs to the young and to sports. Its sandy surfaces are not good for lying down. People go up only in the evening, if a breeze is blowing, to see the sun setting behind the mountains. The spectacle inspires anew again and again, but I can enjoy it only rarely, since I am engaged every evening, working in the hot loft.

The city band under Carlo Taube has developed splendidly, and every day, it presents an hour of music in the open air. Something must be said about this because it is current. The merry art was moved to the courtyard and set up its props and boards there. There are the Strausses, both steadfast bringers of joy, who, with their ensemble, have more than 200 times given the old people two cheerful and often contemplative hours. They perform a colorful mixture of music and dance—seriousness and lightheartedness. Above it all sounds the accordion, which always provides accompaniment when nothing else is available.

Dr. Leo Strauss is an artist of words, whose soul—full of contradictions—never tires and is always creative. He looks like he's suffering, with his long, skinny figure, and narrow face in which only the eyes are alive and which lights up only when a somber verse is recited. The doctor is unique. When he begins in a soft, nearly indifferent voice, one looks questioningly at him, but then one quickly grasps who it is up there on stage wanting to be valued and taken seriously. His cheerful poems are full of wit and spirit; his serious verses and the many sketches and short skits, which are usually written for two, all have literary value that will surely outlast the day.

His wife, who makes the booking arrangements for the Leisure Time department, is exemplary, devoting the entire force of her charming personality to fulfilling her duties. Everything about her is life and movement. The large, bright, blue eyes, the expressive mouth, the delicate little figure, and the art of presentation all combine in her, to make her the darling of Theresienstadt.

Now the artists have left the confines of the *ubikationen* and have gone into the courtyards. In the cool of the evening one can sit there comfortably. A wooden stage is quickly erected, or the edge of the fountain is used—scenery is not necessary. They often perform for 2,000 spectators who delight in the performances and the coloratura of Mrs. Narewczewitz, or Mrs. Eisenschimmel, and whatever all the other blessed singers are called. What an atmosphere, when the twilight imperceptibly lowers its veil and Mozart's arias ring out through it, or the violin of a master sounds in the Czech style. Yes, there are evenings of great expectancy and joy in the ghetto of Theresienstadt, so much so that one forgets where one is.

[…]

* * *

The dry summer has kept the number of deaths low in the ghetto as never before. There are three, four, or five announced each day, not more. Two years ago we had that terrible, murderous period with over 100, 150, and 180 dead. I still see the terrible scene, barely covered heaps of bodies laid on top of each other on the pathetic two-wheel carts. It was gruesome and unforgettable.

[…] Theresienstadt is a town of the living. The dead disappear from sight in less than 24 hours. Dead at noon, fetched a few hours later, and on the next day, a short funeral service at ten o'clock, transport to the crematorium, and the rest is silence. We know only that the urns of ashes are preserved in a dignified manner, but are not displayed.

Perhaps old Jacques Brock's idea—to establish a monument at Weissensee for the "unknown Jew" of Theresienstadt, to which the relatives of all deceased Jews could make a pilgrimage and where an eternal flame would burn in memory of the hundreds of thousands of dead Jews all over Europe—will perhaps become a reality one day, and he who was laughed at will turn out to have been correct. This problem of how to preserve the memory of the 50,000 dead of

Theresienstadt will be a headache for us or the survivors. But a solution will be found for this, too.[63]

* * *

From the series of speakers in the last two months, the name of one man stands out, who belonged among the great of Germany. I had never heard him, and when I was introduced to *Geheimrat* Strauß, a tall, not too broad man, his expressive face and manner of speaking won me over at once. After just a short conversation, I realized that here was a personality of paramount importance.

I asked Professor Max Brahn, who had arrived here recently from Holland, to give a lecture, and he readily consented. He spoke on three evenings about Schopenhauer's life and work: *The World as Will and Representation.* There followed, on two evenings, *Nietzsche and His Work.*

Then, during the so-called "holiday week," I asked Professor Brahn to speak about his life. At first, he was very opposed to the idea; he did not want to see himself placed at the center of an evening. But then he became receptive to my request and said that he was ready.

[...]

* * *

Again, one of the most unbelievable rumors buzzed around the town, and the ghetto guard was at the center of events. My good Kurt Frey, commander and organizer, how astonished you would be, if you could see your corps now! Nothing but elderly, stolid, worthy gentlemen around 50 years old. The young men are put to work everywhere. For supervising and maintaining order in the ghetto, this aged flock is truly sufficient. [...] We are all so very virtuous. Therefore, we finally have been given caps bordered in the correct, the only appropriate, color: blue-white. Now the first step for setting up the Jewish state has been taken—we parade our police under the symbol of our national colors. Shalom! Shalom!

* * *

Our loft Q307 is certainly special. As fond of it as I am, this must be said: When on these hot days the sun beats down on the bricks, it gets hot in that high space, and it is bad for both speakers and listeners. And, nevertheless, my faithful ones come every evening. Although the numbers for the lectures are fewer, the readings are always sold out. We try to provide sufficient ventilation, but the heat can only be driven out with electric fans which we have not got. It is even worse in the crowded halls. We just have to put up with it.

When my visitors have left and I, as the person in charge, want to turn the light off, I am prevented from doing so. A flock of women comes upstairs and, in the twinkling of an eye, arranges the stage and benches as beds for the night, placing mattresses on them. They want to lie down straight away. It must be dark at half past nine on the dot, with no light visible from outside. When I come back in the morning at 8 A.M., everything has disappeared like a phantom, and the laundry already hangs drying on the line in the side area, done by these diligent women at the crack of dawn.

[...]

*   *   *

The Leisure Time organization received the order from the German authorities to record cultural work on film. The project was entrusted to Kurt Gerron, the well-known film actor and director.[64]

The city band at an afternoon concert. A choir concert of Mendelssohn's *Elijah* held in Room BV-241, the first auditorium. The library and its opening hour, the reading room in the Sokolowna, and the revue at the café—there was a lot going on these days. The naturalistic floodlights created a good atmosphere for the cheerful endeavor, and everything was presented in the proper light. Thus, a cultural document came into being, adding to the previous one from 1943 in which the hustle and bustle of life in the ghetto was filmed. There was even a rumor for a time that we would get a cinema, and we could already see in our mind's eye the unforgettable films that would be screened once more here in our ghetto, conjuring up a lost era.

[...]

*   *   *

The largest artistic event, which left all the preceding musical performances in the dust, was the presentation of Mendelssohn's *Elijah*, under the direction of Karl Fischer.

Approximately 80 ladies and gentlemen, who all worked during the day, some doing hard labor, rehearsed for about five months because the conductor could hardly ever assemble the whole choir for a rehearsal. With unbelievable tenacity and energy, this musically obsessed man dedicated himself to rehearsing. Being a tenor himself, he had developed a phenomenal musical ear. He heard every dissonance, and even the smallest deviation was not allowed. He knew each voice and the ability of every individual, and he held the whole together with an iron hand.

The large hall in the Sokolowna provided the choir, which stood on rising steps, with the most beautiful space for the oratorio. The calm, dignified arrangement, with comfortable seating and high ceilings, meant that during the two and a half hours one did not feel confined; everything was festive. The music-hungry listeners had looked forward to this August 15 for weeks. Nobody had been admitted to the rehearsals. The piece was to be worked on without disturbance and presented only upon completion of the great work.

[...]

Theresienstadt may be proud that its inmates came together as such a beautiful community to prove that in the ghetto art can unfold freely despite chains, and no narrow confines and no walls can cripple it. We listeners thank conductor Fischer. He and his work prevailed and presented us with the most memorable hours of unadulterated enjoyment.

*   *   *

I have undertaken to record a series of narratives based on interviews with those truly prominent people living in Theresienstadt about their past lives, people who meant something in the outside world, whose names belonged in the upper echelon. I can only take it case by case because it is not very simple at all to persuade those I want to ask. They do not want to be reminded of the past and decline to speak about it, using age as a pretext, and are, in general, averse. Still, I will not be dissuaded from my desire to wrest a valuable cultural-historical asset from the certainty of being forgotten. I hope to carry out my plan by stages, and I will find the ways and means to win over the personalities whom I would like to interview.

Several great intellects live in the Prominentenhaus[65] Seestrasse 26, and I begin my work there. Visitors have several times brought to my attention that the wife of *Justizrat* Max Bernstein is here. She recently attended the reading of *Cyrano*. I was introduced to her by her escort and expressed my pleasure that she, who is blind, took the risk of navigating the steep stairs. She followed the performance with a lively interest and at the end expressed her appreciation. I requested permission to call on her at home, and now I stood in her room. Two ladies were keeping her company, and a relaxed atmosphere, which did not allow stiffness, prevailed.

First, I had to briefly talk about my life, and then I came to the purpose of my visit. Initially, I received a modest refusal: "What should I say about old times?" Still, I asked if she would answer questions, and if so, everything would develop logically from there. I know the timidity one feels about unfurling one's own life, and I encountered such resistance everywhere. But I found that, just as often, after the ice was broken, there was an almost endless joy in the telling. Here, it was the same. A fantastic life was rendered, evoking most colorful pictures. When I brought our meeting to a conclusion after nearly two hours, the elderly lady was still exuberant and lively, and certainly could have continued. The rich abundance of past decades welled up out of the darkness of the past, and I glimpsed scenes that I will never forget.[66]

[...]

* * *

I stroll along Bahnhofstrasse, the tracks stretching out to the Genie barracks. A goods wagon is stopped there to be unloaded. It is marked: Railroad of the German Reich, direction Kassel. I stand there and look at this messenger from the old homeland. What goes through my mind? Is Kassel a magic word? Yes. On this paved road in the ghetto, it momentarily conjures up times that have faded from me. Kassel, that beautiful city, where so often I lingered happily at the good, modern Hotel Schirmer, where I breakfasted on the garden terrace in tranquillity. Kassel, from which I departed to visit my grandparents in Rhoden, the little town in the Waldeck district, to see the old people and stay for a day or two. Where, during the time that I was in school, I spent holidays every summer. A long train of images forms, linked by the name Kassel, and they all appear to me in such detail, as though I had been speaking about them only yesterday. And all this is called forth by a goods wagon in the ghetto, which a few hours later would roll out toward the homeland.

Four open freight cars stand in front of the Jäger barracks, piled high with coal, a supply for the winter. Every day it is the same picture, the image of strong, industrious figures who transfer the coal to automobiles and deliver it to the cellars of the barracks. Planning in advance, it must have been ordered for now, when we have freight cars available. Later, when the harvest of the root crops begins, the coal run must be completed. Then the indispensable fruit of the earth will roll in to be the staple of our diet.

You old, good freight car, serving Kassel, take my greetings with you when you pull out and go on your way. Greetings from me to all the cities that you travel through on your long journey, and tell them how we worry about and long for the homeland, how we feel connected to it. Particularly now, in face of the terrible adversity that will befall it in the next weeks, when hostile armies will enter German soil.

* * *

It is not entirely simple to set up a monthly program. There are enough speakers available, and most are not content if I can assign only one evening to them. But in order to secure a worthwhile audience in this heat, I often have to refuse. It is my job to be very discriminating.

For me, the fur trader—I stress this characteristic at every opportunity—it is sometimes quite awkward to have to say, "I regret," to a scholar. But what should I do with a lecture on mathematics or one about problems in the education system, or a specialist lecture that is of interest only to professionals? There were two gentlemen who both wanted to speak about problems in *Faust* and said that one evening would not be enough. Good gracious! After the crystal-clear lectures by Dr. Rolf Grabower on this topic, after I have presented *Faust* 50 times, I can no longer allow more lectures about it. We have many philosophers in Theresienstadt. All would like to stage whole cycles of lectures, so as to unlock their fields of expertise to as large and receptive a circle of listeners as possible. I must reject them as well—and the enmity toward the arrogant fur trader grows.

[…]

[The play] *Prince von Homburg*—too Prussian for the Czechs. *Shrove Monday*—officer's milieu. They are unsuitable, despite being exciting and compelling. I have actors suitable for these pieces who would gladly speak the roles, but I must remain firm; I have the sole responsibility for choosing the program, and therefore have to pay attention to the opinions of the majority, not only those of the artist.

More difficult still is reconciling the cheerful, humorous lectures with the requirements, wants, and wishes of the censors, and then producing them in an acceptable way. What is in and of itself harmless has a completely different meaning in Theresienstadt. Here, verses can seem provocative and mocking that really aren't, unless one chooses to see them that way. Everything can be given a political slant. Therefore: always double-check so as not to give offense.

We should be thankful for the literary and artistic freedom that we are allowed. We experience no supervision or constraints whatsoever—everything runs as though we lived in complete freedom. What do we care about what is going on far away, beyond our reach?

[...]

The Plague of Bedbugs

A night of horror. The date is unimportant. I could just as well say it in the plural: nights of horror. I don't know of any book that has covered my theme. It is, plainly said, simply not acceptable to talk about it in polite society, and at home every reader would exclaim, "Ugh! How could you?" and toss the book away. However, in a factual report I am not permitted to gloss over what is unpleasant, and so I must of course also write about this disgusting problem. Because it has indeed become a problem, and a dangerous one, what with the heat and the fact that it has continued for a long time.

At 6 P.M., one begins preparing to "camp" in the courtyard. Anything that is at all suitable as a floor covering is dragged out from all quarters: mattresses that are available for sleeping in the courtyards, short ladders for climbing up to the upper bunks, chairs, footstools, stands. The beds will be built with planks and thoroughly examined for cleanliness beforehand, like the mattresses.

The high, flat transport wagon is a coveted place, and sometimes two people sleep there. In the corridors, the washroom, in the deeply laid cement cesspool—which was decommissioned some time ago and is now kept completely clean—people look everywhere for places to sleep. Now the second act of this interesting play begins. Pillows, cushions, covers, duvets, small rugs, and anything else that is suitable are brought from the rooms. There one sees many things that were once luxury items. Elaborately embroidered sheets, colorful silk eiderdowns, and garish Italian mercerized cotton cloths once brought back from a trip, now light up the courtyards. People construct their beds fervently, because darkness falls all too soon, and everything must be ready. Seen from the balcony, the courtyard looks like a painted picture. The owners of the improvised beds sit and chat as though they were in the garden at home. But at 8 P.M. people begin to prepare for the night's rest. First the elderly people, who are tired after the hot day and allow themselves to be helped, lie down. Then come those who have worked hard. For them, to stretch out and rest is a necessity. People look searchingly to the sky and brush and shake out their bedding once more. Lastly, the young, who are not at all tired, promenade

along the road up until the nine o'clock curfew, and say their good-byes merrily and loudly.

Then, the voices of the house elders ring out in all the courtyards of
Theresienstadt, like the mosque criers in Turkish cities: "Lights out." The reply
comes at once, "It is not nine o'clock yet. Your watch is wrong." Before the parties reach agreement, the clear silvery tone of the small bell chimes the time from
the vicinity of the Genie barracks. The ghetto watch of Magdeburg extinguish
the street lamps.

Now it is curfew. Already the footsteps of the guards going off duty can be
heard. Late pedestrians hurry home; after a few minutes the streets are empty
of people. The fronts of the houses are dark; the dusk lingers, and the first stars
begin to come out. The only life now is in the courtyards, the place where each
house assembles. People sit together enjoying the cool night air, talking about
what sort of food there will be in the morning, and then fetch fresh water for
the night. One feels happy as the loud conversations slowly grow silent, and a
well-deserved sleep comes. On our narrow balcony are mattress upon mattress,
to the extent that there is hardly any room to pass through to get to the toilets.
It is terribly hot in my walk-through room—there is no proper air circulation.
The six toilets nearby often do not flush and do not do much to improve the air.
A shielded electric lamp burns through the night, and that is fortunate. Without
it we would be completely lost.

I made up my bed, which is the top bunk, late in the afternoon. Now I get
some water for washing and drinking water. I shake the covers once more outside and examine the pillows—everything is in order. My bed neighbor is sleeping in the barracks today because he has guard duty. The comrade opposite, who
is a hard laborer, has been lying in bed since 7:30 P.M. and hears nothing of the
noise in the room and the corridor. Below me is a mechanic, who takes a long
time to settle down. The pests all seem to gather around him and, from there,
to move into their positions. I am ready, a white nightshirt, no covers—even the
thinnest linen cloth is too warm.

Now I lie down, stretch out my tired limbs, adjust the pillows, and otherwise want only to let my thoughts wander out into the vastness of the heights.
I remain in this state, sinking into nonexistence. Numbness descends upon me,
and I feel the complete pleasure of falling sleep.

There—I feel it—the first attack. In the neck, on the chest, on the leg, on the
arm, the bedbugs have penetrated everywhere, and their stings are painful. With
my electric lamp, I light up the battleground. I see insects coming from all sides;
they assemble on the pillows. They move around, excitedly, in my nightshirt—it is
as though the heat has driven them mad. I climb over into the beam of light, clean

off my body and my shirt. Naked, I climb back up and begin to pursue the pests. I kill the ones I can catch, but the beasts are so smart and fast that they rush to safety through the cracks in the wood, under the mattress, under the edges of the bed, over to the suitcases stacked up against the wall. (Whose owners do not want their property locked away in the attics. We have protested against this in vain.) Whole armies are under and even inside them. The bed and covers turn red. The ones I can seize, I crush on the wood. One gets accustomed to this, to catching the larger creatures; the small ones cannot be held. They have to be crushed.

After a quarter of an hour the enemy seems to have been driven out, although there is still a specimen here and there. I'm exhausted. I lie down after my body has stopped itching and find nothing more in my hair with the comb.

Within 15 minutes, there is a renewed attack. The smell of human bodies has risen up to the ceiling to lure its occupants. They let themselves drop; one can hear the perfectly aimed fall quite clearly and can catch them. The same picture—renewed battle. One is driven to despair, dead tired and unable to rest. So it goes until midnight. Then I can't stand it any longer. I take my pillow and blanket, put on my gray raincoat, and sit down at the table by the window. I put my head on the pillow and try to sleep in this seated position. But there is still no peace—the bedbugs find me and fall on me. They try to penetrate my coat, which denies them access to my body. Their instinct points them in the right direction—to my neck, to my arms. Dozens assemble on my pillow, which I must clean again and again.

Sleep is not possible. My comrades suffer as I do. Three of us stand in the beam of light and search. It is quite a picture—three naked men, armed with their eyeglasses, searching for and killing the disgusting insects. Outside in the corridor—no one is asleep in our quarter—I shake out my nightshirt and blanket. I take a deep breath and enjoy the light coolness of the night. A glance at the sky. Seeing its splendor, I forget everything. The incredible clarity is overwhelming. It sparkles and glitters. The Milky Way stretches over the house beyond. Shooting stars fall. Magnificent. Magnificent, this majesty of the night.

I take the chair outside and sleep sitting down, no matter if someone visiting the toilet scurries past, just so I no longer feel the infernal itching. When the day begins to dawn, one can lie down; nearly all the vermin will have disappeared, and one's exhausted, beaten-up body may still get one and a half hours' sleep. By 6:30 A.M. at the latest, one is called forth, because coffee is given out only until 7:30, and one wants to drink it hot, after all.

Now we swap stories of this frightful night and determine that there is no rescue from our affliction other than the coolness of autumn. But that still seems so far off. One night's scene repeats itself the next, but it's even worse—the number of bugs has become inconceivably large, waging their war in the heat and bringing us to the point of despair! How long is one to bear this fighting for hours on end? How will the strength that each sleepless night takes from us be replenished?

Not only every room in our house, no, every house in Theresienstadt that is still not disinfested, contains the army of bedbugs of the same size and intensity. We spent so long in the spring pleading with the heavens for heat—now we wish for coolness and yearn for the autumn that will bring us salvation from our torment. Our house should have been gassed a long time ago. It was postponed week after week, and now it seems again that something has come up; the big alterations and restructuring, requiring entire houses to be vacated, have placed huge demands on the exterminators. What is to be done? Work, and try not to despair.

* * *

One may pardon me for this unappetizing topic, but am I to suppress it, send it away with a wave of my hand or dismiss it with a smile? It is of decisive importance for the history of the ghetto, i.e., to its output and performance. This month, despite the heat, which is never taken into consideration, the full effort of each individual will be required. How is that possible after sleepless and tormented nights like these? We wake up harassed, battered, itchy, and feeling not even slightly refreshed after this short sleep. One is hungover, really, morose, feeble, and wanting to catch up on the missed sleep, finding neither the time nor the place to do it.

We want to work, with all our ability, but with the poor nourishment—which is actually varied this month, including some things we did not dare to dream of in the previous year—and the lack of sleep, it is not easy. The spirit is willing, but the flesh is weak.

* * *

On August 29 it finally rained at around six in the evening, but then in the form of a cloudburst. Endless amounts of water fell, quickly forming lakes, a new pleasure for the young. The wished-for cooling down followed and provided a breath of fresh air that was refreshing and free of dust.

In the midnight hour the rain began again. Those on the courtyard were roughly woken from sleep and had to flee with their bedding. It was a mad scene: the elderly who couldn't cope with their odds and ends crying for help; the children calling after their mothers; the young women, scantily clad and not prepared for sudden flight, helpless in the darkness; and the men trying to bring order to the chaos. On this night, those we had envied for being outside had to go into the overheated rooms and, like us, take up the fight.

*   *   *

If Goethe and Heine could write poetry about dealing with the bedbug community, we are also allowed. Is it surprising that the large number of men and women belonging to the poet guild of Theresienstadt eagerly concerns itself with the topic? When the louse infestation was rampant and the resistance mounted, poets of all stripes took up the theme and, now, the new one: the bedbug. [...] I encountered a lot of doggerel on the topic, and I could fill many pages with it. However, I must say that it all lacked the sort of humor that rises above things. It was taken too personally. Verses were composed for the immediate occasion, but none was worth being preserved for the future.

*   *   *

September 1—autumn month. The extreme heat has passed. On Wednesday afternoon heavy clouds rolled in. It took a long time until the rain came. Then there was a flood, heaven having so voluminously donated the longed-for, fruitful blessing. It was high time; otherwise the fields with their promising harvest would have dried up.

There are only extremes in this valley. From heat to cold. No stop in between. One shivers at first going out in the morning and must put on a coat. This wasn't what we wished for. After the cold period of nine months, we had hoped for a long summer, which came only in August and was unusually hot. And now it wants to take its leave. We believed that it would remain with us until October!

There is much unrest in the ghetto these days, a lot of nuisance and work. It is on account of an ordinance to restructure different offices. The Town Hall and the Children's Home were vacated and made subject to other, as yet unknown, purposes. The Court and the Department of Medicine with their many offices were moved into the Magdeburg barracks. Dwellings were made available there, and the semi-prominent had to be otherwise accommodated.

Those who had occupied the upper floors for two years complain a lot at having been turned out of the bright and airy hall-like rooms, with windows and a view over the ramparts and far out to the open countryside, always a comforting and pleasing sight. And now, it was onto the narrowness of the road, up against the walls of the barracks.

The ghetto watch moved its offices into the Magdeburg. The offices have gone into the old entry gate that is situated in the guardroom. The guard itself is finally in Room A7, which had stood empty until then. I'd had to vacate it two months earlier, on one hour's notice, because it was needed "immediately."

In the ghetto "immediately" usually means in four to six weeks, as experience teaches. But it is the same everywhere. One files a request, and it takes so long that one does not need it anymore. Two months ago I submitted a detailed request for a private room. I was assured of approval; a newly furnished house would accept me. Now the restructuring interferes, and we suffer torment in the overcrowded rooms.

My wife's room is a passageway that is situated in the back. All the residents pass through the room countless times day and night, making noise as they come and go. They let the door slam shut, tramp through in wooden clogs, slurp and slap across the floor in felt slippers, or leave the door open. In the next room, an old spinster curses and bickers and is never finished talking. The whole house hates her. Everyone talks too loudly. Six out of the eight beds in the room are occupied, and the women want attention. Can't the authorities understand that those with sensitive ears suffer in such bedlam, lose their mental resilience, and then their will slowly fails because they see no end to these agonies?

There is also the constant disturbance of nighttime rest by the vermin and the nine o'clock "lights out" rule because we lack blackout curtains. After two years in this community, we long for silence and to be alone, because the prospect of another year of such a life is intolerable.

* * *

The second morning of September began with icy cold weather, so that one had to quickly get out the *paletot*[67] for the walk to the coffee dispensary. The black drink is lukewarm to hot, depending on the vat it comes from. Lunch: soup, a portion of meat (really a large, tender piece of smoked meat), 30 decagrams; peeled potato; and half a small cucumber. In the evening there was to be only coffee. Who can imagine our bliss when, as a complete surprise, we received an eighth of soft Swiss cheese wrapped in tin foil, which tasted inexpressibly good.

In the afternoon, the air suddenly turned stifling and humid, and it got even worse in the evening. Walls of black clouds towered overhead and warned of mischief in the night. When I lay down to sleep at nine o'clock, I felt sorry for those who were sleeping in the crowded yard. Hardly a passage remained free. So many people flee into the cool night air in order to escape the murderous bugs.

At about 11 P.M., I am woken up by noise and shouting. A thunderstorm has finally broken. There is no more darkness—the lightening flashes in such rapid succession. Awful thunder intermittently, and then the danger passes. But the lightning continues, fortunately for us, because the electric light malfunctions all night.

The hasty flight from the courtyard offered once again a burlesque scene. The elderly called for assistance, because they couldn't manage to come in by themselves and their beds were completely soaked through from the cloudburst. It was terrible, this flight from the rain and the whipping storm. The tempest continued for over an hour.

In the morning hundreds of sparrows and songbirds lay on the ground in front of the Kavalier barracks, killed by hailstones. The early risers collected the birds, and an assiduous depluming ensued, in order to consume the well-nourished birds for lunch. That's how great the hunger for meat is.

*   *   *

Visit to the Altmann House, next to the high rampart, which contains the central mortuary, a small, inset house belonging to the Aryan gardener Altmann, who still pursues his profession but lives outside the ghetto. The Jewish library is housed there, under the directorship of Rabbi Schön. All the Jewish publications flow into the ghetto library, where they are evaluated. Since books from some of the private libraries of Prague have been sent here, one knew that one would find among them valuable treasures, such as incunabula and rare editions of the Talmud. These are to be earmarked for the large Jewish library in Frankfurt.

One surely can hardly imagine the abundance of Jewish books, which have been printed since printing was invented. These mighty Talmud folios, these works by famous authors such as Rashi, Maimonides, and all the commentators and interpreters of the Torah. There are precious leather bindings, colorful border paintings in the Persian style on vellum, prints reproduced so artfully that it seemed as though they had been set in the most modern *offizinen*.[68] Ancient folios, the pages brown, the corners worn from so much study. And they are all a mystery to me because most are without punctuation. Even when I read aloud, I still cannot understand them.

Rabbi Schön showed me some of his treasures. I am awestruck by the handwritten pages I hold in my hand. In which funeral pyre, in which pogrom did the author pay for his loyalty to Judaism with a martyr's death? Here in these three narrow rooms of the gardener's house lies the history of Israel, preserved for all time. Thousands of books in all languages bear witness to the struggle for God. In light of this spiritual world, which has been built on hundreds of thousands of pages of eternal documents, how can I doubt and always repeat the question, "why?" which forces itself upon us anew each day?

A monument to the past has been established here—to Jewish being, its history, its research and thought, its hopes, and its faith in the future. And over everything stands the mighty word, *Shema* or *Kadoush La' adonai.*[69]

Around this gardener's house it blooms and turns green in full abundance. Every little bit of earth is planted. Above, on the roofs of the ramparts, there are fertile, sustaining gardens. It is a blessed land, a valley through which milk and honey flow.

[...]

* * *

Hallelujah! The thunderstorm drove the heat out, and with it our pests, the bedbugs, disappeared completely. We have slept for two nights—oh joy!— undisturbed and not having to fight. On the other hand, it is decidedly cold at night and especially in the morning, and one has to take out the winter blankets and put on a warm vest. But the sun still has warming power, and it quickly becomes agreeably warm outside. But not in our loft, which is quite drafty with its open windows. It cools down fast and is not a suitable place for clerical work.

How will it be next month when it rains and storms? Then we must look for other quarters. But where? There is so little space, and no one wants to take us in.

Then there is the restless, uncertain activity of wandering around as in the previous winter; it was most unpleasant and certainly not conducive to intel- lectual work.

Well, we will surely see. At the moment [we] have it good. This week, only one lecture. The rest fell victim to restrictions that circumstances demanded. An attempt to substitute them with circles of 20 people, failed.[70] The self- administration is anxious and wants to avoid even the slightest suspicion of deception. So, after one event that was not quite what we had hoped for, we let it go. Strange, when men who understand how to talk in such a fascinating way, who call great knowledge their own, fail, as in this case, to describe their lives when they speak in front of 20 people. It's embarrassing for both sides, who go home with the feeling that it didn't work.

I did not pursue this initiative, regardless of how enthusiastically it was welcomed by our friends, because it could perhaps have been regarded as an evasion of the restrictions. I would have so gladly staged lectures in such an intimate circle, enjoyed at the highest intellectual level. Numerous speakers were at my disposal, but I let it be. Hopefully it will soon be possible to resume our normal activities, which are in demand in the already lengthening evenings.

* * *

At midday it became wonderfully warm. I met Mrs. Elsa Bernstein—she wants no title—this time in the large garden of the house, which is taken up with vegetable patches that form a right angle to the left. Many flowers are in bloom, and there are shining, ripe, red tomatoes; the asters are a blaze of color, and in the trees the apples redden. Mrs. Bernstein sits with her companion at a small table, a folio for the blind in front of her, and reads—a tragic spectacle—with her fingers.

This wonderful, always creatively active woman has lost the weapon she fought with—the pen.[71] Now the hands rest and, with them, the muse. No verse has come into being here, but now, roused by my questions, the past rises once again, expansively, and opens a world to me, one that I certainly knew about but never glimpsed so closely through someone who was part of it. Thus this hour out-of-doors was really special for me.

[...]

* * *

I came from the Jäger barracks, where the Magdeburg outpatient clinic is now housed. Given the authorities' preference for unnecessary modification, reorganization, and resettlement, it is not astonishing that the outpatient clinic on the second floor was summarily dismantled. One finally recognized that the rooms—the smallest in all the barracks—were completely unsuitable and unhygienic. [Still,] a practice that had lasted two years, in which physicians and patients made friends and came to know one another, was wiped out with the stroke of a pen, and the doctors were sent to different places.

One recalls the wonderful arrangement, and the woman with the broken foot who had to be carried up the two flights of stairs. Apparently, there was [at the time] no room on the ground floor for an outpatient clinic. This is how the authorities worked; the doctors could not prevail against "internal administration" and "space allocation." Sick, elderly people had to climb two flights of

stairs and in winter wait outdoors in the drafty colonnade. One could say a lot
about this...but silence is the better part of virtue.

✳ ✳ ✳

There is a manhole on Seestrasse leading into a dark underworld, and before it
stands a man in high rubber boots, long rubber gloves, and filthy clothes. I know
him because he has been one of my faithful listeners for a long time. I stop and
ask him to tell me about his work.

"Admittedly it is the dirtiest, hardest, and most hazardous to my health, but
I chose it because it keeps my family and me from being transported to Poland.
Now I have grown so used to the work that I don't think about it, and when I
take off these clothes, I am another person who belongs to the world above.

"There are 22 men in the sewage-system group. These underground sewers
and their offshoots flow, after the water is treated, into the Eger, and also receive
a rinsing from it. If such a system of ducts is constantly and carefully supervised,
it functions normally. But in Theresienstadt that was not the case.

"The [original] number of inhabitants added up to around 4,000. There was
sufficient support for them, but in the end it turned out that some landlords had
not cleaned anything for decades because they were loath to pay the 300–400
krone that it cost. Thus there were blockages everywhere, and the sewers functioned badly.

"The situation became dire and dangerous when the ghetto came into being.
Fifty thousand people used the sewers and threw anything they wanted to get rid
of into them. Such a senselessness and stupidity, a desire for convenience, and
the lack of discipline quickly made the ducts unserviceable. If we had not cleaned
them, the consequences would have been catastrophic because of the threat of
contagious diseases.

"We crawled in, sometimes on all fours, in order to clean them—one cannot
imagine how filthy it was—but thinking of the ghetto gave us the strength, and
now we 22 men have the sewers in such good order that the huge number of people can use drains, and the danger of epidemics breaking out no longer exists."

I listened with the deepest admiration to this large, strongly built, well-fed
man, who then climbed down the vertical ladder, a miner's lamp on his belt, into
the gurgling, sinister depths.

[One has] respect for these Jews who were businessmen before and who selflessly adapt here. For love of the community they take on the dirtiest work in the
ghetto. The praises for Jewish work cannot be sung highly enough. This work,
which the authorities will hopefully record officially and accurately, should be our

badge of honor, our golden book (as the register of the 12,000 fallen was once[72]) that will record for all time what the Jewish men and women of Theresienstadt achieved together here and what the fighting men achieved in the war.

On the battlefield and in Theresienstadt the Jews put their lives on the line, sacrificed themselves for their people, to make life squashed together in these attics bearable. They did not talk about it; they did not ask questions. They carried out their mission, and many who might otherwise have lived died in the process.

* * *

In connection with this, I should mention September 6, when, without prior notice, a transport of 2,000 Dutchmen from the camp in Westerbork arrived. Unloaded in the evening with the obligatory blockade, they were accommodated in the large Hamburg barracks, where they were searched for contraband. Then came the sanitary procedures: delousing, bathing, and medical examination, lasting throughout the night.

Today, the 7th, the barracks are cleared, but the courtyard still resembles an army camp. Hand luggage is lined up on the ground to be searched at tables, and people stand in groups. Old comrades from earlier transports are here and pleased if they see each other again. More young people this time, good looking, not depressed. The journey took 40 hours, and they saw that the train was bringing them to a peaceful, orderly country.

And, again, the smoothly working organization of Theresienstadt is evident—the 2,000 people were inducted almost automatically. They are already in possession of their ration cards, and the Labor Office sent its officials to put them into service. In a few days they will be distributed among the available *ubikations* and will "belong" to us. From now on, one will hear three languages in the street, and the colorfulness will increase. Nothing surprises us anymore. We come to terms with everything. Soon there will be a new branch of the Leisure Time Organization—the Dutch—because we have Dutchmen in Theresienstadt.[73]

* * *

On my fishing expedition for "personalities," I went to the Prominent House on Seestrasse 20. I spoke to the house elder [ ] about my wishes and was assured of every assistance.

The beautiful house, with its broad, spick-and-span corridors, had the name of the resident written beautifully on each door. My first visit was to the widow of the Danish admiral, Admiral Schultz. A dignified, sprightly, gentle lady of

82 years. She does not speak a word of German, and the conversation is in English. She is herself a Jew, born to Jewish parents in the Danish West Indies, where she grew up. Her father had a business there. When I ask Mrs. Schultz how she came to be married to a Christian high officer, she replied that in Denmark we do not ask about religion when people are in love and want to marry. The elderly lady's hardness of hearing, unfortunately, did not permit a longer conversation.

* * *

In the same house lives Dr. Georg Gradnauer, former Prime Minister of Saxony (1919–1921), and afterwards Reich Minister of the Interior. His sister-in-law is the mother of our singer Edith Weinbaum, the wife of our Alexander Weinbaum, who died all too early in Theresienstadt. She brought the elderly gentleman to lectures, and so I made his acquaintance. After that, it was not difficult to get an audience, and right away he said that he was prepared to talk about his life.

The warm, sunny afternoon tempted us to take our chairs over by the shady wall of the Sudeten barracks—which are taboo for us, open only to the cleaning crews and workmen—and there we chatted easily and informally.[74]

[...]

* * *

With all the upheaval and unrest in the first ten days of September, which affected us all equally, I propelled myself one afternoon toward the Sokolowna for an hour of Schubert in the great hall. Outside was a blue sky; it was pleasantly cool; and the immense hanging vines that nearly block the entrance were wonderful as always—they are the house custodians.

I love to take refuge in Schubert when my soul is in turmoil, when tormenting concerns press too intensely, when thoughts turn to yearnings for what is far away and cannot be reached because everything seems so terribly uncertain and reason finds no anchor. Then the master's sound-images release us from the confusion of the day and lift us gently to those eternal heights, carrying us away from the earth.

The beautiful hall is overcrowded. Silence falls; the doors remain closed. The people are ready to receive. Sonatina for piano and violin. My sonatina, which I practiced with the 19-year-old Ernst Meyer a few months before my departure, was so difficult for me at first, but when I had it in my fingers, it gave me such infinite joy.[75]

This was the piece I heard, and believe it or not, the tears fell from my eyes. I was so moved by this magic that even the first notes conjured up my homeland and reminded me of what I had lost. Three bars—I know every note—I play along with them, while my wife sits in the wings and looks at me affectionately.

Gracious art, what you have always been to me, what you have given me, and how you uplift me here, where you have afforded me a double consolation for the misery and the burden, which you wrap in the great forgetting of mortal suffering!

Then Edith Weinbaum sings *Lieder*. She has developed her voice wonderfully, it flows calmly, fully, and clearly. She leads us into another world. We wander to that infinitely cheerful and easily reached *Elsewhere*, listen in earnest to the *Lindenbaum*, and succumb to the charm of *Mondnacht*, which is so magnificent in this setting. Each of the eight songs is a redemptive message that makes us joyful.

The *German Dances* echoes its melodious sweetness, its melancholy cheeriness, the charming graceful dance, which lets us see gentle maidens in wafting veiled robes, ending wistfully—it brings us a shared reverie. At the end, a brisk *Impromptu*. I awake from dreams. *Hour of music, I thank you!*

Poetry Competition

This had a long, drawn-out prehistory going back to the late autumn 1943. After the terrific success and large participation in my first call to poets to submit their work, I wanted to make it an annual event. No office was engaged in such a venture—idealism is not a characteristic of dignified officialdom. They have other things to do, and must send out circulars and edicts in order to prove that their important and useful existence is necessary. So I was left alone to collect poetry, although I couldn't include all the poets because I could not make an official public request and had to use word of mouth to get the word out, which was nearly as effective.

Approximately 200 poems were submitted, all of which I read, making a preliminary selection, which I would then submit to Professor Dr. Emil Utitz for the final judging. But this completely overworked man, who never granted himself rest, became extremely ill and had to abstain from all activity for many months.

Therefore no decision was made. From month to month, I had to postpone the public announcement of the results, much to the displeasure of those involved.

Finally, Professor Utitz was well enough to make his decisions, and I could announce the date of the readings by the prize winners. This was event No. 497 on the evening of August 3, 1944. It stood under no happy star. My freedom was taken away because the censors interfered and declared a number of the poems unsuitable. Then two of the winners refused to read because they were unprepared, not through any fault of mine, but because the censors had returned the poems to me only that morning. Thus there was a tone of discord in the whole meeting.

I did not agree with Professor Utitz's rankings, but I couldn't do anything about it because a professor of literature always knows more than a fur trader. Professor Utitz gave the first prize to the absent Georg Kafka. I did not agree with this decision. I had wanted to exempt him from the competition and move up the remaining works accordingly[76] That would have been more just. As it was, genuine artists like Sterk remained in a class that did not do justice to their complete works, and they were, with good reason, dissatisfied.

[...]

*　*　*

The autumn month turns up with its whole, proud entourage. For the moment, it doesn't make its presence felt but is gentle, piling up the clouds into the most bizarre formations, which stand out against the bright, deep blue sky. They are a vision of rich marvels that change quickly, transforming, disappearing, while a threatening darkness wells up on the horizon. But it does not approach. It stops as a wall and obscures the setting sun.

There has been no rain in the last weeks, as in 1942, but it's cold in comparison; you can sit outside only when it's sunny. Therefore everyone who can get away assembles every evening for the great solo exhibition up on the bastion, to admire that great state occasion: *Coucher* (preparing for bed) of Lady Sun. She is like a real woman in each instance of transformation, in different costumes, with a varied background. Only the scenery to the sides, the shapes of the mountains, stays more or less static.

All the colors, from the lightest, most delicate pink to the deepest red, are on display as Lady Sun goes to rest. It flames and flickers, it strikes out across the entire horizon, it climbs to the feathery clouds high above. The ball of fire suddenly hangs over the Kegel Mountain, as if wanting to come to rest on its peak. Then it moves to the right, floats dark red in the hazy air, dips into a cloud bank, and pulls free again. This floating and sinking continues for a long time. Now the ball is only half visible. At the same time, the flames blaze all around.

Now the highest cloud tops also glow; underneath they are dark gray, and above they shine in gleaming white. Wherever one gazes—a rush of color, a symphony of color. Now only a small part of the ball is visible, red-hot, like iron under the forging hammer, and then this also sinks. The Kegel Mountains stand, brightness flowing around them. Gradually, the blaze dies down. The evening's veil ascends and spreads out over the distant panorama. But the sky directly above us still blazes and flames. Not for much longer, and then the intensity diminishes, becomes weaker, although a few of the lightest clouds still sail by and receive the sun's final greeting.

Suddenly, it is cool up here. A wind has come up and reminds us that for today the séance has ended. We get up from our blankets. Over on the heights over Leitmeritz, the first lights blink. A majestic glider draws circles in the sky, floats, and then in gliding flight descends into the valley. One is reluctant to leave. Up here is freedom, space, vastness, silence. And down in the crammed *ubikation*, bickering and conflict. One can't breathe down there when one has to return to all that unpleasantness.

*   *   *

In Theresienstadt one may not go dreaming through the streets. So much happens that the "factual reporter" must see. He must have a really good eye and memory in order to be able to write everything down at home afterwards.

And that leads to the big question: Where? In the stone-floored attic Q307, with its open hatches back and front that let such a pleasant draft blow through on hot days, it is so icy cold in the morning that we cannot sit in there. I must look for a small place at home that is cleared for me, and that is not possible every day. So I continue to practice my trade wandering about.

It gets warm enough up there to work only at two o'clock, if the sun is shining. Usually we are not alone, because our stage serves the Strauss Ensemble as a rehearsal space. Serious and cheerful things are played, and there is dancing, even to the accompaniment of an accordion. How long we can keep using this space depends on whether our Arnold Munter can seal the roof against the weather.

*   *   *

I received the following letter:

> Professor Dr. Manes
> Dear Professor,
>
> It is my understanding that in your circle you hold biographical lectures. Dr. Freudenthal's private efforts produced such interesting and inestimable material that, in agreement with him and Professor Utitz, I have been endeavoring

to assemble a sort of archive of biographies for an appropriate project. [...] If this is of interest to you, please be kind enough to let me make an appointment for a meeting at which we can discuss whether a collaboration is appropriate and worthwhile.

I remain respectfully yours.

Your humble servant,
Professor A. Wolff-Eisner MD

What is striking is the style the writer uses, as if it were the good old days. And then, it shows the degree to which I am known or rather not known in Theresienstadt. I am almost ashamed that one refuses to believe that my worthy profession was a fur trader, and therefore confers a title on me, because they cannot imagine that a man in my position is without an impressive, elevating title. So I sail around here in Theresienstadt almost like an impostor with all sorts of titles, and the best proof of this is the letter.

*   *   *

Death notices and funeral times are posted at five o'clock every afternoon on the gate of BV. In recent weeks, the number rarely went over ten. On [September] 11 nobody in Theresienstadt died, on the 12th, one person. This fact must be recorded and most thankfully stated. It is the triumph of the physicians and all public health authorities who lead the fight against illness and death.

*   *   *

There were two sensations in the mess. The first was unpleasant. When we wanted to hurry to the 12 o'clock meal, the air raid siren sounded, and we had to wait in a courtyard until the all-clear signal returned us to freedom. Then people got log-jammed outside the hall because two hungry shifts were pushing to get in. So the door to the holy place was closed, and we had to wait for three-quarters of an hour before we could go inside.[77]

Then we were rewarded. There was soup, which was granular because it contained an abundant supplement of pearl barley. And now, the sensation. Sweet-and-sour cabbage, potato, and a rather thick—just 10-cm-long—sausage, with mustard. We were speechless. Absolutely, this was peacetime fare. We ate the delicacy slowly and reverently—for the first time in two years...sausage.

We get vegetables nearly every day, sometimes as coleslaw, or cooked, or sweet and sour; still, they are the long and sorely missed vegetables. Sometimes, more rarely, we may also get half a cucumber, a very desirable enrichment of our very monotonous diet. But the bread we get is tasty and good, and not one single time did we need to return it because it was moldy. This remains an enormous advantage over 1942, when we had to exchange it regularly, which involved a lot of running around. And since we are on the subject of bread, let me describe a visit to the bakery of Theresienstadt.

*   *   *

Theresienstadt is the land of unlimited possibilities, offering a much wider field than the United States ever can. A stately man, approximately 50 years old, comes to speak with me about a lecture.

Dr. Ludwig Jacobi, a lawyer, had lived in Berlin. We agree on a lecture with the theme *Through Palestine with a Backpack*.

I ask, "What do you do here in Theresienstadt? Do you work at the Court?"

"No. For the last two years I have worked as a baker at the central bakery."

"Splendid. You are very welcome. Please describe, if your time allows, how baking bread is carried out."

"We are approximately a hundred men, who work in three shifts per eight hours. Sacks of flour are delivered from the central provisions store, which are first sifted and then sent to the large mobile basins in which the dough is mixed. It stays there until it has risen. From there it goes into the kneading machine, and after the kneading process, it is divided according to weight and placed on a conveyor belt, which passes under a four-cornered block that holds an adjustable iron plate that forms the dough. The press shapes the dough into sausage-shaped pieces that are placed on boards of twelve meters and put near the oven to rise.[78] These pieces are constantly brushed with water to prevent a skin from forming. This would allow the carbonic acid from the fermentation process to tear up the bread instead of allowing it to rise. It goes into the oven, arranged in tiers, for 40 to 50 minutes, and the baking is complete. The hot bread is again coated with water to maintains its color and gloss.

"For two hours after leaving the oven, the bread is very sensitive; it must remain on the board and cannot be squeezed. Then it is delivered to the warehouse, where it is stored for about three days before distribution.

"Only pure rye flour is used in Theresienstadt. All the stories about adulteration in times of shortage are the fantasies of idle gossips. Each shift, depending on the demand, produces from 200 to 300 loaves. In an emergency, the bakery is capable of producing the entire supply for 35,000 inhabitants. If the delivery from outside fails—it can happen—everything possible is done so that the people receive their normal quantity of bread as usual."

* * *

September 15. The wind has turned. It has become warm and summery again; even in the morning after getting out of a warm bed, one no longer shivers on the way to the washroom but stops on the balcony and looks up at the sky, which is golden and shining, promising a wonderful day. Even our "office" under the Theresienstadt roofs is usable, and one can write at the table, without seeing the ghost of pneumonia creeping in. Our efficient interior decorator Munter promised to make the room watertight. He has been promised some mattresses for this purpose, and so there is a chance that we may keep our beloved stage.

After the meal one doesn't want to spend the rest of the break in the crowded room, where people are cooking and there is the endless rattling of pots. The blanket, that faithful assistant, is put over the arm, and it's up to the bastion. There, on the first slope, one can lie on an incline, as though on a *Kavalec;* it's not too soft, but one can still get lost in far-flung dreams. Mine lead me to that faraway rocky island, my beloved Helgoland. There for many a year, my wife and I lay on the covering and protective small slopes, which once held cannons. The wind always blew, and from down below came the quiet sound of the rushing surf.

Sun, the bluest sky, and wind are also up here on the bastion, and one closes one's eyes, takes the beloved's hand, and feels wondrously woven into the past. At this midday hour there are only a few people on the wide expanse of the bastion, which opens out into the distance and allows me to see far across the land. It is completely quiet. The sun is hot. One must protect oneself.

A reprieve before the storms come and tear the foliage off the trees, and then, oh, we will again see the bare branches of the brushwood in the town hall square for endless long months. We want to enjoy these last days of the departing summer and to appreciate the gift of each hour that nature in her goodness has granted us, and which reconciles us to our being.

* * *

Today, a long, loaded train stands on the track by Bahnhofstrasse, ready to depart. The cars are loaded with sections of huts that were manufactured here, and the last one carries balls of tied-up rags, secondhand clothing, and remainders of all manner of spun fabric that was collected here. And new life will bloom from the ruins.[79] I walk past the cars; they provide a piece of contemporary history. One belongs to "Italy," the other, "France"—"*Chevaux...Hommes*" is marked on it. Cologne...Frankfurt. A whistle sounds, and the train gets under way. *Take along with you my greetings and wishes to my beloved homeland, you turning wheels, you, that touch the ground as you rush by, greet it, wherever you arrive, several thousand times!*

[...]

* * *

The lecture series must not disappear from our field of vision, because it is indeed the scaffold around which my whole existence is wrapped, it is what makes the day worthwhile; everything else is secondary and can perhaps be pushed onto a different track. The 500th evening still resounded for a long time after the event; I let the "repertory pieces" be read over again, but although they filled the cashbox, we did not have a full house. I sold 200 tickets at 3 [krone] easily and without any advertisement, just placards in three places, but either people hoarded them or forgot the day, and so not more than 150 to 175 people showed up, enough to allow the room to appear well-filled, but without exceeding the limit set by the [ghetto] police.

Iphigenie, Nathan, Faust I and II, *Sappho* [Grillparzer], *Cyrano,* and *Talisman* were read. In between, Dr. L. Neuhaus spoke, Professor Max Brahn, Dr. Rolf Grabower, Mrs. A. Auředníček. Then in September: a new ordinance that all lectures had to be submitted to the authorities in Prague, namely texts, poems, and the lecture schedules. This required extensive clerical work; consequently, some of the meetings had to be canceled. This hit me very hard because my whole program was disrupted and I could offer my faithful visitors something only once a week or so.

[...]

There was a break over the holidays[80] during which religious services were held in the large halls and even in my loft. There is not enough space for all the inhabitants to all join together for one hour of prayer because the working people are supposed to have one at five-thirty in the morning. During the day they may not rest and have to be on active service, rightfully; such are the laws of necessity. The holidays commenced with a dignified celebration in the mess hall at 7:30 P.M. Around 2,000 people filled the room, and to the left, the stage, with the lectern bordered in green, was visible to all.

An organ recital by Paul Haas[81] ushered in the hour. Then the Jewish elder stepped up to the lectern for his lecture: *Thoughts on the New Year 5,705.* Dr. Paul

Eppstein spoke in his sure, calm way, by way of introduction about the work of the collectivity, and expressed his thanks. Then he proceeded to describe the current situation that culminated in the longing for clarity [about the future]. He most urgently and seriously warned about the lack of discipline and the danger it posed to the life of everyone if each individual did not apply himself to the work to which he was assigned. Theresienstadt ensures survival only through the strongest work effort. There should be no talk, but work. All speculation about possibilities must cease.

We were on a ship in front of the harbor, but we could not enter because a barrier of mines prevented it. Only the ship's officers knew the way, which was narrow, that would lead to safe land. The ship could not pay attention to deceiving signs and signals that came from the land. It must remain outside and wait for instructions. One must have confidence that the administration was doing all that was humanly possible to ensure the security of our existence. In this way, we should go seriously and confidently into the New Year, with a firm will to hold out and to fulfill our duties.[82]

The service ended at around eight-thirty, and one went out very thoughtfully into the darkness, but with head held high because the starry sky shone above in the most magnificent splendor, and raising our eyes up to it gave us the courage and confidence to live on.

*   *   *

When I still led the Orientation Service and had a lot to do with the office of the Social Welfare Center in Room 76, I became acquainted with a researcher, who had shared some findings with me. She was delicate and youthful, with blond features, very exuberant, with unusually light, bright eyes, which looked energetically and at the same time merrily at the world. With a leather bag under her arm, she stepped out rapidly to her duties in the various houses. Thus we became acquainted, and today I sit out in the most beautiful weather with the elegant, well-groomed young woman in the garden of the Prominent House Seestrasse 26. She is Ellie von Bleichröder, and she reports on her background:

"I am the granddaughter of Gerson von Bleichröder, who was born in 1822 and died in 1893. He was the son of the founder of the Berlin banking house, Samuel Bleichröder. A hereditary title was conferred upon him in 1872. I am not able to tell anything about my grandfather, because he died before I was born. I am the daughter of James Bleichröder, born in 1869 and died in 1937, the eldest son of Gerson Bleichröder.[83] I was born on my parents' property, Drehsa near

Bautzen, where we stayed in the summer. Otherwise [we] lived in the Dresden villa. I went to school there and enjoyed good and challenging instruction.

"My mother ran a large house, and the whole of musical Dresden, the opera with all its prominent artists, kept company there—at the pinnacle stood Ernst von Schuch and Richard Strauß. Who can name all the people I became acquainted with during those informal evenings? Backhaus, the great pianist, belonged to our intimate circle, and with so much music around me, it was natural that I turned toward it and chose the piano as my field of study.

"Then I married early and gave birth to a son. Our marriage was not a happy one, and I ended it.

"Then I dedicated myself to my own interests, which centered on the German Reform Movement, and embraced everything that served to promote health in the broadest sense of the word. [...]

"It is my purpose in life to dedicate myself to these ideas in their broadest form, and to help people who are suffering, as far as my strength and experience will allow. I may at some point perhaps be active in my grandfather Gerson's foundation, Schloß Seelösgen, on the lake of the same name near Frankfurt/Oder, a home for 100 children who were raised there until the age of 15, as per its regulations.[84] Now it [the foundation] is a home for the blind, after the aim of the foundation was changed. My stepmother, Marie von Bleichröder, still directs this beautiful home today.

"I came to Theresienstadt in July 1942, and reported to a cleaning crew as my first service. Then I became a researcher at the social welfare office, and now I work in the same capacity for the post office. I dedicate myself completely to helping the suffering in whatever way I can. My days are full, and I am pleased to be allowed to carry out useful work here."

* * *

This afternoon is already my third time in the garden, and around me sit about 50 children of all ages, listening to what this old uncle has to say. He tells his stories in a way that all the children can understand, even the smallest ones, and they pay rapt attention. On the first day, I told them of the journey of the [ship] *Columbus* and described the beautiful ship. I led the children from Bremen to the port, through the Weser across the North Sea to Southampton, and from there, a short excursion to London.

"Who governs England?" I asked. I got three answers: Churchill, a lord, a king. Even the older ones did not know more. But after I finished, the inquisitive boys asked many questions. They were very interested in the ship and its machinery.

On the second day I told *Stories of the Old Grandfather Clock*,[85] and on the third, when I was actually only there for an appointment, the children surrounded me and pleaded: I should tell them a story; it was a holiday; and they had nothing to do. I couldn't say no, and so we sat down in the garden, and I described my North Cape journey.

Holidays

They are here again, the religious celebrations, with their rousing, uplifting, contemplative hours of reflection, retrospection, and prayer. These days are important in the ghetto because they lead people of all orientations to one goal: knowledge of Judaism, homecoming, and turning to God. External appearances announce the Holy Days.

There was a special distribution of food donated by the Red Cross of Switzerland—noodles, cheese, cookies—rationed according to age. Also, the meal is very slightly richer though food is not more plentiful, and we sat at tables covered with white tablecloths. But otherwise it was business as usual. Everybody had to work, and there was no holiday for the workers.

The religious services in the usual rooms are overcrowded. At the last minute, the service in the attic L319, which has been presided over for the last year by the house elder Selmanowitz, was moved into the large hall of the Sokolowna. Over 1,000 people could listen to the wonderful choir that was singing under Durra's confident direction. For those of us from Berlin it was an hour of wistful memory, as all the melodies that sounded in our ears were ones we had heard for two decades in the synagogue on Lützowstraße. It was a greeting and a benediction—both a reminder and an admonition to accept the divine providence and to put our faith and hope in God.

In addition, there was the soft, beautiful voice of Kurt Messerschmidt as cantor. He never overdid it, but he often added artistically to the antiphonal singing and achieved an effect of profundity. The atmosphere was reverent; there were no disturbances, no coming and going, and no one showing off by singing too loud. It was a sincere commemoration. The only thing that was missing was the sermon, the pastoral words giving solace and encouragement. We had to let our prayers and singing suffice.

In this beautiful room, the altar and the Torah shrine had been set up with dignity, with its black background, white drapes, and curtains bearing a large, bright Star of David embroidered in gold. The sun was bright and warm, and so, despite all the restrictions, the two days were celebrated properly and framed by the good wishes that everyone called out to one another, outdoors and at home: "All the best!"

It is idle to speak of the Jewish inclination to the theatrical: The history of the theater of the last 50 years indeed boldly celebrates the many names of Jewish directors and actors. The cities of Vienna and Berlin are where they attained international fame and spread the German theater to all continents. There are enough books about it, and many artists have published their memoirs, which balance truth and poetry. They are amusing to read, and those who witnessed the decades they describe will be able to tell whether the accounts deviate too much from reality. [...]

Solemn Interlude

Thus it began. In the early morning, while one was getting coffee in BV, it was said that those in the registry had worked through the whole night. The well-informed took this as a bad sign and murmured something about prospective transports. At lunch I asked the police commander's deputy whether he knew anything about the rumor—the answer quickly came: "No. Those were the usual monthly lists, which have to be submitted to the Department." Thus again, idle gossip, latrine rumors. Since there was no further evidence, we accepted the information.

The High Holy days began. I took note of this and called the lectures *Contemplative Hours.*

As in past years I asked Dr. Baeck to take the first evening, but he unfortunately declined because he was too busy. In his place Dr. Leopold Neuhaus spoke about the concept of atonement. On the second evening, the Danish Chief Rabbi Dr. Max Friediger, made himself available, selecting as his topic *The Four Archangels: For He Offers His Angels.* As a third speaker, I got Rabbi Heinz Meyer from Berlin, who spoke on *Faith and Prayer*, and as the fourth, Dr. Salomonski from Berlin, whose talk was called *The Meaning of the Jewish Holidays.*

Friday evening remained free, and that was good, because in the meantime a quiet rumor that had gone around, without confirmation, turned out to be true. As I returned from Rabbi Meyer's lecture along the dark road home, I heard, at the gates of the Hamburg barracks, "Roll call at eight o'clock, called by Dr. Eppstein."

I followed the stream of people who accumulated in the second courtyard, whose large square was two-thirds full. One could see only outlines of things;

the arcades and windows were densely occupied. The sound of buzzing, like a swarm of bees gone wild. Suddenly a strong arc light ignited—in it one saw Dr. Eppstein, ready to speak. People on all sides called for quiet. [...] It took a long time for the uproar to subside, but then loud talking surged again from the back. It was the Dutch, who had been brought from the first courtyard.

Then Dr. Eppstein begins, as reasonable calm sets in. His voice is not strong enough; one understands only isolated sentences, and while those standing nearby try to pass his words along, they remain incomprehensible. Eventually, we know what this unusual speech is about:

"The Department has requested a work transport of 5,000 men aged between 18 and 50 years. They must be dispatched within the shortest period. We are assured that they will return after six weeks upon completion of their required duties. Only the most extremely urgent and justified objections are permissible. The selection will be made on the basis of age only and will include all men, regardless of any important position they may hold. Maintain discipline. This has to be. Make it easier for us, this difficult task—already doubly hard since it is imposed on us during the highest holiday."

A tremendous din followed these words, which quickly collapsed in upon itself and yielded to silence, which was broken only by the reverberating sound of footsteps shuffling over the stone ground.

That took place on Thursday evening. On Friday one tried to obtain details—in vain. What we understood was that all men in that age range should prepare their luggage, packing as light as possible, only what they could carry. There were no official announcements again on Saturday. Everyone had to be at the ready to respond to the narrow, colored name-slip, which was so familiar. Complete uncertainty—who would be released and at which name the summons would stop. Early on Monday morning the house elders brought in the slips and handed out the numbered tags to hang around one's neck. With that, the official act was complete. Now one could do nothing but wait for the call.

On Monday the Durra choir was supposed to sing psalms to mark the end of the days of penance and to serve as a bridge to Yom Kippur.[86] Arnfeld was to recite them. Actually, I had not intended to call either these or the Sunday lecture off. But, since both the Messerschmidts were summoned and also a number of the husbands of our participating women, I unfortunately had to cancel the events.

One cannot imagine the changes that follow routinely from the notion of transport. The second courtyard is declared a *Schleuse* and cleared of all residents. It is difficult to describe what it takes to accommodate 2,500[87] people and their very extensive belongings. The elderly must be helped with packing and moving. Everything must be taken out of the room in which one had comfort-ably settled (by Theresienstadt standards), with a stool, table, and wall shelf—the foodstuffs had to be taken, and nothing could be left behind.

Everyone is preoccupied, trying to get a space for himself on the floor. And in the meantime it has become cold, and the floor proves to be a stopover that is not good for one's health. But it has to be, and it is accomplished. The transport department deploys its auxiliary workers, and so the barracks stand ready on the date ordered. On Tuesday the first 2,500 of the transport are to move in [to the second courtyard].

At the same time, we were called up as helpers and told to appear at six-thirty in the morning in Room 241 in BV to receive our orders. Since, after two years, I knew how things worked in Theresienstadt, I didn't get worked up about it and arrived at the familiar room shortly after seven-thirty. Approximately 200 men and women were already waiting. They were mostly office heads, whose age made them available for this duty, men from the court, the Leisure Time Organization, the internal administration. After an hour, I went to see to my colleagues and requested that information be sent to me about what I was wanted for.

What I now learned was very bad because the call-up included many of my associates. My secretary Sedelmeyer, whose physical condition had so far exempted him from any hard labor, had to go. The actors [Friedrich] Lerner, Dr. [Georg] Běhal, [Georg] Roth, [Friedrich] Schönfeld, the pillars of the ensemble, were taken from me. I had announced that many of them would be speaking in October. And the Leisure Time Organization itself had to give up [nearly] everyone, from the secretary, Dr. [Hans] Mautner, to the humorists [Bobby] John, [Hans] Hofer, [Ernst] Morgan, [Walter] Lindenbaum, and Smetana. Only a few actors remain, thus making it impossible to put on the plays that we had performed with such great success.

In the office of the Leisure Time Organization they sat: distraught—unem-ployed. All the work of organizing the program had been in vain. A proposal for each lecture has to be submitted in triplicate, and the plays, if they are new, must be submitted to Prague.[88] The copying places an enormous burden on the office staff, already weakened by the numbers being transferred to production. With the increased paperwork and the reduced number of personnel, one really has to put one's nose to the grindstone to be able to submit everything by the deadline. The efficient women were up to the task (the two smallest ones, nearly dwarves, Dr. Joachimsthal and Mrs. Bronsiek).

More bad tidings followed. The conductor Fischer had to go and also the great Dutch singer [Machiel Gobets] with his Siegfried-like build; the pleasant actor Stein, a humorous man from Cologne; indispensable members of the town band, along with the conductor Professor Carlo Taube; the second violinist of the Ledeč quartet, Dr. Henry Cohn. I mention these names only to show how just one order destroyed everything we had worked so hard for two years to build.

The hard necessities of war! Even the strengths of the Jews, that were proven here and found to be useful, have to be deployed somewhere—we do not know where; there is no communication—to work for the defense of Germany! Five thousand strong and willing workers will serve again wherever they are placed, with no holding back. No force or threat of punishment needed.

For nearly three years the Jews have put their ability, their will, and their skills to the test in the ghetto and before that in all the factories [that they were called up to work in]. One thing that can and no longer will be said about us is that we Jews only understand trade. This is definitively over [...]. I need only to think of our tenant, the attorney Dr. Curt Liebert, who for two years went at five o'clock every morning out to the battery plant in Niederschönweide, where he had to handle lead, and worked himself to an early death. [...]

The slips have been delivered to all 2,500 people of the first transport, and it will soon be revealed how many additional substitutes will be called. Street life changes the moment the engagement begins—the main road, that normally densely populated evening promenade, is deserted. The focal point is the Hamburg barracks, through the left wing of which the influx of men now begins.

The familiar routine is repeated. The luggage is brought in by every available means of transportation, from baby carriages to carts, pulled, of course, by human beasts of burden. One can bring only what he can carry. Depending upon one's strength, this will be a large backpack, with plates and dishes fastened to it; a smaller pack [carried] on the chest; in the left [hand] is a tied-up bedroll; and in the right [hand], a suitcase so heavy it is almost impossible to lift. At the gate, the helpers jump up to assist, without being asked, once one's name has been entered on the list. Large posters tell the incoming in which rooms they are to spend the night.

Down below, the transport staff is furiously busy at the information counter and in the administration's room behind it, where the answers to all questions are decided. The outpatient clinic does exams day and night; all the offices work without a break. Anyone deemed not fit to work or severely ill is sent to the head physician, Dr. Reinisch, whose decision [regarding fitness to work] is final and not contestable.

The post office receives powers of attorney [from the people leaving]. Workshops are set up to take care of emergency shoe and tailoring repairs, and missing articles of clothing and warm covers are handed out. The kitchen works continuously to ensure that there is enough food.

The *ultima ratio* is to apply to the Jewish elder, to appeal to SS Obersturmführer Rahm,[89] who has to decide, if the reasons for it are grave enough, whether substitutions can take place, even at the last moment, just before boarding the train. Stories, entire novels are told to this receptive gentleman, and he has to be able to reduce them to a single sentence. He has approximately 100 requests to deal with, and cannot spend a lot of time on any individual.

Slowly the courtyard fills, and people disperse to their storeys and fill the arcades. The number is everything. One cannot determine, however, where, say, to find a Mr. Meyer, since the list is not in alphabetical order. Only chance brings us together with the one we are looking for.

Night falls, and now everything becomes really difficult. The only strong sources of light are at the entrances. From outside heavy traffic between the storeys and the street. Wives are also allowed in; they bring a hot meal to the men and want to embrace them once more. Holding onto each other tightly, they walk in the courtyard, stand in the arcades, and help with sleeping arrangements. Whoever nabs a bed has it good. Below there are only straw mattresses, and if you don't get one of these, you must spend the night lying on the luggage.

At 9 P.M. complete calm descends—everyone in the ghetto must then be in their *ubikation*, and the streets are empty. Only at the open gate of the *Schleuse* is there activity throughout the night because the people who have been called up are constantly arriving. All helpers and those on duty must be at their posts by rota through the night, because there is a steady stream of men who are making requests and asking for information. The first night is generally calm—the strenuous efforts of the upsetting day have drained everyone's energy. [...]

Theresienstadt sleeps, but it is a restless sleep, not undisturbed as it has been in the last months—notices are still being served, and those who are called must start packing immediately.

The new day begins early, even before the darkness fades. All the various rumors that went around, and to which one clung so gladly, are proven to be incorrect.

The long row of carriages stands at the station road. And already the call begins for the first hundred to board with their luggage, followed by another hundred, and then a third. They leave through the rear gate, where the ghetto watch officiates, loudly calling out each number and crossing it off the list.

The relatives go with them up to the gate. One last embrace, and then the heavy backpack—carried to this point by the helper—must be heaved up, and the hands are no longer free to wave good-bye or shake. The compact line of prisoners, marching heavily, passes through the vault of the gate and disappears.

The station road is strongly barricaded, and only the ghetto watch can lend any help. After the departure, all ties are cut, and the relatives can go home; the parting is over. It was easier this time than usual. Because official assurance had been communicated: work transport for approximately six weeks. Thus the atmosphere really remained very good; one did not go out depressed, but as if the change were desirable. If the age limit—meaning those up to 58 years old—was adhered to more strictly than usual, this isn't surprising. After all, it is about physical labor—and not office work, like here. But one kept a stiff upper lip—I did not see even one person who did not remain absolutely calm and confident.

The train carried 2,500 men. Otto Zucker, engineer and member of the Council of Elders, assumed the leadership [of the transport]. He was one of the most peculiar figures among the men who headed up one of the many branches of the administration. Zucker, a man of 43 years, was born in Prague, studied there, and worked for several years in Berlin in construction, an enthusiastic Zionist and fully dedicated to its ideas. A compact, broad build, the head large, angular, full dark hair, eyes that stared intensely, energetic mouth, the whole reminiscent of Beethoven. No one had ever seen him laughing, always serious, offhand, and not forthcoming or obliging.

His style could be clearly seen in the way he implemented the dissolution of my Auxiliary Service of the Ghetto Watch. To my objection that I should be given one month's time he had only the answer, "When the administration makes decisions, they cannot be discussed any further. They are to be carried out." When he took over as supervisor of the director of the Leisure Time Organization, I had hoped for his support, he being a highly educated university graduate. But I found only the opposite. He was against the inclusion of *Nathan*, considering it stuffy and dated, and he wanted me to put on plays by Jewish authors. His attitude was not surprising, since he absolutely belongs to the Czech cultural realm and cannot adjust to a German one. I explained very firmly to him that I was too old to change and he had to take me as I am.

Strange, we so rarely had anything to do with each other, yet he was always against me, although he said to me each time that he appreciated my work and thought highly of it—however... Thus he had forbidden my comrades' savings bank, which amounted to about 10,000 krone, consisting of contributions from comrades and the donations of our friends—despite the fact that the heads of the legal department and the bank had given their consent.

Zucker changed his office repeatedly. After him, Dr. Eppstein assumed the overall direction of the Leisure Time Organization, but he was hardly concerned with its internal affairs (why should this overstretched man take on another burden?) and delegated the actual administration of it to Mr. Moritz Henschel, former chairman of the Jewish Community of Berlin.

In closing, I would like to say that this headstrong man Zucker did not have many friends, but everyone respected him because he was known as a man of honor and averse to all patronage. The official history of Theresienstadt will have much to say about his far-reaching contribution. His departure is an irreplaceable loss for the ghetto.

✳   ✳   ✳

The departure of the 2,500 took place on the day after Yom Kippur. The remaining men were called up immediately afterward, and the same process was repeated. Then came the big surprise. There was an announcement: 500 women would be called up; they should report immediately, and it would only be wives or fiancées (in the broadest sense) of men who had left in this transport. [In a few hours they were assembled. The younger people who had had to give up their fiancées felt sheer joy—they would now be reunited.][90]

Again A7 was besieged and stormed. Brides pressed to follow their beloved. Women with children here or with single parents who would be alone were in turmoil. It was not an easy decision to reach, but some just went along out of a craving for adventure. Two years in the ghetto made the desire for change very understandable, in particular among the young and beautiful. Then, one leaves the five-year-old child in the lurch and follows the beautiful, oh-so-blond lover.

A husband is called up, an attorney and homeowner [...]. His wife—once spoiled—who had proved herself in a remarkable way as the head of the warming kitchen of our house for one and a half years, immediately says that she and her adult daughter will go along. They are enlisted.

One of the finest intellects among the rabbis has to go—Albert Schön; his spiritual face is, oh, unfortunately, so pale and delicate; he seems to have lung disease. Likewise, the young rabbi Heinz Meyer from Berlin, who held services in L319 and was open to modern ideas.

In the midst of all this tribulation, I personally experienced a great pleasure. Many of my listeners came to thank me for the many beautiful evening hours that I had given them in these two years. Again and again, they expressed appreciation for my accomplishment and gave their thanks. So many men of rank and high caliber and highly cultured women spoke to me: It meant more to me than any medal of honor.

Such words create an obligation. I want to continue, to put my whole being into it to the very end and maintain the high quality of the evenings, in spite of the fact that so many participants are missing. Now I must look for new people, and I think that there are still enough "brains" here, so that there will be no lack of speakers. One must only seek them out and connect with them. The "greats" do not come forward of their own accord.

On Saturday, September 30, the call-up order was carried out. It was not yet known when the departure should take place. That depended on the arrival of the [train] carriages. The night passed calmly. Not until ten o'clock the next morning did the long train arrive, only cars with compartments, and the boarding of the train began. It ended at four o'clock. The thoroughfares were strongly barricaded. Walls of people stood at a distance and waved good-bye.

And many tears are still shed by those left behind, because we are, after all, at war and aren't certain where people will be placed. They are now again drawn into the events of these days, exposed to English bombs. Here security; over there, more disturbed nights again, which we no longer know. May the work of the 5,000 be valued as much as their dedication and consciousness of duty, as always.

A great good fortune—the weather stayed dry; on just two days was it ice cold in the early morning. Then the wind turned and blew warm again. Today, October 1, it's quite warm, and one could spend the afternoon outside on one of the quiet benches. [...]

A hard week lies behind us. Yom Kippur was overshadowed by the sad events of these days. Many men and women fasted; they could not be in a prayer room, but they held fast to the beloved old custom, even though they had to work from sunrise to sunset.

In spite of being called up on Yom Kippur. Kurt Messerschmidt had declared himself ready to serve as cantor. He performed this beautiful function in his distinguished way, with a great deal of musical artistry, accompanied by the Durra choir. An atmosphere of solemnity was achieved. The audience surely left the Sokolowna hall feeling elevated, festive, and confident.

In the dark sky, the first stars blinked, eternal heralds of the kingdom of heaven, which will come to this earth, one day when war is declared an epoch that humanity has overcome. But for us the question is, where will we spend Yom Kippur next year? In the secure Theresienstadt? Or will we be involved in fighting the battles of this war, forced to leave the land that has almost become a dear home? Who is in a position to answer this?

*   *   *

[…]

The difficult day drew to an end; it stayed dry and warm. The streets emptied early—a hard week lay behind the men and women, who in most cases had done duty day and night in the service of the transport. [Now they can] enjoy the evening a little, look at the trees, which carry their full foliage, which is barely tinged with autumn color. The wind is quiet, a pink veil of light clouds in the sky. In the garden of the home on Südstrasse the children still romp around, rushing about and frolicking themselves into exhaustion. Above, on the bastion, the last visitors—silhouetted against the starry sky—also walk toward home. The gate of the Hamburg barracks stands open and unguarded.

There is a linden tree in the second courtyard. […] There are a few fresh, bright green leaves sprouting on its bare branches. I brought this miracle to the attention of many people, and they regarded it reverentially. The young green on the old, dead wood shall proclaim the eternal passing and eternal return; it is a symbol of hope and freedom from suffering, reuniting all who are separated!

[…]

Of course, many tragicomic scenes also unfolded, because "affairs" overlap and become entangled as colorfully in the ghetto as everywhere in life. In Theresienstadt, the relations of the two sexes is no exception, and pairings occur in a light and jaunty way, as is only possible here.

Again, the entire apparatus of the *Schleuse* was in operation, and on Sunday the train could leave promptly in the direction of Germany.[91]

Already on Monday a new sensation rushed through the town. All the relatives of the 5,000, up to age 65, should immediately make themselves ready to be transported, in other words pack and perform the usual formalities—the house elders learned about this in a circular. Those listed on the family register should prepare for one of the transports departing one after the other. The call-up should begin on the night to Tuesday, October 3. According to our estimates, around 10,000 people will be affected by this unexpected measure. Right away, in every house, people adjusted to the new situation.

It is more difficult for the women who have small children to care for or have to take along several six- to ten-year-olds. Packing is difficult and time-consuming because they have to ask about each piece—urgently needed or not? You can bring with you only what you can carry. How should a mother get organized when she has three children to bring along, and what about the young women, who in two years have acquired almost a dowry's worth of dresses and clothing?

Or what of a friend, Dr. Walter Bacher, who was much envied for his private library comprising about 100 of the best books, which he brought here from Hamburg (and—just think—they were actually delivered to him)? He has to leave this treasure here, and I am asked to take it under my protection, which I am more than happy to do. Among the books, I find James Joyce's famous work *Ulysses*, in two beautiful leather volumes, and I will read it here in Theresienstadt, of all places, because I hope to have time left for this purpose. And yet another joy: *Die Heilige und ihr Narr! (The Saint and Her Fool)*.[92] But everyone must leave behind many of their belongings: The suitcases and boxes, the bags and packages lie abandoned on the empty beds and will be handed over to the appropriate authorities.

Theresienstadt is in constant motion—day and night. There are no more hours of calm. But in the offices the many desks yawn; there are only a few people present, who have nothing to do and wait eagerly for new information. We also certainly know nothing and, indeed, live only on what we hear in passing.

The call-up order was distributed, and those concerned ready themselves before moving into the billet. Supposedly, the train would depart during the night. Those in the know were skeptical that it would happen on time, remained at home, and slept once more in their [...] beds, avoiding the noise and chaos of the *Schleuse*.

This time leadership of the transport was shared by Salo Krämer from Prague, the member of the Council of Elders, who was an eager visitor to the lectures and supported me, as only he could, and Franz Kahn, head of the lecture activities [of the Leisure Time Organization], one-armed leader of the Zionist movement in Prague. I said good-bye to them in the evening, and saw the chaos in the otherwise well-maintained dwellings in BV—it wasn't pretty.

Wednesday [October 11, 1944] dawned icy cold. The clocks had to be put back an hour at midnight, and with it the summer, the summer of our discontent, is officially ended. [...]

The transport proceeded chaotically this time in that people weren't called by number, and therefore the crowd pushed and shoved with their bulky baggage trying to be among the first allowed through the narrow gate to the train.

Many children of all ages were included. [...] The administration had provided very well for the children: Each of the little ones received 20 decagrams of chocolate, 6 decagrams of margarine, 10 decagrams of sugar, a *buchtel*, and hot boiled milk. [...]

In the meantime, the first cards arrive with a message reporting safe arrival and "news" about work and the usual food.[93] All the participants showed cheerful countenances.

A woman who is about 75 years old explains that she is going to join her only son.

Now the courtyard clears; the rooms on both floors are cleaned, and then the gates open again to receive the next transports. The biggest gift, however, is the dryness and the sun, which at lunchtime gives us the warmth we miss.

* * *

October! Autumn month. It has sent two of its representatives—the first is a demanding master who comes bringing cold and fog. [...] The other appears around lunchtime as a charming gentleman, elegantly dressed—green is still his favorite color—but he is also fond of brown, in hues from red to bright gold. The sun accompanies him everywhere and tries to make up for what it failed to do in the morning—to give us some warmth. [...]

We gratefully enjoy the grace period that nature has given us; we can still be outside until five o'clock, when there is work to do: We have to get the evening meal—that doesn't take very long; if you live close to Magdeburg, the lines are short. Water must be brought in and wood chopped in order to get the stove in the kitchen working. The *ubikations* are not allowed to be heated yet, but the little stoves serve more for warming up meals than for heating. Now the skills of the men are tested in trying to solve the most difficult problem: getting the wood and coal. Every day, four or five railway cars arrive—today there are about 14, piled high, standing at the station road—and our efficient workers have to unload them at night. Wagons pile the coal in front of the cellars of the barracks, in big heaps; the houses also get such loads, and so the coal supply seems assured.

But wood! That is a cross to bear! The little bit of kindling each individual receives is "for the birds"; it is barely enough to light the fire. So that means, be on the lookout for wood everywhere; once a day one really must have a hot meal, and the rest of the food that is given out is only lukewarm. And we manage because we can light the cooking stove in our room twice a day.

* * *

The transport continues.

This time the war wounded had to go up before the gentlemen of the Department, and it was they who determined who had to leave Theresienstadt.

And then those who were in, or had been in mixed marriages were summoned and asked about their family circumstances. On Thursday, [October] 5th, the ones who had stayed behind after the last transport [the substitutes] were again called up and had to prepare to leave with the rest, starting at 6 A.M.[94]

Already, the courtyard of the Hamburg barracks is brightly lit, and the helpers and officials stand ready to receive the arrivals. I was also called up to help but was sent home again in consideration of my age because there was only heavy night work to do. No, I no longer wish to stay up all night, no longer have the strength for it. I need to go to sleep early in order to husband my energies; I simply can't stay up late anymore.

My friends were of the same opinion. [...] They are ten years younger than I and gladly take the night duty, which nearly always consists of sleeping because a transport has never yet been dispatched during the night, possibly in the early morning hours. Then the Jupiter lamps[95] light up; the arcade and the courtyard come alive; and a jumble of voices and loud calls begin. People shuffle out of all the rooms and down the stairs with all their luggage, and then they stand there for hours until their number is called. Then the waiting people push themselves forward slowly, step-by-step, to the gated entryway, which is lit up as bright as day and admits the crowd. A last wave, a look around, and the railway car is ready for boarding—*addio* Theresienstadt!

Those who were called up have been in the *Schleuse* since Friday evening—they were supposedly to go in the night. Friday passed, and nothing stirred in the courtyard. The rear gates remained closed, indicating that the transport wasn't ready. Those called swarm out, fetch things they have forgotten, buy what they need in the shops, and in the evening must be back in their assigned rooms because checks can be carried out at any time. In the ghetto itself everything is at a standstill, with the exception of the operations outside that have again begun in the usual way. The group makes its pilgrimage to change shifts outside in the southern area, where in the huts the night activity is carried out by hundreds of industrious hands.

The transport leaves in the night from Saturday to Sunday at [ ] o'clock.

*   *   *

It is infinitely difficult for me to write about a subject that is of the greatest importance in Theresienstadt, and has a great impact on all affairs. I went back and forth for a long time about whether to mention it at all or whether to just make a few passing remarks that would say nothing and conceal much. [Yet] we cannot, as observant inhabitants of Theresienstadt, avoid this subject because it intrudes into all the *ubikationen* and is an essential part of daily life for nearly all people who are beyond puberty.

I wanted to call this section "Morality in Theresienstadt." I discussed this topic with many men my age and tried to get them to share details of their experiences and observations. Judges told me about the fates of the 700 children—they came without parents, without relatives—and the ghetto cares for those who will never know the warmth of a mother's love. Attorneys spoke only of divorces, thefts, insults to honor, and other misdemeanors, which were all too frequent. The house elders said: "Yes, we experienced all sorts in these two years, but to tell…No, why stir up dirt? One knows enough anyway to fill volumes." From the physicians: "*Nihil humani me alienum puto.*"[96] And no more information could be brought out of them, but what they told me about the health of the young girls who come to the outpatient clinic did not allow me to research further into this area.

I am personally ignorant in these delicate areas. When all one's days are spent working, and the evening hours as well, almost until sleep comes, there is little time left in which to worry about [romantic] affairs in Theresienstadt. Every now and then an all-too-colorful story is reported, like this one:

It was in January—the husband comes home unusually early from night work and finds his wife and her beau, who happens to be a well-known actor, in an unambiguous situation. He takes the clothes, which have been placed carefully on a chair, and throws them out the window—and her beau out the door. The beau had to run to the police station wearing only his vest, in January. Lucky that it was dark.

Or, in the office, two "ladies" slap each other. They have been with the same man and believe that in this way they can secure him as all their own.

And this last true story: An attorney from Berlin who is in a most agitated state comes to the court to request its assistance. His only daughter, 17 years old, is with the transport, following her boyfriend. In order to accomplish this, she had said nothing to her father about her intentions. Her mother is dead; the girl does not have adequate supervision. Nothing can be done; one cannot bring back the girl forcibly. As I said—volumes.

No, I will not write this chapter. I would have to become very, very bitter and tell truths, which the gossips of Theresienstadt are spreading far and wide.

Whom God gives an office, he should also give—where "love" is concerned (although I, as an old idealist, use this word in the present context most reluctantly)—the requisite understanding; more still, the proper restraint. It won't do that one makes laws for the others, punishes them, and dismisses them from service for small misdemeanors, and at the same time takes the view, "do as I say, not as I do" in private life.

I cannot go along with the apologetic drivel: The ghetto engenders different laws and ways of life. No and once again no. It is precisely here that we have to uphold the fundamentals of Jewish ethics. Are we to wash our dirty laundry before the eyes of the authorities who are watching us closely? [...]

Don't say that the separation of the sexes—husband from wife—encourages ethical laxity and the exercising of freedoms that would have been impossible at home. We men were at war for three and a half years. The married ones guarded against taking the opportunities that were offered so readily—such as in Warsaw and other large cities. We had a sense of dignity and knew what we owed our wives.

At that time, it was the belief of the German officers that most Jewish girls, despite the flirting that they were not averse to, did not give themselves. And Gronemann[97] writes about Vilna, "These girls let themselves be invited to coffee, stuff as much as possible into themselves—at home they have nothing to eat—and when they are full, they disappear."

If our young people, who work hard and are in the fresh air all day long, take their right to friendship and love and choose the way themselves, we must stay out of it. The youth in Theresienstadt live according to their own laws. They live under constraint, inhibited in their development, and do not know the youthful pleasure of going to a dance or hiking, so they have to carve out their existence in a different way. There is a lot to be said on this subject, as the heads of the youth welfare service could tell you.

*　*　*

This prominent man [Dr. Arthur Eichengrün] had been brought to my attention several times as being one of the most interesting men in the ghetto because he was the greatest inventor in our German chemical industry. I knocked on his door several times at the house on Seestrasse 20, but without success; the door always remained locked. Its inhabitant took advantage of the wonderful weather to find rest outside [of the house].

Today, I probably came a little earlier than usual and gained admittance. But, on account of the housecleaners, he was still in bed. Quickly donning a house jacket, a blanket over his knees, he offered me a seat, and the interview began. It was not easy for me to start. The person opposite me was a scholar, researcher, and examiner, and he also wanted to know from me whither this journey. This was understandable because he had probably in his entire life not had the time to tell stories. Surely, he has never sent his thoughts backward, but only forward. Three-quarters of the day, his brain went in new, unknown directions; he perceived, pondered, and raised speculative problems, allowing himself no peace until they were solved, the goal reached.

After hearing only his first few words, I appeared infinitely small to myself. How can you dare to approach such a great intellect, to question him, and ask him to spread out his life before you!? But, I told myself, in this milieu you are allowed to carry out this rather impudent undertaking because you want to serve the community by showing what great intellects live here in the ghetto.

Outside, this would have been a matter for scholars; they would have marked October 1, the 50th anniversary of the day that led the young scientist to IG Farben[98] by writing long papers [about it]. Festschrifts would have appeared, and on his golden anniversary, the University of Erlangen would have held a magnificent ceremony to celebrate him and renew his doctorate. The whole scientific world would have flocked around this famous son of Germany and paid homage to the man who gave the world aspirin. Here in Theresienstadt, he was commemorated only by the nurse who cared for him every day, who placed autumn flowers and a cake on the table.[99]

[…]

✳   ✳   ✳

When I came home, the latest notification had already been posted everywhere:

> All persons up to age 65 must prepare for transport and have luggage weighing up to 30 kg ready for call-up on the night of Saturday to Sunday, October 8. Bedrolls and washbowls may not be carried. The call-up will proceed only when the written order is given to the individual by the house elder.

This new and frightening proclamation struck the inhabitants of the ghetto like a bolt of lightning out of a clear blue sky. We had reckoned that work transports would still go up to the age of 60, but we were completely unprepared for the extent of this. It meant evacuation of everyone but the old and infirm. Petrified, we sat in our room, which soon became like an information booth. Our house, Q211, mostly accommodates women, and they now vehemently demanded advice and assistance.

The first call-ups came toward the evening, and the enormous sorting and packing began. What has to be left behind from two years' accumulation? How does one choose? Which method of rolling and tying everything up is the most secure? Our Julius Weiler, himself called up that night, worked as a calm, thoughtful helper. He packed the ladies' backpacks and knew all the right words to say. His courageous wife still cooked and baked potato dishes for the trip, and at the end made the room "spick-and-span."

It has become quiet in the house and the courtyard. The noisy Brockmann children, who got on our nerves from the first thing in the morning until the last thing at night, have gone. The mistress of the warming kitchen, Dr. Löwenstein, left with her husband and daughter, and a sign on the door reads: "Closed." Our rooms, once noisy and overcrowded, are nearly empty.

What a transformation! What *Sukkoth*, what a Simchat Torah celebration![100] A hard week lies before us. We, too, will prepare for departure. We are in no way safe, because every hour can bring new orders.

* * *

Approximately 2,700 people [who were getting ready to leave] moved into the barracks; there is a steady stream of people in and out because if no count is taken and inmates are obliged to be in their rooms, the gate is not guarded. Once the transport begins, things are very strict.

One notices the first signs—the Czech gendarmes close off the station road. From that moment on, the call can take place at any minute, and boarding the train can begin. On Sunday, the original date, complete calm. There were some exemptions and rearrangements, but they do not change the number. Only the reserve have any hope, anyone who gets a high number can reckon on being dismissed, if not too many are excused because of illnesses or exemption. The night passed undisturbed. The morning dawned hazy; low clouds covered the sky; it drizzled continuously, settling the dust on the road, which was welcome.

This transport deeply affects the existence of the ghetto, and if the transports, with the numbers of three times 2,000, are really carried out as announced, Theresienstadt will exist only as an old folk's home, in which 70-year-olds belong to the youngest group.

In every corridor I meet dear friends or acquaintances whose call-up is worn on a tag around their neck. One does not need to ask, "You too?" Here is Wilhelm Sterk, the Viennese poet, on whose behalf I tried to intervene that afternoon after he appealed to Dr. Murmelstein. [...] The small, splendid Mrs.

Mansbach, once the big wheel in Room 76; the little girls, whose recitations were so charming; the beautiful Miss Schönemann, who made her debut as Sappho; Miss Bick, so fresh and cheeky as Lieschen, Gretchen's friend at the well.[101] And so many from my audience who come up to thank me and to shake my hand once more.

In between, children of all ages play and make noise, using every cart and clamoring loudly through the corridors on both floors. There is a great bustle outside the kitchen—large portions of food are being given out, and one is not mean. At four o'clock in the afternoon there is still no change in the situation.

[...]

* * *

In the *Schleuse*—to which I have admission—I couldn't do anything to help. People had adapted to the situation and had only one desire: that the train would arrive so the usual procedure could begin.

The warm weather continued. At five o'clock the gendarmes moved up and closed the station road, indicating that the departure would likely be soon. And so it was. The order was issued in the rooms to get ready for the call. Teams of helpers, strong chaps with white caps, stood ready to carry [luggage] where necessary. Boarding began at about seven o'clock and ended after midnight.

Sixteen hundred people went with this transport; the rest stayed behind and have to be ready for the next one. Good-bye, all my beloved friends—may you feel the same duty to work and remain strong and courageous, just as [you were] here in Theresienstadt, which you leave with heavy hearts.

* * *

[...]

We were allowed to rest for one day, and then the preparations began for the next transport, which had been announced. Since the ghetto was informed about who was to go, there were no surprises and, above all, no rushed preparations. Those who thought they were going took care of their affairs and packed. Bedrolls were again permitted; a few kilos more did not matter. When I saw what most people schlepped, I realized how generous the German authorities were and how tolerant they were about people taking too much.

On Wednesday, October 11, the barracks began to fill again, although many of those who had been called spent the night "at home," coming in at 9 A.M. for the count. After the meal, toward one o'clock, everyone had to go to the billet. The administration functioned perfectly; nothing was left undone. The officials have been at their posts since noon yesterday—transport direction, information, post office, outpatient clinic, doctors, all the auxiliary personnel, the young helpers, the fresh girls in their gray and brown work trousers.

The buxom Liesel courageously carries the heaviest backpacks. As often as I see this really beautiful, blond girl, her lovely, pretty, and still self-confident face, which I have now known for two years, gives me pleasure.

The morning passes calmly, but there is brisk activity everywhere. The warmth of the sun tempts one to linger in the courtyard, and people are still wandering around the town. Some are hoping to secure their release through an audience with Dr. Murmelstein or a member of the Council of Elders. A waste of time. Only the Department is in a position to grant release, and I know that each justified complaint is heard. Nothing is rejected outright. Even before boarding the train, one can still present oneself to the head of the Department and press him for a decision. One is not completely defenseless, but the reason must be convincing.

This time the transport includes:

Philipp Kozower—Head of the post office
Dr. Walter Löwinger—Head of accommodation and office allocation
Arthur Weisl—Commander of the ghetto watch
Leon Neuberger—Deputy commander of the ghetto watch
Julius Grünberger—Engineer
Karl Stahl—Engineer, head of the supplies office
Dr. Desider Friedmann—Head of the bank
Field Marshal Lieutenant Johann Georg Friedländer

to name only a few of the prominent.[102]

There is a large number of my acquaintances. If I were to name everyone who stretched out their hands as I went around the rooms to thank me for the lecture evenings, I really would have to fill several pages. In this heartfelt and sincere gratitude that is expressed at each transport, I experience how the humble amateur work of a fur trader was appreciated by the simple and the scholarly, and that makes me joyful and happy.

Every good-bye is difficult for me. It is quite certain that I will never see them again.

There, my dear couple the Strausses sit on their luggage. He, cheerful and merry in his blue work suit (the good one is underneath). She is smart, as always, but has obviously been crying. We chat once more, reminisce about the two years we have known each other and the work that brought us closer. But now the dear doctor will no longer get round to writing the Theresienstadt poem with the Fontane-like refrain that he promised me: "Yes, I'd still like to live to see that."

They pick up their luggage, which I assume contains more literature than important articles of clothing. What poems and sketches, of every kind, the two have tirelessly produced here! May they both find an agreeable place to continue their work, and may their call "See you in Vienna" be realized.

Dr. Martin Kraemer approaches to say good-bye, that stately, slim man, that indefatigable poet, who last week still wrote an expansive opus about all the personalities in Theresienstadt. He is a colorful personality: doctor of law, *Hofrat*, cavalry captain in the reserve, and a highly decorated war veteran. And his wife, Valerie, Duchess of Alençon, is the granddaughter of Empress Elisabeth's sister, who burned so miserably in Paris.[103]

Rabbi Regina Jonas, 42 years old, graduated in 1922, and then seven years of study at the Academy of Jewish Studies [Lehranstalt für die Wissenschaft des Judentums], became a rabbi in 1930, active in pastoral care in hospitals and convalescent homes. She took many official trips throughout Germany to preach and hold services in the smallest communities, the only woman in Germany to choose such a career and succeed in it—because she possessed all the competence of her male colleagues. Here in Theresienstadt she was not able to assert herself properly. Here, one was too pious and not tolerant enough. She accompanied her old mother, from whom she did not want to separate.

From the attorneys: Dr. Joel Kamp, from Bielefeld, a well-known defense lawyer in Westphalia, who earned his laurels in sensational murder trials [...]. He met an unusual fate. He was separated from his daughter in Amsterdam, found her again here after a year, only to lose her again now. Unfortunately, all his efforts [to get a release] were unsuccessful, and there was nothing he could do but to come to terms with the fact.

Melly Weiß, the charming diseuse and singer, is the daughter of Adolf Weiß, director of the German Folk Theater in Vienna (mother, Irma Wachtel from Hamburg), an opera soubrette and the sister of the well-known singer Weiß. She waved at me through the window; she had spotted me on the street and wanted to bid me adieu. She is a lively, very well-maintained, self-confident artist, who traveled all over Europe to sing and speak in seven languages. Her repertoire ranged from classical to musical comedy. In *Faust* she spoke the part of Helena. But she kept from me at all costs her date of birth—she was too vain to reveal that.

Many of my old comrades from the Orientation Service also had to go: Hugo Weinmann, once my deputy, and his wife, who was still being treated following serious surgery; Nathan Mayer, Libowski, Neumann, Steinberg, Lewitt. The head of the women's section, Mrs. Frič, was leaving with her husband, who had held a high position in the supplies office. One of my most eager listeners, Mandelbrod waited upstairs for the call, in the same room with his beautiful daughter and his delicate, blind wife, who bore her hard fate so patiently and very calmly, faced traveling, once more, into the unknown.

I want to close the list. It is too painful for me, because there are just too many who will leave my field of vision forever.

I help out below, as much as my strength will allow. The train advances one car at a time, as each is filled. Then they are counted, and the travel provisions are passed inside. Thus the Theresienstadt episode concludes, and 1,500 people pull away, [heading] to an unknown destination.

*   *   *

Friday, October [13]. Overnight, the great magician autumn made his entrance in Theresienstadt. Most of the trees have changed color, transformed into all shades of yellow and brown. [...] In the afternoon we sit for two rather enjoyable hours in the still-warm sun at the sheep pen, where one is protected, and only a few people pass by.

The children are led in groups by their caregivers to the redoubts and can cavort on the lawn. The mountains are mostly covered with snow. In the gardens the harvest is being brought in. I receive some small samples: recently matured ears of corn that taste wonderful boiled in saltwater, also tomatoes or a small cabbage, which is for us a welcome contribution to the meager midday meal, feeding us twice. The menu has remained the same in the last weeks. Extract soup; potatoes with different sauces; more rarely, vegetables; and once a week a *buchtel* [...]. The soups that are given out in the evening are mostly thick and are therefore satisfying. Meat comes in the form of meatballs or canned blood sausage and liver sausage. This is usually enough for three evenings, if served sparingly. Bread, sugar, and margarine are served regularly and on time. Today,

60 decagrams of good jam was distributed, a long-awaited and much-anticipated event.

It has become quiet in the offices; most of the workforce is gone. At the moment there is nothing to administer; things are completely unsettled. One does not know if the age limit will be held at 65 or raised to 70. The next transport is supposed to go on Sunday, followed by another, but this is as yet an unconfirmed rumor. For me there is only one thing: to calmly continue my work as usual, and to be composed and ready, when our time comes.

After the several days' break occasioned by the transport, I was able to resume [my interview] and add another chapter [to his life's story]. In the interim Dr. Gradnauer had made notes and prepared.

At the beginning [of the interviews] the gentlemen are a little bit reluctant, but once they get warmed up, they take a sort of wistful pleasure in looking back, and then they become intensely engaged in remembering the faded sequence of events that took place half a century ago. Now, they fancy writing a book: "About My Life," but that is impossible with all the to-do [of the transports]. So for the present, this biographical deposition of mine has to suffice. If fate allows the old gentlemen to keep their health, they will dedicate themselves to the enormous task when they are in more favorable circumstances. [...]

* * *

The evacuation continues at an accelerated pace. The entire administration is presented to the Department [i.e., the Germans], and they will determine who will go with the next transport and who will remain here for the time being. All measures taken [to date] lead one to conclude that only the old people who are mobile, and thus able to quickly prepare for the transport if necessary, will remain here. The sick are to be sent on a transport now, which indicates that my conjecture might be correct. Preparedness is, once again, everything.

On Saturday the 14th [of October] the inflow to the *Schleuse* began, and the processing took place in the usual way. Many people who have become very dear to me are included. All of them approach and thank me for my work over the past two years, emphasizing what I have given to them and that they do not want to forget me.

There is the genteel, distinguished *Hofrat*, Dr. Paul Langer, from Vienna, who in his hometown had been the director of the revenue office. He was a well-educated man who knew literature well and was one of my constant visitors.

Trude Pick, the pretty, youthful director of the department of "allowances," who was mobbed every morning by hundreds of applicants and claimants and had to decide, without assistance, how much to give and to whom. She and her aides examined and wrote indefatigably, and made grants generously, for as long as there was something to give. She was a tireless worker who never got ruffled. She should have remained here, but because her mother was going, she accompanied her.

The Strebinger family, my oldest listeners, had a firm place with me. He, working in the employment office, always helped me out with writing materials and was most enthusiastically interested in the development and continuation of the lecture series. He frequently brought me fruits from his garden—cabbage, tomatoes, corn. He came with these beautiful "allowances," even if it was late in the evening.

Rabbi Dr. Salomonski, from Berlin, who had to let his son go two weeks ago, now followed him.

Dr. Phil. Walter Unger said good-bye to me; he was a unique personality who had given lectures for me on several occasions. He had had his greatest success when he spoke about the growth of the Kempinski Company in Berlin.[104]

He was born in Berlin on August 21, 1894. His father was a banker and a partner of Kempinski's. He completed his *Abitur* [final school examination] in 1913, and then took part in the 1915–1918 campaign, earning the Iron Cross 1st class; he was also second lieutenant in the reserve. Studied in Grenoble, Berlin, and Freiburg; in 1920 earned a Ph.D. with a dissertation on number theory, his favorite topic. Joined the Kempinski Company and was made partner in 1924. He directed the finance department of the giant enterprise. He was interested in India and Near Eastern culture, and he gave deep and searching lectures about these topics to small audiences. Recently, he had studied Gaelic and Celtic in order to translate a work written in these languages: *Figures from the Earth*, which he set in verse. A splendid person who will, hopefully, realize his personal and literary plans.

My choir conductor Willi Durra also has to go, while his young wife, an efficient draftswoman and excellent caricaturist, remains here.[105] When I called on Durra to succeed Alexander Weinbaum of the Auxiliary Service of the Ghetto Watch, it was only in order to provide him with an environment in which to pursue his valuable activity. In a short time he assembled a double quartet, and what he accomplished with this small, efficient band is registered in the annals of the arts in Theresienstadt. He was a charming, engaging man, always calm and conciliatory, who completely lived for his art, wrote out all the music himself, and studied with each singer separately, until he had taken the amateurs to where he needed them. Knowledgeable and highly musical, he simultaneously conducted and sang the bass part himself. It was particularly beautiful when he sang with his wife. Now the choir is scattered to the wind, and their beautiful art will give us no more pleasurable hours. It was a wistful parting for many of us, although we all have the prospect of seeing each other again, in the new, large camp in Germany.[106]

The day was warm and partly sunny, the greatest gift the sky could have sent. At two o'clock in the morning the long train left the station road, the bright electric lights were put out, and the many helpers who had unceasingly exerted themselves in their blessed work were permitted the rest they so deserved.

*　*　*

Theresienstadt has a different face—the streets are empty, the elderly walk, not to say creep, silently along. Our young people have for the most part gone away to work somewhere. The war, which until now had not touched us, now extends its greedy paws toward us, too, in our seclusion.

If our life is, once again, changed from the ground up, this is the bitter imperative, the hard necessity of the final battle, which draws on everyone who still has the use of their limbs.

I can understand that one takes 15,000 workers from here in order to use their forces there, where they are needed. I don't believe that they will stop at 65 years—I reckon that those up to age 70 will be utilized, and that we, who at the moment feel safe, should prepare for the call-up, at least mentally, and hold ourselves ready.

It is warm on this peaceful Monday. We are just glad to have one day without the nerve-wracking call-up. But the registry is already at work preparing the narrow, colored, flat 1-cm-wide slips, which are affixed to the summons.

At midday there was an air-raid alarm, which lasted for two hours and prevented us from fetching our meal. After the "all-clear" signal, we had to line up for a very long time, advancing to the counter inches at a time to get soup, 30 decagrams of potatoes, and sauce. In the evening there were coffee and five small, unripe tomatoes, which taste very good cooked and sweetened.

When one meets acquaintances whose age one does not know, it is a doubly happy greeting: "Oh! You are still here?!"

In the Leisure Time Organization it is bleak and empty. Only Dr. Cohn, from Breslau, sits at his table and waits in vain [to audit] the accounts from the evening events. Everything has been canceled, and when I am out, I am so often asked when I will take up the lectures again. I can only shrug my shoulders.

If anything is to be offered at all, the organization will need to be rebuilt. Rabbi Weiner, Dr. Mautner, Dr. Kahn, Professor Kantorowicz, and most of the office ladies are gone. Only Mr. Henschel reigns, from his beautiful private apartment on the second floor of BV, but he hardly has any vassals.

If something is to be offered, it can only be based on my example [i.e., by organizing lectures]. All the musicians and singers are gone; even Professor Ledeč waved his Kalabreser in a parting gesture.[107] Only the piano and the spoken word remain. Whether we will get around to doing it or not is more than questionable. I myself hope to help out in the sick rooms. Professor Stein, the director of the department, wants to use me there.

Q307 is changed. The elder who was so attached to me [...], Polack, has gone away with his wife and daughter, as have most of the occupants of this well-maintained house. Only the old bookbinder, engineer Löwinger, who makes a hobby of this handicraft and tinkers and binds a great deal—all these volumes in which I write have been made by him as well—now lives all alone in the once overcrowded, and now abandoned, ground-floor room. The Strausses resided across from him and produced and rehearsed their pretty [theatrical] sketches and poems there. Next door, the fat Meyer, once a wealthy cigar trader in Cologne, and a few others from Cologne who had arrived together, went together. In parting they said, "It all has been going well, and it will continue to go well."[108]

The loft stands empty. The poster listing the cast of *Cyrano* still hangs on the wall. All the cast are gone. I can only dedicate a sad thought to them, who have now forever disappeared from my horizon.

*   *   *

On Sunday [October 15], [Rabbi] Dr. Salomonski[109] delivered one of a series of lectures for the days of prayer and repentance. On Monday, as a solemn prelude to the Day of Atonement, the Durra choir was to sing psalms, and Arnfeld, with his powerful voice, was to recite. That didn't happen anymore. Since last Sunday's event, which was only poorly attended, all meetings have been suspended. No matter how often I am asked, I can give no answer; there is no point at the moment to even discuss it.

So I can dedicate myself fully to the task of describing the men of importance and the work in Theresienstadt. The latter will be difficult because most of the men who knew me and could provide information are no longer here. And there would have been so much to report about everything that has been achieved here. This whole book may be nothing less than a lofty hymn to Jewish achievements. The German authorities set up the correct principle: self-administration.

Thus whatever we wanted, we had to create for ourselves. To a large extent, the necessary materials were supplied—for example, timber—but it was left to Jewish hands to make something out of them. For creating this necessity, we are thankful to the authorities. It was only because of this that the energies that had slumbered in those who formerly did mental work were awakened, and if the upper age brackets are today being summoned, this is right and proper. If the ghetto is to remain for the old, it must mobilize the remaining forces to try to take the place of those who have gone.

All new orders, which are not always comfortable for the individual, must be viewed from this perspective. If we now create for ourselves our modest life, we will be allowed to live here; if not, we must be part of the great resettlement drive, which leads to the unknown.

Thus I turn to a really interesting task—describing the lives of people who made something of themselves and have something to say.

I begin with the attorney Ernst Moos, from Ulm. We became acquainted while sitting next to each other in the provisional office of the transport management, and started to chat. I was pleased to hear the cozy Swabian dialect, and given that I know well all the beautiful cities of southern Germany, like Regensburg, Augsburg, Ulm, and Tübingen, from my travels, we had a lot in common and could talk about our beloved homeland. During yesterday's air raid, we had enough time, and this splendid person told me about his life.

"I was born on April 12, 1884, in Ulm. My father was a manufacturer and wholesale merchant and, like my mother, reached the age of 74. My mother's family was quite prominent. My grandfather, whose name was *Geheimer Kommerzienrat* von Steiner, had his domicile at Castle Laupheim, near [Ulm]. When the Commander's Cross of the Order of the Crown of Württemberg was conferred on him in appreciation of his service to the state, he was raised to the hereditary nobility.

"My grandfather was the founder of the Württemberg Vereinsbank [a bank]; the leader of the German Party, stood as a candidate for the Tariff Parliament,[110] and a man who put all his time and ability at the disposal of the state, wherever he was needed. And he was needed.

"My great-grandfather was wealthy and, likewise, very respected. He bought Castle Laupheim from Baron von Welden, who could not keep it because he was badly in debt. Over the gates, engraved already long ago: 'Into this castle, no Jew steps.' Oh irony of fate! The owner had to yield, and a Jew moved into the castle, which has remained in the family to this day. His great-grandson Uli Steiner (half Aryan) is the owner. So much for my ancestors.

[...]

"After the [First World] War I opened my practice again, strongly determined to keep myself out of any political activity. I was of the opinion that Jews should hold themselves back and not enter the arena of [the wider] public life. I have stuck by this until this time. I was always influenced by the ideology of Naumann, the land reformer, and grounded myself in his political doctrine.[111] [...]

"I worked intensively on Jewish affairs, became the leader of the Jews of Württemberg. I established the *Kulturbund* and represented the Jewish community until recently."

*   *   *

In this context I would like to express my attitude toward politics. Political education was never talked about in our youth, least of all at school, and except for the Social Democrats, the political parties had no time at all for young people. They were left to find their own way; it did not occur to anyone to create youth associations for [the purpose of] political education.

Thus my generation hardly knew the word "politics," and we knew nothing of the events in the world. The debates in the Reich and state parliaments did not concern us. When we were old enough to vote, we supported our father's candidate. We did not go to election meetings; doing so was a waste of time. During my ten years of traveling, [my knowledge of] politics was limited to what I read in the newspapers. I had no political orientation abroad either, because there one spoke about politics even less.

When I established myself permanently in Berlin, I joined the district tax commission of my borough and had to examine appeals. I enjoyed that because I became acquainted with people and conditions that until then had been unknown to me. I was actually [...] under consideration as a city councilor. The war came, and I remained in Russia until December 1918, and was a soldier until March 1919 because I, along with my captain, Gess,[112] from Constance, had to close down the field bookshops. Then in May 1920, I founded the Association of Berlin Furriers, remained chairman for seven years, and then assumed the deputy's position and in my free time dedicated myself completely to technical reporting for the trade newspapers at home and abroad.

So it was this extensive work—from 1928 to 1930 I belonged to the steering committee of the Leipzig "IPA" [International Fur Goods Exposition]—that kept me completely tied up and away from politics. I also possessed no natural bent or inclination for it. I understood nothing about it and always refused to discuss political things.

I have kept it that way to this day.

* * *

Hugo Friedmann, born April 10, 1901, in Vienna; his father was Jacob Friedmann, consul, bank director, and well-known Midrasch expert and researcher.[113]

Friedmann grew up in a strictly religious but wealthy household and could devote himself completely to his interests. Grammar school in Vienna, *Abitur* 1920, and then to university, to study law and art history. Changed over to industry and, in order to learn everything from the bottom up, worked three weeks as a boilerman in the textile mill, and a worker in the business. After this thorough training he became departmental manager, 1922, in Teplitz-Turn. In 1925 he set himself up independently in the knitwear industry. He was active in professional associations in Austria and associate judge at a court of trade. Besides these moneymaking activities, he was a servant of art and knowledge as art adviser to the Jewish religious community; lecturer at the Jewish college for adult education, department of the history of art; honorary gallery guide at the art-historical museum; and curator of the Jewish museum. Personal interests: bibliophile and art collector. After the Anschluss,[114] he was departmental head and deputy head of the religious community in Vienna.

When the library in L3 was opened in Theresienstadt, Friedmann became the acting director, while Professor Utitz was responsible to the [German] authorities.

Here, his organizational ability and his great professional knowledge proved itself. He knew every author and their work; he was as much at home in the area of belles lettres as in rigorous science. He knew the collection by heart and could always say whether or not a requested book was available. No friend of bureaucracy, if the library had been run according to his ideas, it would have developed faster and better and been a greater blessing. Professors always act with the best intentions, naturally, but hold things back terribly. We businessmen see things differently; are practical men.[115]

[...]

Friedmann had to leave his library in the beautiful rooms of Parkgasse 14, which he had so splendidly arranged according to subject—making everything easy to find—to travel into the unknown with his wife, son, and daughter.

* * *

[…]

Wednesday, [October] 18 [1944]. No sun the whole day. The arrangements for tomorrow's transport continued until the afternoon, and the billeting followed at once; the gates were besieged and are crowded with carts. As usual, the young and the old work again as a team, ready to help. In the evening it starts to rain heavily. One guesses that the departure will take place tomorrow. The order comes that everyone must be gathered by the afternoon—anyone who is missing and has to be found by the detective department must leave their heavy luggage behind. Many friends are included. The health service to a large extent, among them my devoted listener Professor [Dr. Ernst] Herzfeld, from Berlin. Dr. [Wilhelm] Dreyer with his splendid wife. He headed the department of war wounded extremely well, and now, because he is too young, he himself must go. But he will be able to continue his work in the new ghetto, like all the rest. *So here's to all of you who were so devoted, working both day and night. Indeed, much too little has been said or made known to the public about your accomplishments.* I must reiterate it again and again, this ought to be my main undertaking, this recording of the work of the ghetto that in later times will offer evidence of the assertive Jewish will.

The transport left the ghetto at three o'clock in the morning.

* * *

On the night of Tuesday to Wednesday, October 18, 1944, *Geheimrat* Professor Dr. Strauß, from Berlin, died of a heart attack at age 76. In the afternoon he was still hale and hearty, speaking animatedly, interested in everything. In the last few days many people approached him, hoping to receive exemption from the transport through his intercession—that had upset the old gentleman very much, and he suffered visibly from the dissolution of the health service, for all his staff and nurses had been taken for deployment in the new work place.

[…]

Geheimrat Strauß had given me his friendship and engaged with me in the most kind and unforced manner. He was greatly interested in my efforts. […] He often came with his wife to the lectures, heard all the plays enthusiastically, and was never sparing with words of appreciation.

He, himself, participated in my lecture series with great pleasure. The last time was to commemorate the 100th birthday of Robert Koch. His descriptions of the great Berlin physicians from around 1900 were extremely lively, as were those of his travels in the East.

He was planning two new lectures and was looking forward to them because they led him back into the past, which he loved.

He spoke standing behind the table, declining the comfortable upholstered chair. Sometimes the lecture lasted one and a half hours without tiring him even minimally. During his lively speech one completely forgot that he was 76 years old.

[...]

On August 25, 1944, he wrote in my album:

> *Docendo discimus* was always a great inspiration to me during my academic teaching.[116] Here this becomes further strengthened by another feeling: the uplifting consciousness that by sharing my knowledge and experience with unhappy, oppressed companions in fate I give them comfort and stimulation. Therefore I will long remember, both as a lecturer and a listener, the hours I spent in the Manes circle. Much luck for further successes.

* * *

[...]

Friday, October 20, 1944. At night it rains as it did intermittently all day, which was quite dark. Mrs. Von Giżycki let me know that she was going to practice in the Sokolowna at nine thirty, and I arrived punctually. The house lies desolate, the weeping willows—still untouched by the autumn—guard it; the gates are locked. The caretaker, an elderly lady, the mother of Dr. Fantl, has remained behind. Steps echo in the empty corridors and the halls. The chairs in the terrace hall are set up in rows ready to be used, but, I fear, they will not be used anymore. Desolation and silence will descend on these lovely rooms; we are robbed of what we had begun with such love.

Today, two sat and listened, entranced, to the playing—the sounds of Mozart, Schubert, Beethoven; for an hour they lead us to another world, a world, eternally beautiful, sober, cheerful, and bathed in the sunlight of genius.

We forget the terrible burden of these sad days of farewells; we let ourselves warm up to the sweet pictorial quality of Mozart, the mournful songs of

Schubert, who laments in his sonata but quickly moves beyond that to take us into cheerful, greening realms, where peaceful contentment expands the chest and gives joy to those with open hearts and minds.

The first four notes of Beethoven's concerto: Fate knocks at the gates—open up, you people; hear how a life unfolds with its heights, depths, with whooping joys, the highest bliss, delightful love, burdensome care, oppressive grief. But always the heights are recovered. Although in between the dunning four notes can be heard, a reminder that fate can suddenly close in, but it cannot hold you down because the stormy desire to go forward toward exhilaration, the joy of being, is so rousing that all oppression is dispersed, and divinity triumphs.

Professor Herman Leydensdorff, from Amsterdam, who came here six weeks ago and has worked so far in the Hundertschaft, was the partner of Mrs. von G. On an unfamiliar violin he played perfectly, with sweet tones, and his *cantilena*[117] made us feel blessed and warm.

A wonderful hour that gave us hope and strength.

[...]

*   *   *

Monday, October 23. Another hard day of sad farewells. Dear people left us, aged up to 65. The familiar scene: two days and nights of preparation. It was not cold and didn't rain, which was a great advantage. The provisions worked out, except on Monday. Then, the days of departure. One had reckoned that the train would depart in the early morning hours, but it was delayed until five o'clock in the afternoon. So the participants had to wait without anything warm and had to be satisfied with what their friends brought them.

Two men whom I held in high esteem were affected, and I deplore their departure publicly: *Justizrat* Jakob Wolffing, head of the finance department of Theresienstadt, a man who bore a resemblance to Wilamowitz-Moellendorff, the Greek scholar: the rosy, smooth, fresh complexion, the snow-white hair. He spoke with a slight suggestion of a South German accent and was distinguished socially by a very special amiability. Born on November 22, 1876, in Würzburg, *Abitur* 1895; he studied in his hometown. A junior lawyer in Munich. Established himself in Grünstadt near Pirmasens. Became a notary. Moved to Aachen in January 1936 and remained there until evacuation in 1942. He was able to make himself useful here as a member of the Council of Elders.

The second, whom I was fond of, was Dr. Ernst Podvineč, who looked after the children's home and now had to go with a large number of his wards. Working, taking care of things up to the last minute, he gave me yet another good supply of vegetables and tomatoes from his large garden. I was so grateful to him.

Born October 2, 1900, in Golčuv-Jenikov, Bohemia, he studied in Prague, Berlin, [...] and Vienna and established himself as a physician in Iglau in 1929. He had to retrain [after the German occupation] and chose horticulture as a new occupation. He came to Theresienstadt in January 1942 and was infinitely useful working as a physician. It was hard for him to leave the children's home that he had created so beautifully, and which now had to be closed. All who knew this good person sincerely regret his departure.

We helpers were busy all day, and in the afternoon there was still excitement because, again, people who had been called up did not come but hid themselves. Such a stupid, absurd endeavor. They harm the community, possibly exposing it to justified sanctions by the [German] authorities, and ultimately will have to give themselves up because they do not have ration cards. Today, October 24, 30 such fugitives have already been apprehended and taken into detention. They must accept their punishment now, and nothing can save them.

The children remain untouched by all the suffering that each transport brings. The baby lies in its little basket and slumbers. The little ones are dressed warmly, and a six-year-old proudly shows me his backpack, which he is allowed to carry on his back. The older ones play in the corridors and in the courtyards, and their happiness is contagious. Joy and suffering live close together here in the barracks.

On the small tree in the center, which has seen the many thousands passing by, the delicate, bright green leaves still hang, despite night storms and rain. They should remain for us a symbol, referring to a future that is still concealed from us, which could nevertheless turn toward life again.

* * *

Today, October 25,[118] nature's transformation is nearly complete. Brown and gold dominate; the birch trees look enchantingly decorated, and the chestnut trees again flaunt the color gold as they prepares themselves for winter's sleep. The dying is unmistakable; leaves pile up everywhere, and the sweeper does not have it easy keeping the paths clean. The children no longer pick up the chestnuts that fall into their laps. They are only desirable while they still hang on the trees and must be skillfully brought down by throwing things.

Now soccer is played everywhere *en miniature*. The young have made themselves a big rectangular board out of pasteboard or wood, with a batten on each side. The goals are painted in, and the game is played with large buttons that are snapped [as in tiddledywinks]. They sit with red faces, surrounded by their comrades, and get excited, as if they were playing above on the bastion.

Today in the ghetto it is again a big day for cleaning. Every house will be cleaned from top to bottom, and the rooms scrubbed and cleaned. Once again there is to be an inspection, and thus the order. Also, a census of the residents is to take place at night, and everyone must be in their beds and not sleeping in some other room. The poor house elders have night duty and must remain available between 11 P.M. and two o'clock. Temperature mild, and windless.

Otherwise there is nothing to report from our districts, we are getting back into our work slowly after the efforts and yesterday's commotion off duty, and can dedicate myself to writing and discussions, and discover how quickly the day goes past.

[...]

Humor in Theresienstadt

It is a paradox, to want to speak of humor in Theresienstadt, a town that overflows with suffering, depressed, homeless people who bear an infinitely heavy, undeserved, hard fate. But still, one hears in the afternoons and evenings the little bells of the fool's cap ringing out brightly, which are donned by many actors to brighten up the gray of the days and the evenings, and to unleash liberating laughter. In Theresienstadt, in the beginning, strangely enough, there was humor.

The Leisure Time Organization strove, when it took up its many promising and encouraging activities, to present light fare in order to lift the mood. It found men and women who enthusiastically embraced this challenge in presenting their amusing programs.

The married couple Hans and Liesl Hofer provoked storms of laughter when they conversed. [...]. Then Bobby John took over, the only comic who looked and sounded Jewish, satirizing himself and spoofing. Then there was Ernst Morgan, the piano humorist, who played splendidly and performed humorous parodies of opera. In the beginning, when there was no piano, he played duets with Bobby John. Then the humorist Walter Steiner was often heard; he was good, old school, the way we liked it, which today seems somewhat dusty.

Then there were two real men of letters who had something to say to us: Paul Blum and Leo Strauss. The latter's wife, Myra Strauss, was a born [cabaret star], and she performed charming, perfect cabaret. These three performed mainly their own creations, and it may really be said that the Strauss' poems became legendary in Theresienstadt.[119]

[…]

I begin with the most distinctive among the literati: Professor Dr. Phil. Paul Blum. In Theresienstadt he is the house elder in one of the prominent dwellings. Born August 16, 1884, in Brno [in Czechoslovakia]. His father was a major importer of hemp from Russia, Italy, and Manila. *Abitur* 1902. Studied in Vienna, German studies, in addition to art history and philosophy. After the exams, he was an upper school teacher and, at 20 years old, was already a lecturer at the college of adult education in Brno. He went to Paris to study and was interned there following the outbreak of war and was moved from camp to camp, spending the longest period in Guérande, Brittany. He was freed in March 1919. Afterward, he again taught in Brno and also made extensive lecture trips, which led him to Prague, Vienna, and many other cities. [He often spoke on the radio.] He came to Theresienstadt on December 2, 1941.

I present an extremely well-received performance, which fittingly shows how one brings humor to Theresienstadt: a letter of farewell.[120]

Geneva, the…

Dear N.,

With the unrestrained candor for which you always praised me, I answer your question, as to whether you might hope to bring me home soon as your wife, with a flat "No." Everything is over between us, finally and irrevocably.

I have, as you rightfully must admit, excused you with great indulgence and affectionate patience for all these months and bore, again and again, what you liked to refer to as the "Theresienstadt cinders," in the hope that these cinders would gradually crumble away and that you would finally stand before me again in the way that I knew and—oh—loved you in *anno* 1941. This hope, unfortunately, proved to be false, and now my patience is at an end. It truly has been granted for long enough.

How much I have had to overlook from you in the course of these months. I excused it as force of habit, when you, a few weeks after your return, instead of greeting my old aunt from San Francisco, a proud American, asked her with which transport she had arrived, what her number was, and where she had left her bedroll. I made the same excuse for your quirk of using laborious capital letters in numerous tender letters, which you have written to me on all possible occasions since your return, and that you always end these billets-doux with the same formula: 1,000 hot kisses from your, adoring N. Aa b x/IV—1617.

Now, as I said, all of this was bearable, because it more or less took place en famille. But I began to have serious doubts for the first time about the possibility of living together with you, when at the *table d' hôte* at the Hotel du Lac in Montreux [Switzerland], you tried to eat the beefsteak with the spoon and afterwards suddenly jumped up, took the plate in your hand, ran to the kitchen window, and demanded in a loud voice, "seconds." Furthermore, the next morning you threatened to denounce the hotel manager, a perfect gentleman, because he had not set up a "toilet guard" between two and four o'clock in the morning, and then, in a strict tone, instructed him to send the bedclothes from our room to the disinfestation area.

That at first you doffed your hat almost to the ground in front of the elevator boy, for the reason that this was a basic duty toward anyone in uniform, and later passed him with a derisive smirk, because the compulsory greeting had been rescinded, I could still just about understand. Uninitiated people, thus all the hotel guests and personnel including the elevator boys naturally considered you ready for a mental hospital.

And this was also naturally the impression the waiter Jean had on that day, when you lunged at him with a knife, only because he had recommended pearl barley soup as a first course for dinner. Even now I blush when I think of the pitiful role that you played at the birthday dinner that our mutual friend, the banker Marcel Abéles organized in his magnificent palace (Quai des Eaux Vives). It was most unfortunate that he called upon your supposed social skills in asking you to arrange it. You justified his trust in you by calling shrilly to the guests, who were from the cream of Geneva society, "Line up for food," herded them in two lines out of the salon to covered tables, and then with the excuse that you had to cancel the ration cards, went from table to table and cut the date, May 5, out of the exquisite menu cards with your pocket scissors. That you took the soggy cigarette stub from your mouth in the smoking salon after dinner, and pushed it between the horrified lips of your neighbor, the host's daughter, with a gesture of invitation, was also not likely to strengthen our social position.

What was even more outrageous, however, was the circumstance that, every time after a visit to a stranger's house you came to me and—always with the same radiant expression—opened your briefcase in order to extract from it gloves, scarves, alarm clocks, and also thermos bottles, drinking cups, and, as occurred just yesterday, the lid of a pot. You explained, with cynical pride, that you had "sluiced," as you called it, the aforementioned articles from the waiting room of Dr. X, the office of Mr. Y, and the kitchen of Mrs. Z.

My dear N., I have endured it for seven months, and I cannot bear it anymore. *Adieu, adieu pour toujours.* Be happy! Best you should look for a woman from Theresienstadt. She will understand everything, and therefore forgive everything, even if sometimes during a break in the discussion you suddenly sing out dreamily, "Do not forget to wash your hands after the toilet and before the meal."

In the arms of the right companion you will soon have forgotten me.

Your heavily disappointed,
　　Juliette

That is an example of the Theresienstadt spirit, but Professor Blum brings splendid, finely polished verses, which were often reminiscent of his favorite poet,[121] whom he often spoke about and recited. His French was wonderful, and he had been assigned to speak Riccaut when the transport canceled my plan to read, as a farewell presentation, *Minna von Barnhelm*.[122]

* * *

Dr. Leo Strauss, born January 21, 1897, in the theater building in Teplitz. His father was the composer Oscar Straus; mother, Nelly Straus, née Irmen. Being settled was unknown to him; he attended 24 schools. Nevertheless, *Abitur*, Vienna 1915. Study in Vienna, philosophy and law. At eight years old he had his first poem published in the school bulletin; school essays already in newspapers

EPILOGUE

At this point the Factual Report breaks off in mid-sentence. Philipp and Gertrud Manes were put on the last transport from Theresienstadt to Auschwitz on October 28, 1944. Their subsequent fate is documented in testimonies by Theresienstadt survivors. Alice Ehrmann (later Alisah Shek) was seventeen at the time, noted this in her diary in Hebrew script on October 28, 1944:

> Loading wagons, instructions [...] 2,038 persons, in cattle trucks 50 and more. Günther[1] had the last tiny hatches nailed shut with metal plates and one has to crouch on the baggage heaps without an atom of air and light for 24 hours, with one bucket for 50 people [...] Ghetto is being reorganised. End of transports for now. All are too tired to start again, but we shall do so after all.[2]

Zdeněk Lederer states in his book *Ghetto Theresienstadt*:

> Transport Ev.
>
> October 28, 1944...2,038 prisoners. This was the last transport from Theresienstadt to Oświęcim [Auschwitz]. It arrived on October 30. About 240 men and 140 women were selected [and many of them sent to other camps], all the others were gassed. They were the last victims of the gas chambers, which soon afterwards were demolished [...]
>
> Number of survivors [of this transport]...137.[3]

The figures given by both Alisah Shek and Zdeněk Lederer compare well with Danuta Czech's information published much later in her authoritative *Auschwitz Chronicle*. An entry for October 30, 1944 reads:

> 2 038 Jews arrive [...] from the Theresienstadt ghetto. There are 949 men and boys and 1,089 women and girls in the transport. After the selection 217 men

are sent to the camp and given Nos. B-13754–B-13970. 132 are put in the transit camp. The remaining 1,689 people are killed in the gas chambers.[4]

The subsequent entry for November 2 reads: "Killing with Zyklon B gas in the gas chambers of Auschwitz is probably discontinued. The selected prisoners are shot to death in the gas chamber or on the grounds of Crematorium V."[5]

What happened in Theresienstadt after Philipp and Gertrud Manes' deportation to Auschwitz is described in a survivor's report by Professor Jacob Jacobson.

After the last transport had left towards the end of 1944 only 11 000 Jews remained in Theresienstadt [...] The town appeared desolate, in poor condition; the inhabitants were in despair. Yet, more quickly than was expected, life within the Ghetto returned to normal again. The inhabitants, particularly the women, had to work still harder [...]

The SS Command tried to wipe out all vestiges of the past. They did not want to be reminded of the many Jews who had been sent to Theresienstadt and had died there or had been deported from there. The urns with the ashes of the dead were suddenly removed, nobody knows where. All files and registers for the period up to January 1, 1945, together with all photos of former Ghetto inmates, had to be handed over to the Camp Commander.

The SS continued to display their authority. They tried to maintain the fiction that they still had faith in the continuation of their power. Yet they could not conceal their nervousness. War still raged [...]

On April 20, an unending spectacle of horror began. Without interruption, men and women from [other] concentration and labour camps streamed into Theresienstadt. Within two weeks, about 15 000 Czech, Slovak, Polish, Hungarian, German, Dutch, French, Italian and Greek Jews had trudged to Theresienstadt. Miserable, half-starved people, often desperately ill, they carried their dead and dying with them and brought spotted fever into the camp [...]

On April 29, [...] M. Dunant, a representative of the International Red Cross, arrived in Theresienstadt. The town was placed under the protection of the International Red Cross [...] On May 5, the SS Commander left. Theresienstadt had ceased to be a Ghetto under SS rule. The Jewish elder, Dr. Murmelstein, resigned and was replaced by a provisional council, consisting of representatives of the various national groups. Dr. Baeck represented the Jews from Germany, Minister Meissner the Czech Jews, Professor Meyers the Dutch Jews and Dr. Klang the Austrian Jews [...] Our danger had now passed for good."[6]

NOTES

Editor's Introduction

1. Similar arrangements were in place in all the major Nazi ghettos. One motivation was to give the Jewish victims a false sense of independence and security and so make them easier to control. Another was to reduce the number of SS and military personnel tied up in running the ghettos.
2. This was on the orders of the Jewish self-administration, although the reasons are not clear.
3. Gerty Spies, *My Years in Theresienstadt*, Trans. Jutta R. Tragnitz (Amherst, N.Y.: Prometheus Books, 1997). First published in German, in 1984. Gerty Spies continues: "I do not think that anything survived of his reports and perhaps these lines are the only witness to his devoted activity. He surely took his writings with him, on the way from which nobody returned." Gerty Spies was unaware of the survival of the manuscript.
4. Yehuda Bauer, *Rethinking the Holocaust* (New Haven: Yale University Press, 2002).
5. Leo Baeck, "Life in a Concentration Camp," *The Jewish Forum*, March 1946.

Prologue

1. This refers to the birthday of P.M.'s wife, Gertrud Manes, née Elias. From 1939 P.M. had kept a war diary, which he intended his children to read at a later time. The last pages of this diary are close in content to the first pages of this report.
2. For two months before his deportation, P.M. had been drafted with other Jews to work in the F. Butzke factory at 75 Brandenburgstrasse, which manufactured nuts and bolts.
3. Jews were required by the Nazi regime to list all their property, and this was enforced through Jewish community organizations.
4. At this time Jews were permitted to use public transportation only to travel to and from work, but they were not allowed to sit down.

5. During his school days, P.M. and his parents lived at 1 Brandenburgstrasse.

6. Annemarie and Eva were the daughters of P.M. and Gertrud; Rudolf and Walter their sons. Lilli was Walter's wife. By the time P.M. and Gertrud were deported, Eva and Annemarie had escaped to Britain, Walter and Lilli to Shanghai, and Rudolf to North Africa, after living in Paris for a number of years.

7. The Old People's Home on Grosse Hamburger Strasse, a center of Jewish life in Berlin, was founded in 1829. In 1942 it was taken over by the Gestapo and used as a gathering place for thousands of Berlin Jews awaiting deportation. The building was bombed during the war. Out of all of the former inhabitants of the Old People's Home, only one survivor from Theresienstadt returned, in 1945.

8. The cemetery with Mendelssohn's grave was destroyed by the Nazis.

9. The Grunewald rail station, now part of Berlin's S-Bahn network, was at this time a freight station and the departure point for thousands of Jews suffering deportation.

10. The Weissensee Cemetery was erected in 1878 as the fourth Jewish cemetery in Berlin. It remained relatively unscathed during the Second World War and is today the largest Jewish cemetery in Europe.

11. After the Aryanization of his business, Manes was still an employee at the fur company Georg Petkowitsch, until this was forbidden to him. We know that P.M. helped his "successor" continue the Aryan business, but are unsure whether this successor and Petkowitsch are the same.

12. Schupo is an abbreviation for Schutzpolizisten (policemen).

Part I   1942

1. In his authoritative work on Theresienstadt, Adler describes *Schleuse* (sluice) and its derivatives as "central words of the camp language at Theresienstadt." The word was initially used by the SS for processing the arriving inmates and did not relate to any specific place in the ghetto. "Sluicing" normally meant that bags were searched and smuggled goods were confiscated, and later it came to mean "appropriate," analogous to the word *organize* in Auschwitz and other camps. For a detailed description, see the glossary in H. G. Adler, *Theresienstadt*, page L.

2. "Abandon all hope" is a quote from Dante's *Inferno*.

3. The number is unknown. It has been estimated that up to 58,000 were incarcerated in the ghetto at one time.

4. This must mean the people from the stables opposite, who had arrived earlier.

5. P.M. had often happily visited Hamburg. It was his wife's hometown. He described his memories in detailed unpublished writing that are in the archives of the Wiener Library, London.

6. Sir Morell Mackenzie (1837–1892) was a renowned throat specialist, who treated the crown prince and, later, Kaiser Friedrich. In 1888, his book *The Fatal Illness of Frederik the Noble* (*Die tödliche Krankheit Friedrichs des Edlen*) was published. Mackenzie's diagnoses and treatments were severely criticized by German doctors.

7. *Freizeitgestaltung* was the official Leisure Time Organization of the Jewish self-administration in Theresienstadt. Manes was attached to it from February 1944, but the tension between him and the organization is reflected in the text.

8. Leunawerke, near Halle, was a large chemical works owned at the time by IG Farben. It was the biggest producer of nitrogen in Germany and produced "Leuna petrol" from lignite.

9. P.M. and Fritz Janowitz established a close friendship, almost a father-son relationship, which is clear from a letter of farewell Janowitz wrote to P.M. just before he was deported to Auschwitz (included in an album dedicated to P.M.).

10. The Blue/White (Blau/Weiss) was a Zionist youth organization that emphasized the learning of Hebrew and Jewish history and tradition. It educated members toward settlement in Palestine.

11. The Makkabi Federation was a Jewish sports organization, named after Judah Makkabi, who in 168 BCE led a revolution against Syria.

12. An account of the ghetto is found in the second chapter of H. G. Adler's *Theresienstadt*. As Adler's table overview shows, November 14, 1941, was the date of the first transports of 340 prisoners from the Protectorate to Theresienstadt. Jacob Edelstein and 32 colleagues followed on December 4.

13. Despite his being a central figure in P.M.'s narrative, there is no biographical information available on Frey.

14. *Ubikation* is a term in Austrian and Czech military language meaning "quarter" or "accommodation."

15. P.M. wrote an unpublished manuscript, *The History of Field Bookstore* (*Geschichte der Feldbuchhandlung*), in which he described this period in his life, and in Theresienstadt he reflected on it often. The manuscript is in the archive of the Wiener Library.

16. P.M. means that between noon and 2 p.m. it was not possible to consult the records that allowed him to identify where the lost people should go, so he arranged to give them lunch.

17. *Genie* is a military term connected with engineering.

18. *Der Stürmer* was a notorious anti-Semitic newspaper edited by Julius Streicher.

19. The rough-hewn timbers gave shelter to plagues of bedbugs, hence P.M.'s comment.

20. *Chevra Kadisha* (Aramaic): a holy association, mostly voluntary, for rendering loving service in illness, deaths, and burials.

21. It is not clear whether this was in the stables or the barracks.

22. The Sokolowna, or Sokolhalle, in the part of the ghetto known as Kreta, was a clubhouse with a gymnasium, originally used by the Czech *Sokol* (Falcon) Gymnastics Club. Until 1944, the Sokolowna served as a hospital. Then in the wake of the "city beautification," it was transformed into a "community house." We assume that the Institute for Bacteriological Investigation is the Laboratories for Bacteriology, especially bacterioscopy.

23. The later process in the delousing facility is described in the section "*Mors Imperator.*"

24. After the destruction of Czechoslovakia in September 1938, the country was divided up: Slovakia was made nominally independent, and Ruthenia was occupied by Hungary. The Czech parts became the Reich Protectorate of Bohemia and Moravia and were occupied by German troops on March 16, 1939.

25. However, in later passages Manes mentions a few gifts.

26. Adler describes this as a "tripartite body to monitor the proper use of food and food distribution."

27. Czech for "caution!"

28. Joachim von Ribbentrop (1893–1946), who would later be foreign minister, married Anneliese Henkell, the daughter of the sparkling wine producer Otto Henkell, in 1920 and was the Berlin representative for Henkell.

29. The Garrison Cemetery, which formerly served as the burial place of the Berlin Regiment, was changed into a park in 1867.

30. More drawings by Henriette Lehmann-Laizner can be found in P.M.'s manuscript and his albums.

31. Composer of *The Chocolate Soldier* and *La Ronde*, among many other operettas and films.

32. The heavily ironic poem *Als Ob* (As If) depicts the unreal, make-believe quality of life in Theresienstadt. One line of this poem, *Als obs ein Leben wär* (As if it were a life), serves as the title for this book. The charming poem *The Yellow Star* tells of a meeting of two gentlemen, a Jew and a non-Jew, in the Vienna Prata.

33. Several poems by Ilse Weber can be found in the German manuscript of this book and in the volumes dedicated to P.M. held at the Wiener Library, London.

34. This was the first Jewish holiday that P.M. marked by an event in his Lecture Series, but Rosh Hashana and Yom Kippur preceded it.

35. Hanukkah is the eight-day Festival of Lights to commemorate the consecration of the temple by Judah Maccabees. The candleholder of eight flames (menorah) is lit (on each day one candle) in memory of the Miracle of Light in the sanctuary when a day's supply of oil lasted for eight days.

36. A literary cabaret founded in Berlin in 1901 by Ernst von Wolzogen.

37. "Emperor Death."

39. P.M. used "gassing room" with the meaning of "disinsectization" or "delousing area," without knowing at this time what the term has come to mean today. Gassings did not take place in Theresienstadt. There was, however, a plan to kill the last inmates of the camp before the relinquishing of the ghetto in 1945. One of the methods for killing was also gassing. Two Jewish engineers were charged with the design and construction of a gas chamber, but Rahm, the last commander of the camp, finally opposed the construction. See Walter Laqueur, ed., *The Holocaust Encyclopedia* Yale Unversity Press (New Haven and London: 2001), pp. 239–240.

40. Jewish prayer for the dead.

41. This passage, with its interpretation that the ghetto mirrored war prisons, was contrary to P.M.'s thoughts, and a manner of wishful thinking; perhaps it was also a defensive gesture toward an eventual censor.

42. According to Adler, in September 1942 the restructuring of the ghetto into a currency economy was announced, although the ghetto money was first circulated only in May 1943. A system of payment for work was instituted in November 1942. The building of the café is mentioned in the daily report of December 6, 1942. Adler writes scornfully about these measures and says that the inmates regarded this as a cynical pretense on the part of the SS. In the following passage, P.M. seems to take it seriously. In the reading of these passages, it must be considered that P.M. wrote at the time the events were happening, while Adler and others wrote about it in hindsight, or based on reported information that was not available to camp inmates.

43. Katharina (Käthe) von Mendelssohn-Bartholdy was born in Berlin on September 24, 1870 (1876 according to other reports). She was the great-granddaughter of Abraham Mendelssohn and married the lawyer Dr. Felix Wach, who was a senior civil servant in Saxony.

44. She was the granddaughter of Gerson von Bleichröder, not the wife of his descendant, as is apparent from her brief biography written in 1944.

45. H. G. Adler writes about the postal traffic in his book. It was promised that twice a month writing a card would be permitted, but this promise was never kept. In a limited mail connection with the Protectorate, a card with 30 words written in block letters was approved in January 1942, but this was only on paper, and the news did not come to fruition. Here P.M. thought of one card for more than one month, but would later insert the number.

46. The inmates in Theresienstadt knew almost nothing about Auschwitz-Birkenau and what happened there. Of the men in charge, Leo Baeck knew about the murder of European Jews, and he made a conscious decision to keep the knowledge a secret.

47. "Remain unbowed" is a quotation from Goethe's *Lila*: "Remain unbowed / Show strength / A call to arms / Hither the gods."

Part II   1943

1. An Austrian term for "stamp," originally coming from the Italian.

2. See note 36 on page 272.

3. These were songs that formed part of the cabaret.

4. At this time P.M.'s activities were unofficial, and he feared attracting negative attention from the Jewish self-administration, of which the Leisure Time Organization was part.

5. This is a further reference to his ambiguous relationship with the official Leisure Time Organization, which viewed his activities with some reservations.

6. The date of the second performance cannot be traced exactly, but was probably on February 1.

7. A scene in *Faust* in which Gretchen bows before the *Mater dolorosa* and asks for assistance.

8. This was a new performance space for P.M. A description of the preparations of the Deutsches House for the ghetto watch follows on p. 94.

9. Latin quotation from the *Satires* of Juvenal, meaning "It is difficult not to write a satire."

10. Evidently P.M. got permission to read *Nathan* through proving himself flexible and cooperative in regard to some other project.

11. *Hundertschaften*, groups of 100 men, women, or youths. They were grouped together, where possible, according to aptitude. They were led by a *Hunderschaft* elder. The strongest men and women formed *Cadre-Hundertschaften*. See Adler, page 378, for this and other work organizations.

12. The folder presented to Manes is not extant. The *Hatikwa* was the hymn of the Zionist movement and is now the national anthem of the State of Israel. It was originally written by Naftali Imber (1856–1909), composed by Samuel Cohen, and first published in Jerusalem in 1886.

13. Adler also records the escape of six inmates in April 1943. Three were recaptured. He cites the penalties imposed by Commandant Seidl (a ban on leaving the barracks and the use of lighting, and a ban on leisure events), which were not lifted until May.

14. Karl May (1842–1921) was the author of popular cowboys-and-Indians and other adventure stories for boys.

15. By "two other religions" P.M. means Protestant and Roman Catholic.

16. It is evident that in this paragraph P.M. contradicts what he has written above about religious freedom. It seems that there he referred more narrowly to the freedom to mark Passover by eating matzoh rather than bread.

17. Martin Buber (1878–1965) was a religious and social philosopher. Buber sought a renewal of Judaism in the spirit of the Bible and the mystical religious movement of Hasidism originating in eighteenth-century Poland.

18. *Der gute Kamerad* (The Good Comrade), a traditional lament of the German Armed Forces. The lyric was written by the German poet Ludwig Uhland in 1809. In 1825, it was set to music by the composer Friedrich Silcher.

19. P.M. left a space for the insertion of the name. Probably he intended the Institute for the Scientific Study of Judaism (*Hochschule für die Wissenschaft des Judentums* in Berlin).

20. Theresienstadt had generous provision of beds for the sick arranged in various locations, but of course lacked the proper supply of necessary medicines, and the

physicians and surgeons were powerless to tackle the malnourishment that underlay so much of the sickness and disease.

21. A German-language newspaper. This must refer to the relatively short period during the "Town Beautification" program, in preparation for a visit from the International Committee of the Red Cross, when shops and a café were set up in Theresienstadt.

22. *Bonke* (plural: *Bonken* or *Bonkes*), meaning any false rumor, especially any that seemed favorable to the ghetto inmates. If any report or story was characterized as *Bonke*, this meant that it should not to be taken seriously (quoted from Adler, p. xxxv).

23. The Zeughaus, or armory, in Berlin was a prominent building, constructed on Unter den Linden around 1700. It has been reconstructed and today serves as the German Historical Museum.

24. These masks were created by the sculptor Andreas Schlüter (1664–1714) and were a prominent feature of the courtyard.

25. P.M.'s son Walter and his wife Lilli lived during this time in Shanghai as refugees.

26. These diagram(s) and notes for *Suggestions for a Handbook for Pharmacists* came from Theodor Behnsch, "former resident of the Pharmacy on Arminiusplatz, Berlin NW 87, Turmstrasse." They are archived today at the Wiener Library, London.

27. Manes was writing in 1944. Here he combines material from 1943 and 1944.

28. This portfolio is not extant.

29. For Frey, this "calling" to Auschwitz was a death sentence.

30. A Czech military term, meaning "camp bed." In Theresienstadt it was used for the two- or three-story bunk beds that slept four, six, or more people and were made of rough-hewn timbers.

31. Meaning "Diversity is pleasing."

32. A short biography of Anna Aurědničekova follows in the original document.

33. Lynkeus was the pseudonym of Josef Popper (1838–1921), the Austrian social philosopher, engineer, and inventor.

34. Rosh Hashanah, the Jewish New Year, which falls on the first day of the seventh month in the Jewish calendar. Yom Kippur (Day of Atonement) is the tenth and last of the Days of Repentance beginning with Rosh Hashanah. The two days are the highest of the Jewish Holy Days. Yom Kippur would play a special role in the following year, 1944.

35. This was a separate event from the Hanukkah lectures of December 24, described on page 000.

36. The Jewish Cultural Associations (*Kulturbünde*) were self-help organizations of Jewish artists, set up after 1933. The most important were in Berlin, the Rhine-Ruhr area, Hamburg, and Munich. In 1936 the 36 regional and local organizations formed the Reich Union of Jewish Cultural Associations (*Reichs Verband der jüdischen Kulturbünde*). This was replaced in 1938 by the Registered Jewish Cultural Association in Germany (*Jüdischer Kulturbund in Deutschland e.V.*), which was dissolved on September 11, 1941.

37. German Jews deported to Theresienstadt were "advantaged" in that they were not sent directly to death camps. The Nazis recognized certain categories: the old, decorated veterans of the First World War, and the prominent and well-known, whose abrupt disappearance might cause comment. Theresienstadt served as a holding place for such categories, until the Nazis felt it was safe to murder them.

38. P.M.'s words are not quite clear. In fact, there were some transports even before autumn 1943. However, these were not yet the beginning of the large-scale transports that took place in connection with the "Town Beautification" in 1944 or those of autumn 1944, which are described in the last part of this book.

39. P.M. is clearly deluded about the fate of those sent out of Theresienstadt. However, no certain information was available to the inmates, and his optimistic view may have been representative of at least a large portion of the ghetto population.

40. P.M. is referring simultaneously to this early transport of 1,000 people and the later ones that took up to 2,500.

41. According to Adler, Löwenstein's downfall occurred on August 16, 1943, shortly after Commandant Seidl was replaced by Obersturmführer Anton Burger. Possibly the SS were suspicious of a "paramilitary" unit in the ghetto. Kurt Frey was soon to be "transferred."

42. The reason why it had to be written out every third day is unclear.

43. A quotation from Friedrich Schiller's poem "Die Glocke" (The Bell).

44. *Sic transit gloria mundi*, meaning "Thus passes the glory of the world." This is sung at the papal coronation ceremony.

45. *Faust I*, Verse v b860.

46. Play by Ludwig Fulda (1862–1939), a German-Jewish writer and translator (*Cyrano de Bergerac*) who committed suicide in Berlin.

Part III: Section I   January–July

1. In fact, P.M. does not revert to this topic.

2. Hamlet's last words.

3. The Ordnungsdienst (OD) was a sister organization of the Ghetto Watch responsible for lighter duties. See Adler's comments in various chapters.

4. Quotation from Friedrich Schiller, *The Conspiracy of Fiesco in Genoa*, Act III, Scene 4.

5. Department responsible for copying documents.

6. The Reich Association of Jewish Front-Line Soldiers (*Reichsbund jüdischer Frontsoldaten*) was founded by Löwenstein in 1919 and had about 40,000 members at its peak in 1925. They were organized in 16 regional associations with around 500 local groups.

7. *Sulamith, eine Zeitschrift zur Beförderung der Kultur und Humanität unter den Iraeliten*, first published in 1806 by David Fränkel (1779–1865) and Joseph Wolf (1762–1826). It was the first German-language periodical specifically for a Jewish readership. In

1810 the word *Israelites* in the title was replaced with "Jewish Nation." It ceased publication in 1848.

8. An allusion to King John of England (1167–1216), whose epithet was "Lackland" because he had not inherited any land. He accepted the Magna Carta and was the eponymous protagonist of Shakespeare's *King John*.

9. Eppstein was at this time elder of the Jews and had nominally taken over the leadership of the Leisure Time Organization, which was managed by Moritz Henschel.

10. *Ducheten*: an Austrian term meaning "quilt."

11. The so-called town beautification was undertaken in preparation for the visit to the ghetto of the International Committee of the Red Cross.

12. It is generally thought that the town beautification started in May, and Manes himself later gives May 1 as the starting date. However, his manuscript suggests that some beautification work was already under way in the second half of April.

13. Adler also reports three prizes and five consolation prizes (p. 168) but does not give the details reported here.

14. The "prominent" were a category of privileged inmates, people who had a public profile in Germany and even internationally. They enjoyed better conditions and were less liable for transportation to the death camps. Many survived.

15. Adler also mentions three transports in May 1944 and gives the even more precise number of 7,503. The Theresienstadt memorial books show that the transports departed on May 15, 16, and 18, respectively, although this does not rule out the possibility of the call-up coming at two-day intervals as mentioned by Manes. Auschwitz and Poland were not mentioned; the destination given was Birkenau in Upper Silesia, ostensibly a family and labor camp.

16. In other words, those being transported asked those staying behind to notify their children.

17. "Refusal" meant that the appeal was rejected, and the person was transported; "decision" meant that the appeal was accepted, and the person was exempted from the transport; doubtful cases were handed over to the Jewish self-administration.

18. A larger number were called up than were needed, in order to secure the quota for the transport after the appeals had been dealt with. Those who were "surplus" to the quota were then released back into Theresienstadt.

19. This refers to Karl Rahm, the commandant of Theresienstadt, and is a rare positive judgment of his character. Whether Manes was naive or writing cautiously in case his notes were examined is unclear. Adler (p. 776) cites this passage as illustrating the former.

20. It is unclear exactly what was done with the harvest, but we assume that it was taken by the Germans.

21. Whitsuntide, or Pentecost, is a major Christian festival, falling on the 50th day after Easter.

22. Shavuot, or the Festival of Weeks, is a harvest festival falling between Passover and Sukkoth.

23. Goethe's *Urfaust* was preserved in a copy prepared by the lady-in-waiting Louise von Göchhausen and was discovered and published by Erich Schmidt in 1887.

24. Maskir (more usually Yizkor) is one of four annual memorial services, performed at Yom Kippur, on the last day of Succoth, the last day of Passover, and the last day of Shavuot.

25. In other words, P.M.'s Room A7 was taken over by those processing the shipments of sardines.

26. It is unclear precisely what this department was. The builders' yard apparently accommodated a number of manufacturing workshops, of which the cardboard-packaging department was one. Evidently it produced cardboard packaging for a variety of purposes, and P.M. was able to get a supply of waste pieces for his own purposes, as described.

27. The events put on by the official Leisure Time Organization.

28. Adalbert Stifter (1805–1868), poet, painter, and author of novels and novellas.

29. Two large German companies.

30. In the course of the town beautification, the Camp Command (*Lagerkommandatur*) was renamed the Department (*Dienststelle*), presumably to strengthen the impression of a Jewish civilian self-administration. P.M. adopted this term, which he had previously used in the generally accepted sense.

31. P.M. refers to the visit of the International Committee of the Red Cross, which took place on June 23, 1944. The delegation was made up of Dr. M. Rossel, from Switzerland, and Frants Hvass and Juel Henningsen, who were both working in Denmark under German occupation. The delegation was received by a high-level German reception committee, who arranged a carefully stage-managed inspection of the ghetto. Dr. Eppstein addressed the delegates in a speech approved by the Germans. Dr. Rossel's subsequent report has never been published, but there is no reason to doubt that the town beautification and the visit succeeded in concealing the true nature of the ghetto.

32. The weights of the bread were left blank by P.M. and have been inserted using information from Adler. In fact, the exact rations varied. The "S" indicated heavy labor (*Schwer*); the " N" meant nonworkers.

33. As P.M. explains later, the loft was actually used for drying laundry.

34. From a later comment it appears that they were not much more than planks.

35. This is a modified quote from Schiller's *Wilhelm Tell* whose the second part reads "if it does not please his beloved neighbor."

36. Norderney is an island off the north coast of Germany. Westerland is a town on the island of Sylt. Both were fashionable seaside resorts.

37. The Teutoburg forest was the scene of a famous battle between the "Teutons" and the Romans in the year 9 CE.

38. At this point in the manuscript, P.M. left the number of Jewish topics blank. Later he presented Rabbi Weiner with a document entitled *500 Lecture Evenings of the Manes Group*, in which he gives the number of Jewish topics as 82.

39. P.M. had evidently been criticized for his secular orientation and lack of familiarity with Eastern European Jewish culture and tradition.

40. All of this was part of the "town beautification."

41. The ghetto guard had its "own stage" in the Deutsches House. Kurt Gerron (1897–1944) was an actor and director who made the infamous film *Der Fuhrer schenkt den Juden eine Stadt* (*The Fuhrer Goes the Jews a City*).

42. The Süd barracks were outside the main garrison toward Bauschowitz.

43. Compare with the report on the first lecture by Professor Klausner (p. 61 of this translation.

44. Apparently, rather, his grandmother's brother (Großohm), Simon von Geldern (1720–1774 or 1788), traveler and adventurer, great-uncle of Heinrich Heine.

45. The term for Jews who were forcibly converted to Christianity in sixteenth-century Spain and Portugal.

46. Berber tribe in Morocco.

47. (In Arabic, Abu abd Allah; called El Chico, the Small One) as Mohammed XII, the last Moorish king of Granada (1482–1492). Chaoñen is the holy city of the Rifkabyls, in the formerly Spanish part of Morrocco.

48. Founded in Naumburg in 1894, it was the first organization to archive and document the philosopher's life and work. It is located today in Weimar.

49. Also *Kehillah* or *Kahal*; meaning "Jewish community."

50. Historical comedy in five acts about the author and free thinker Cyrano de Bergerac (1619–1655) by Edmond Rostand (1868–1918). It premiered in 1897 in Paris and was translated into German by Ludwig Fulda.

51. These lines were probably written around July 20–22, 1944, several weeks after the invasion of France, and at the time when the assassination attempt on Hitler failed on July 20. We do not know whether P.M. knew about these events. If so, he probably would not have dared to mention them in his writings. Fellow inmate Thomas Mandl reported that a friend of his was able to listen to the radio because he had to repair an SS car with a radio installed, and so heard about the attempt immediately (this is quoted in Viktor Ullmann, *26 Reviews of Musical Events in Theresienstadt*, edited by Ingo Schulz [Hamburg, 1993]). Regarding Manes's reference to "the gift of "a bit of freedom," it should be noted that this was written during the weeks of the town beautification.

52. This must refer to the time before the First World War.

53. Obviously, it was a shop for leather goods, but the name is not legible in the manuscript.

54. This refers to the Austro-Prussian War.

55. In the German and Austrian armies at this time, men liable to military service could opt to serve 12 months, instead of the usual two years, as reserve officer candidates. To qualify, they had to have reached a certain level in school and be prepared to pay for their own accommodation, food, and equipment.

56. In writing about sentenced criminals, P.M. uses the official language of the ghetto and has no idea about the true purpose of the "Little Fortress." Adler describes it

as a concentration camp housing political prisoners, mostly Czech: "Jews had little expectation to stay alive there. As a punishment, ghetto inmates were also committed and nearly always killed or transported to Auschwitz." Paul Eppstein was among those killed there.

57. P.M. may have written this troubling sentence with an eye to a possible censor. He was conscious that inmates spied on one another for the SS and that he might be betrayed at any time.

58. P.M. is referring to the time when he was active establishing the field bookstores during the First World War.

59. A humorous weekly magazine published 1886–1944.

60. These manuscripts are no longer extant. However, Mrs. Hochstetter was the first recipient of P.M.'s chronicle, the manuscript of this book (see also the "Introduction").

61. P.M. uses the word "*Liegehalle*," literally meaning "open-air wing" or "solarium."

62. Frisians are an ethnic group of Germanic peoples found chiefly in coastal regions of the Netherlands.

Section II   August–October

63. These remarks provide evidence that P.M. did not have knowledge of the extent of the murder of European Jews. In the summer of 1944, the number was already in the high millions. It is nearly certain that P.M. went to his death without knowledge of these dreadful facts.

64. Much has been written about this film. See, for example, Käthe Starke, who used the working title of the film, *The Führer Gives a City to the Jews*, as the title of her book about Theresienstadt.

65. P.M. refers here to the *Prominenten*, a class of privileged ghetto inmates, who lived in substantially better conditions than the others.

66. This was the first of five interviews in which Elsa Bernstein spoke about her life, her husband Max Bernstein, Gerhart Hauptmann, and many others.

67. A man's coat; an outmoded term originating in fifteenth-century France, when it meant a cloak worn over a suit of armor.

68. From the Latin for "workshop"; refers to large printing operations and also private presses.

69. *Shema Jisrael*, a prayer that expresses the unity and uniqueness of God; also, the confession of a martyr, often spoken as a last prayer before death. *Kiddush La'adonai* is sanctification through (divine) names.

70. Nothing more is known about this circle. Perhaps there were lecture evenings in small circles.

71. Blindness was not the end of all writing for Elsa Bernstein. After her release she was in contact with friends by letter and worked on her memoirs, which were lost. They were found by Rita Bake and Birgit Kiupel and published. According to the introduction: "This manuscript, from notes likely made by Elsa Bernstein in Theresienstadt [...] was drafted with a typewriter for the blind." (Elsa Bernstein, *Das Leben als*

Drama, Erinnerungen an Theresienstadt [*Life as Drama: Memories of Theresienstadt*] [Dortmund, 1999].)

72. This refers to the 12,000 Jewish servicemen who died in World War I.

73. In fact, since April 1943, a series of transports from Holland had arrived in Theresienstadt. Out of approximately 5,000 people, only a quarter survived.

74. Georg Gradnauer's biography is the longest one that P.M. recorded. On account of its length, it is not repeated here.

75. In the year before his deportation, P.M. took violin lessons from a young musician, and this probably also helped somewhat.

76. We understand this to mean that Manes thought that Kafka was such a superior poet that participation in the competition was unfair to the other entries.

77. This could have been a real air raid siren. But we also know that the authorities sounded the air raid siren when filming, in order to empty the streets of "spectators" who were not involved.

78. This and the next sentence are unclear in the manuscript and have been repeated here slightly changed. Likewise, in the last part of this description of baking, the longer word-length was later replaced.

79. Friedrich Schiller, *William Tell*.

80. Rosh Hashanah and Yom Kippur.

81. Paul (Pavel) Haas, Czech composer born in 1899, killed at Auschwitz.

82. Eppstein's speech, given on September 19, 1944, excited a lot of attention. Adler brings to his text nearly the same words as Manes, but speaks of 1,220 listeners. It stands firm that on September 27 Eppstein was arrested, probably under a pretext, and, as later came to be known, was shot on the same day in the Small Fortress. Dr. Benjamin Murmelstein became his successor. It is important to note here that this speech was given a few days before the announcement of the transport of the 5,000 described in the next chapter. The announcement, through Eppstein, followed on September 23, 1944.

83. For the history of Gerson von Bleichröder and his family, see Fritz Stern, *Gold und Eisen: Bismarck und sein Bankier Bleichröder* (*Gold and Iron: Bismarck and His Banker Bleichröder*) (Berlin: Ullstein, 1978). James was Gerson's third son.

84. Today the Przelazi Palast School and the Agawa Recreation Center in the province of Gorzów in Poland. There is an unpublished chronicle of the castle by Karl-Heinz Graff that strongly differs from the description given here.

85. P.M. originally wrote this story in Berlin for his children. The manuscript is in the archive of the Wiener Library in London.

86. Manes probably means the end of Rosh Hashanah, the Jewish New Year, which occurs some days before Yom Kippur, the Day of Atonement.

87. In the manuscript Manes writes "1,500," but clearly this is a slip of the pen.

88. Presumably, to the SS headquarters there.

89. SS Obersturmführer Karl Rahm. Rahm (1907–1947) was the last commander of Theresienstadt (from September 1944). He is mentioned only once more by P.M., but not by name. Rahm was sentenced to death and executed in Leitmeritz in May 1947.

90. This sentence originally appeared elsewhere in the manuscript but has been placed here for chronological clarity.

91. Manes was deceived—the transports went to Auschwitz.

92. A sentimental best-selling novel by Agnes Günther, published in 1913.

93. These cards were part of the deception; the Nazis forced the victims to write them before killing them.

94. This paragraph indicates that the German authorities are now directly involved in the selection from the start. Also certain (relative) privileges are now dispensed with, such as those for wounded veterans of World War I and Jews married to non-Jews.

95. Powerful light sources also used for filming and onstage.

96. From *Heautontimorumenos* by the Roman playwright Terence (Publius Terentius, ca. 190–159 BCE): "Homo sum; humani nil a me alienum puto" (I am human; I think nothing human is alien to me).

97. Sammy Gronemann (1875–1952), attorney and writer, interpreter for Yiddish in World War I, wrote *Hawdoloh and Tattoo: Memories of the East Jewish Stage, 1916–18* (*Hawdoloh und Zapfenstreich, Erinnerungen an die ostjüdische Etappe 1916–18*; Berlin, 1924). The quote refers to a sentence spoken by an anti-Semitic German sergeant.

98. IG Farben was the big German conglomerate that combined a large part of the chemical industry (it was dissolved after World War II).

99. In the manuscript there follows the first of two parts describing the first 30 years in Eichengrün's life. In the years 1999 and 2000, 100 years after the launch of aspirin, there was a lively debate on the question of how much the "invention of aspirin" was attributable to Eichengrün or to his colleagues. He certainly was closely involved in the process.

100. The tabernacle celebration (*sukkoth*, the plural of *sukkah*, is Hebrew for "tabernacle"), also simply called "the celebration," is a festival of joy. Simchat Torah (Hebrew for "joy of the teachings") is the last day of the tabernacle celebration.

101. Figures in Goethe's *Faust*.

102. This suggests that the opinion that the "prominent" were protected against deportation is not entirely right. However, compared to the majority of inmates in the ghetto, a relatively large percentage of the prominent in Theresienstadt survived.

103. Empress Elisabeth's sister was Sophie Charlotte (1847–1897), who was married to Prince Ferdinand d'Orléans, Duke of Alençon. She perished in a great fire in a Paris bazaar, one year before the empress was murdered.

104. Kempinski was a famous hotel company in Germany. Today an international hotel chain carries the name.

105. On October 15, Durra wrote a thank-you note to P.M. on two pages of one of the albums. A portrait of Manes opposite the title page of the Factual Report is signed "Durra" and was probably drawn by his wife.

106. It is not clear why Manes believed the camp was a new one in Germany; possibly, a rumor was circulating. He was of course deceived; the destination was Auschwitz.

107. A wide-brimmed, soft felt men's hat, originally from Calabria; since about 1848 called a Hecker-hat after the revolutionary politician F. Hecker.

108. Manes here mimics the Cologne dialect spoken by these people, which cannot be rendered in translation.

109. This was on the day before Salomonski's deportation.

110. "German Party" was the name of the National Liberal Party (Nationalliberalen Partei) in Württemberg (1866–1919). The "Tariff Parliament" (Zollparlament)" was established by treaty in 1867 as the Parliament of the German Tariff Union (Parlament des Deutschen Zollvereins).

111. Friedrich Naumann (1860–1919) was a liberal politician and parliamentarian.

112. Gess was the superior officer and a friend of Manes in the First World War.

113. Name for the rabbinical interpretation of the Bible.

114. Anschluss: the annexation of Austria by Nazi Germany in March 1938.

115. Manes is comparing Friedmann and Professor Utitz in this sentence, to Friedmann's advantage.

116. From Seneca's letters (VII 8): *Homines dum docent discunt* (While men teach, they learn). The entry in P.M.'s album is given verbatim.

117. *Cantilena*: literally "little song"; a passage of melodious, songlike character; a moderately vocalized, synchronous, mostly solemn melody.

118. This is the last date in the report. The following pages must have been written during the last three days before P.M.'s deportation.

119. *As If*, the poem from which this volume takes its title.

120. This letter has been preserved nearly verbatim in other sources, such as the collection of Karl Herrmann, where "N." appears as Nathanael.

121. It was very likely Christian Morgenstern.

122. *Minna von Barnhelm*, a German comedy by Gotthold Ephraim Lessing, produced in 1767. Riccaut de la Marlinière is a character in the play, who speaks a mixture of German and French.

Epilogue

1. Hans Günther, SS Oficer, director of the "Central Office for the Settlement of the Jewish Question in Bohemia and Moravia."

2. Translated from German. Alisah Shek, *Tagebuch*, in *Theresienstadter Studien und Dokumente 1994*, Prague 1994, p. 173f.

3. Zdeněk Lederer, *Ghetto Theresienstadt*, Edward Goldston & Son Ltd, London, 1953, p. 242. The book was commissioned and written in Prague before the Communist takeover in 1948 but only published in English (translated by K. Weisskopf) when Lederer had left Prague after the coup. Lederer also wrote the article *Terezin* in *The Jews of Czechoslovakia*. Vol 3, ed. by Avigdor Dagan, Gertrude Hirschler and Lewis Weiner, Vol. 3, Philadelphia & New York 1984, p. 104–164.

4. Danuta Czech, *Auschwitz Chronicle 1939–1945*, 1st American Ed. New York, 1990, p. 742f (previously published in Polish and German).

5. Information about the methods of murder in Auschwitz can be found in *Nazi Mass Murder: A Documentary History of the Use of Poison Gas*, ed. by Eugen Kogon, Hermann Langbein and Adalbert Rückerl, Yale University Press, New Haven and London, 1993 (previously published in German and French).

6. *Terezin—The Daily Life 1943–1945* by Dr. Jacob Jacobson, with an annex *The Russians in Theresienstadt* by Professor David Cohen (Amsterdam), published as *Jewish Survivor Report 6 of the Jewish Central Information Office* (later Wiener Library), London, March 1946, p. 17ff.

INDEX